WHALERS
NO MORE

W0259466

A History of Whaling on the West Coast

W.A. HAGELUND

HARBOUR PUBLISHING

Whalers No More

Printed in the USA

Published by Harbour Publishing Co. Ltd.
Box 219, Madeira Park, BC
Canada, V0N 2H0

Financially assisted by the Government of British Columbia through the British Columbia Heritage Trust.

CANADIAN CATALOGUING IN PUBLICATION DATA

Hagelund, William A. (William Arnold), 1924–
Whalers no more

Includes index.
Bibliography: p.
ISBN 0-920080-02-2
ISBN 978-1-55017-760-2
1. Whaling—British Columbia—History. I. Title
SH383.5.C3H33 1987 639.28'09711 C87-091388-3

Dedication

This book is dedicated to my father-in-law, Fredrick S. Greenhalgh, and to the memory of my father, Emil Hagelund—both seamen, both men in the truest meaning of the word.

Contents

Preface

This account of whaling was written because an old man held determinedly on to a dream long enough for me to realize that when he and his dream went, we would have lost an important touchstone with our country's historic past. That man was Max Lohbrunner, and his dream was to refit the old steam whaler *Green* to go to sea again. It was an impossible dream, but for almost twenty years he nursed it, and it became his vital spark of life.

This book can make no pretense of being a statistically correct record of whales, or even of all the companies involved in taking them. The information offered is of only sufficient depth and accuracy to create interest in, and to give understanding of, one of the almost forgotten pursuits of man.

Events are listed chronologically where possible, for many factors influenced both the whales and the companies of men involved in taking them, and they must be related, one to the other, to be appreciated. Where possible, all information has been double-checked; credits for photographs, when in doubt, are given to those who supplied them. The author's opinions and comments throughout this work, though based upon personal knowledge and observations, should not reflect upon the character of anyone who supplied material for this book. Any errors due to insufficient depth of research are those of the author.

This book is the legacy of all those now-silent men who, by their deeds and belief in a honest day's work for a day's pay, created this great country of ours. It is bequeathed to the present and future generations so they may have better understanding of that vital ingredient that is necessary in all human beings who sincerely wish to make this world a better place in which to live. Freedom and security have never been considered a birthright, but must be continually worked for and, if necessary, fought for.

Acknowledgements

Much credit must be given those people who helped me compile the data and pictures for this book. Leonard G. McCann, in his role as curator of the Vancouver Maritime Museum, has been both an enthusiastic supporter and a procurer of many old and rare pictures and notes. Robert L. Spearing, Lawrence Balcom, Harry Osselton, and Winston R. Garcin expended personal effort in providing many facts and pictures. William S. Lagen offered much personal information on his family, arranged for me to peruse his family's whaling company files and records, and also supplied equally rare old family pictures.

Captains Arnie Borgen, Allan Heater, D.B. MacPherson, and Jim Goodwin provided technical information and pictures for this account. Norman Hacking, former marine reporter for the Vancouver *Daily Province*, supplied information. C.H. Watson contributed his personal reminiscences and pictures of whaling. Of special note was the assistance given by Hector M. Cowie, former manager of Coal Harbour. For the vessel information my thanks to C. Stannard, G. Willson, and C. Honour. For additional pictures, my thanks to L.C. Hume, Orval Forrest, R. Gustavson, J.D. Williamson, and the Vancouver *Sun*. Thanks to Mrs. Suzanne Dodson, who reviewed the manuscript.

Information is also gratefully acknowledged from the following organizations: Vancouver Maritime Museum, British Columbia Provincial Archives, Victoria *Daily Colonist*, Washington State University, San Francisco Maritime Museum, Fish and Game Department of California, Dr. M. Bigg and his staff at the Pacific Biological Station and the Fisheries Research Board of Canada, and the Puget Sound Maritime Historical Society.

During the interval of compiling this work and preparing it for publication, I regret to advise that a number of the contributors have gone by the board, as the old sailors phrased it. I appreciated their generous help and am indebted to their memory. May Orval Forrest, Hector Cowie, Arnie Borgan, Dode MacPherson, Alan Armour, and Laurie Balcom rest in peace.

Introduction

People today, especially younger people who have heard only the viewpoint of the popular protester, are appalled that a man such as I could ever have been a whaler. They probably would be even more appalled if I were to tell them of my specialized skills as a naval commando. Yet they easily excuse the latter, as it had to be done for king and country so they could be born free. Being a whaler appears to be not so easily justified in their eyes. "How could you have done such a terrible thing as kill a whale?" a young acquaintance gasped in disbelief. "Why, you love dogs and cats, and even children!"

My explanation, that whaling had been just as justified in keeping the wolf from the door as had our activities during World War II, appears inconceivable to them in this day of abundant waste. I try to explain that whaling, like mining, logging, and fishing, was necessary as the only means at hand to produce, or to generate coin to purchase, the materials needed to develop our country into a self-reliant nation. The whales provided medicines, food, building and craft materials, and oils and waxes of such fine quality that they lighted the darkness of the world for hundreds of years.

Whaling has never been the pursuit of the well-found, wealthy, or complacent. Quite the contrary, it has always been the pursuit of the very poor, the very hungry, and mostly, the very desperate of men. When the Basque followed the Black Right whale out of the Bay of Biscay into the tempestuous North Atlantic, or when Captain Hussey dared to harpoon the first Sperm whale off Nantucket, thus leading the infant American country into becoming the greatest nation of whalers history has ever recorded, they were driven by a dire need few people of today can even imagine, or would ever wish to experience.

The story of man, most puny of earth's creatures, stalking and attacking the largest of earth's known creatures within the mysterious seas which cover much of this planet's surface, lends itself to fanciful imagination, never quite credible to the hunter on solid land. The romance persisted up to the turn of the century, when the advent of modern whaling, with its harpoon cannon and steam-powered killer ships, changed the whaling scenario completely. With these small vessels the contest was really not one of man against the whale, but of man against the unpredictable seas, for the ships and gear were designed and built to take the largest and swiftest whales of all—the sleek Finback and the giant Blue whale.

The industry has also had the effect of bringing out both the best and the worst in those who pursued it. Courage, tenacity, and feats of seamanship were virtues unstintingly accredited the whalers, but they were also guilty of greed and waste. Wanton killing of the whales for their highly prized whalebone and head oils during the nineteenth century was caused more by avarice than by a limitation of equipment to utilize most of the whale. The methods pioneered by the more thorough Dutch whalers a century before, at Spitsbergen, were ignored in view of the abundance of fat-rich whales upon the ocean's vast horizon.

It was not until Sven Foyn had invented and perfected the whaling cannon and killer ship, and Ludvic Rissmuller and Nils Kvaerner the equipment to process the catch, and after hundreds of dedicated scientists had discovered ways to refine all its products, that we finally received the total gifts the whale had to give. But in almost all instances, these products were soon superseded by coal or petroleum substitutes of equal or superior quality. When whale products became less critical to our needs, whaling became more difficult to justify, both economically and morally.

The whalers' accomplishments and exploits fill this book, yet, unfortunately, much of the earlier information has already been lost and can never be recorded, due in some small part to the thoughtlessness of their families, but, in the main, to the upheaval of our times, that span two World Wars and the Great Depression. For many, like myself, whaling provided the greatest sea training a young man could ever hope to receive, and the price was agreeable to most of us seeking a worthy career. The lessons of hard work and dedication to the ship were set before us every day by the examples of our peers, and we followed without question and without doubt.

No one would seriously trade the comforts and opportunities we enjoy today for those that are often credited to our yesteryears. For our youth, by all means, if it were possible, but for the harsh realities of those hungry, lean, cold years? No sir! Certainly not me!

Chapter One

North to the Charlottes

I was a youth during the Great Depression, and a mill fire, which left my father jobless just when thousands were looking for work, placed my family in dire straits. My mother, a homesteader's daughter from the prairies, and my father, a fisherman's son from Norway, never bemoaned their plight. We lost our home but not our dignity. Hospital bills incurred by my mother's lengthy ill health took us years to repay. But they were all paid. We owed no one a debt and we worked for all we got. Worked harder, perhaps, than most people, because we knew no other way than hard work to earn our keep.

We picked berries, mostly wild berries, and my mother cooked or preserved them. What she didn't put down for the winter months ahead, we peddled door to door. We picked apples, windfalls and those from abandoned orchards, and these were made into apple butter which was often the only spread between the thick slices of homemade bread she put in our school lunches. In winter this was alternated with beef or bacon dripping to help fortify our rather lean bodies. Even the winters were colder during those days, and God knows our cheap denim trousers and thin coats did little to keep out the cold. I've waded to Lynn Valley school through waist-high snow, and our rented house was so cold at nights the windows froze thick with ice. Yet we never considered ourselves desperate, and had it much better than some.

My father cut wood, huge logs that required me on the other end of an eight or ten-foot cross-cut saw, and demanded liberal doses of kerosene and water on the blade to cut the pitch bind. After the logs were split into cordwood, carted by a horse-drawn wagon to our place, and re-sawn into stove wood, what we didn't need for our winter woodpile was bartered for things we did need: eggs, potatoes, vegetables, and fruits. My mother used some of these to make pickles, preserves, and salad dressings, and these were carefully bottled and sold by my father, who walked countless miles each day to peddle them.

There was no money for toys. We fashioned them, and sleighs, skates, and scooters, from bits of tin and wood, using a red hot poker from the kitchen stove to drill holes, and an axe or pieces of broken glass to shape them. To get a dollar or two at Christmas with which to purchase a present for our parents, we fashioned wreaths from holly, monkey vine, and cedar boughs and cones found above the valley, and peddled them to the same good people who had bought our berries. Later I had a paper route that started five miles away from our house and covered another two miles before I could turn my tired feet homeward each night.

Yet I envied no one. True, I hungered for many things, but what we had we enjoyed and willingly shared with our friends. Work, hunger, and cold have been no strangers to me, but that didn't cause me to like them any better.

When I turned fourteen my father managed to get a fishing boat, an old double-end Columbia river boat with an equally old Easthope engine in it, and I spent the next two summers out fishing with him. It was a memorable time in my life. The kinship we forged together as we wrested a living from the sea provided the experience I needed many times in the years ahead. At sixteen I joined a small marine towing company as deckhand, breaking up log booms and towing scows within the harbour limits. When I turned seventeen I journeyed to Esquimalt with Roy Gustavson, a friend of my own age I'd met on the waterfront, in hopes of joining the navy as seamen, but our age denied us the opportunity.

I was a tall, rawboned lad, lean as a whippet and hungering for adventure and a square meal with about equal zeal. I had never seen a whaling ship before, but when we gazed across the harbour at Victoria and saw those grey and black ships, I knew what they were and, more importantly, I knew I wanted to sail on them.

Roy and I hurried around the harbour with youthful excitement, trying to imagine what life aboard a whaler would be like. Fearful that, at any moment, a loud voice of authority would boom out and order us away, we skirted the office area of the Consolidated Whaling Corporation and made our way down to the dock, where we found ourselves close to the man obviously in charge of the freight being hand-trucked aboard two whalers.

Their funnels were belching smoke and steam, ready for immediate departure, so I puffed up my courage and, in the most salty language I could muster, asked him if there were any berths open for two good, experienced seamen. Good fortune stood with us that day, for unwittingly I had approached the mate of the whaler S.S. *Blue*, a man of considerable understanding, and the protege of Captain Andy Anderson, the best-liked whaling master and certainly the best gunner in the fleet.

After a quick, startled look that accurately assessed our degree of saltiness, and with only a hint of a twinkle in his eyes that bespoke the humour of the situation, he confirmed our worst fears. They did have a full crew, as did Captain Harry Anderson of the *White*, moored alongside them.

Unable to conceal our disappointment, we turned to walk away. Then the mate had an afterthought, and called us back. The *Brown*, he suggested in a fatherly tone, which was lying at the far end of the dock, might require a couple of good seamen. Her mate was away at the ship chandlery but should be back shortly, and she was due to sail in ten days for Naden Harbour at the north end of the Queen Charlottes. He told us to wait and talk to Finn John.

The strange name caught my fancy. Whaling, I was to learn, was an exclusive fraternity, with each member earning a special nickname such as Paper Nose Frenchie, Montreal Mike, John the Baptist, and Uncle Harry.

While Roy and I were still reeling from our last-minute reprieve, the mate of the *Blue* invited us to board his ship and have a cup of coffee while we waited. Coffee? To us, it was nectar of the gods! With a mug in one hand, and a thick piece of the cook's chocolate cake in the other, Roy and I stood upon that cluttered deck, breathing the coal smoke, the moist vapours of steam, and the musky odours of tar and cordage, our eyes inspecting every detail, while our hearts beat mightily with hope.

All too soon the coffee and cake were gone, and the ship ready to sail. We said our thanks to the cook and mate, and finally to the heavy set captain, for allowing us aboard. He grinned and asked us to do him the favour of letting his lines go from the dock. A favour?! This was the greatest compliment we could have received, and we scrambled recklessly up onto the dock to fulfill it.

As the boat backed away from the dock, the captain called gruffly across the opening spread of water, "You lads! Go see Finn John. I'm sure he can use you."

This was more than we had ever hoped for. A recommendation of such magnitude from a commanding whaler like the captain of the S.S. *Blue* was instant intoxication to our senses, and we stood conversing in admiring tones as the small steamships swung nimbly on their heels and headed down the harbour and out of our sight.

Only then did we turn and make our way across the façe of the dock to where a lone vessel lay, only her bridge and top works visible above the bullrail with the ebb of the tide. There was purpose in our strides, and my long legs covered a greater spread of the dock's time-worn planks than Roy's shorter ones, forcing him to trot. Our hearts beat less excitedly as the ship came more into our view.

Never have I seen such bedraggled weariness in a ship. Paint peeled from every part of her. All her rigging sagged. The canvas and rope seizing, weathered and rotting, flapped from the wiresplices they were meant to protect. Her ratlines, leading up to the foretop barrel, hung broken or unlashed to the shrouds. The frayed edges of the tarps, lashed with rotting ropes over her funnel and ventilator, stirred in the first breath of the midday breeze. Scuttle and hatch lay open to the elements. Bits and pieces of rotten wood and rope, rusted gear and rags, were strewn everywhere. Except for the fact that her black hull had been freshly painted, and the ring of tools was echoing up from her open engine room skylight, she seemed readier for the boneyard than the bounding main.

It was not until later that we learned she had lain idle and neglected for four long years beside this dock, waiting for one last chance to go whaling. In retrospect, it was appropriate that she, so old, so weary, and yet so anxious to feel the rush of the North Pacific under her forefoot again, should be crewed by novices so eager and naive as Roy and I.

We stood a little undecided, trying to see, beyond her neglected ugliness, a ship as meaningful and well-found as the *Blue*. Our unguarded evaluation of the ship and the unlikelihood of our sailing on her was interrupted by an apparition that rose into view above the gunwales of the ship's lifeboat, a few feet above our heads. To our first startled glance he looked like a big angry walrus, complete with brown-stained drooping moustache, brown Indian wool sweater, and brown fedora hat pulled down over his eyes, casting his tanned face in a shadow from the weak sunlight behind him.

"Vell! Vhat the hell do you two vant?" he growled sternly down at us.

Our choked reply "a job," brought forth a derisive grunt, followed by a humourless chuckle that threatened our shaky self-confidence. "We've got experience," I added, a little lamely.

"Experience, eh? Vhat experience you got? Ever been vhaling?" Slowly lowering himself onto the lifeboat's thwart, he grinned down at us, the sternness gone from his face.

Swallowing mightily as the importance of this moment fell upon me, I told him about myself, how I had fished with my father and

William Hagelund, age 17, aboard the Brown *in 1941.*

worked on the tugs, then added a little bit about Roy, who could only nod and grin back at the mate. I carefully refrained from mentioning the navy, and when he asked our age, stated without hesitation that we were almost nineteen.

He pulled out a pipe, and, after worrying the tobacco in the bowl with the end of a large wooden match, flicked the match against the edge of his work-hardened thumbnail and puffed noisily and a little wetly till he had it belching smoke, casually asking us between puffs if we could scrape and paint, if we could splice rope and tie knots, and if we knew how to steer by compass and had good eyes. Stretching the truth, we nodded, eager to match his standards of a good seaman, and his grin deepened till we could see the blackened yellow stumps of his teeth.

Standing up and pulling back the hat from his head, he scratched the thinning white hair it exposed while his sea-puckered eyes gauged our worth. "Vell, maybe ve give you a chance. You vant to vork to get this boat ready? Clean up all this goddamn mess?"

When we nodded and gasped out a relieved yes, he put his hat back on his head and heaved himself out of the lifeboat. Then, with more agility than I supposed possible for one of his age, he sprang across from the boat rack to the bullrail of the dock, and beckoned us to follow as he set off towards the office.

Pausing at the counter to ask the aging bookkeeper if the manager was in, he motioned us to wait there, strode over to a frosted glass door, and disappeared inside without benefit of a knock or word. We held our breath in the deathly silence of the ancient office as Finn John's rumbling voice from the other side of the glass door was stridently outmatched by a loud sharp voice raised in protest.

The bookkeeper ignored the growing storm of noise and scratched away in his ledger, pausing after every few words to dip his tall pen in a large bronze inkwell that had been stained a rusty purple by countless drips of india ink. After an exceptionally loud outburst of angry voices, of which the words, "Too much! Too much boy. We can't afford that!" reached our ears, there were footsteps, then the door opened a crack and a bony head with piercing dark eyes stared out at us for an unblinking moment before retracting itself inside as the door clicked shut.

Easing our tension, the voices resolved themselves into a low rumble. We glanced around the darkly panelled office at the pictures of whaling ships and whales that hung upon its walls, moving over to inspect the pictures more closely and discuss their significance to our aspirations, unaware that the bookkeeper had stopped to watch us. We turned, a little startled, when he spoke up in a voice as crisp as the paper he wrote upon.

"That's me," he chuckled, pointing at the picture in front of us, showing a man seated in the mouth of a whale. His eyes twinkled above the glasses perched on the end of his nose. "I sailed with Finn John on the *Black* that year. That was over twenty years ago," he added.

Pleased with our respectful attention, he came over and explained the stories of the other pictures, naming dates and people which had existed before I was born. Then he counselled us on our good fortune should we get hired by Finn John and go whaling with him. "Work hard and keep your eyes and ears open. Work never hurt anyone, but ignorance does. Finn John may be a hard taskmaster but he's also the most able teacher. You'll be seamen, real seamen, if you stick it out for a season with John. When you get back, believe me, you'll rate a seaman's berth on any ship!"

Finn John came out of the office then, and angrily motioned us to follow him outside. At the gravelled driveway he paused. We thought he was going to tell us to get the hell home. Instead, he suddenly flashed us a rueful grin and grunted, "Vell, I've got you two for ten days to clean up the boat and get her ready. Ve vork ten hours a day, every day from seven to five, till it's done. You get two-bits an hour, but nothing if you swing the lead, ja?" We nodded, happily relieved, and replied as earnestly as we could, "Thanks, mister. You won't be sorry."

"Ve'll see, ve'll see," he chuckled.

We worked as we had never worked before. We cleaned bilges, the coal bunkers, and the hold. We chipped and scraped paint, and then laid on new paint. We cleaned up the horrendous mess on deck and carried it ashore. We greased and oiled the easing gear, the steering gear, and the anchor gear. We served and seized the rigging, and hoved it down hard. We re-lashed the ratlines and tried out the lookout barrel on the foretop for size. As the ship began to sparkle and shine, it was time to get up steam. We were sent up on the dock to shovel aboard ten to fifteen tons of coal.

It was a distasteful chore we would become hardened to but would never enjoy, and it rained during the whole time we worked at it. Grit from the coal stuck to the watersoaked handles of the old shovels so that it ground into our soft hands till they blistered and broke into running rawness. Even the simple act of lifting a cup of coffee became a feat requiring both hands, and the handling of a knife or fork was painfully awkward.

We lodged at the Salvation Army hostel on Johnson Street, and ate our early morning breakfast of hotcakes and our late supper of Salisbury steak at an old Chinese restaurant across the street. We washed down a bag lunch of sandwiches, bought at the same cafe, with water from the old dock hose. The ship was without heat or comfort, and the only shelter for us was in the hold. The messroom off the galley, in the only deckhouse built on the ship, was below the bridge and had room for only four. The mate, engineers, and seamen claimed this. They were proven sailors; we were not. We didn't complain. We were anxious to prove our mettle, and were well aware that after a week's work cleaning ship, wearing the only clothes we possessed, we had nothing to entice sociability from Johnny, a well-scrubbed and cleanly dressed blond Norwegian lad, five years our senior and a veteran of two seasons in the Antarctic. Paddy, the second engineer, and Cec, the chief, were too busy to really take notice of us, but Finn John seemed more tolerant of us the dirtier and smellier we got.

Our two firemen joined us on coaling-up day. Willie, a big, ham-fisted Norwegian, scolded us for our filthiness, and Harold, a Victorian father of two young daughters, advised us to use the shower and washing tubs at the Sally Ann, where we could hang our clothes up overnight to dry. We tried out the advice that evening, but the lack of heat in the hostel, and the humidity from the rain outside, left our clothes still wet when we shrugged into them in the morning darkness.

With steam up and the deck winch proved out, we were ready to take aboard the whale lines. Six bales of new manila rope, approximately three inches in diameter, were joined together with carefully tapered long splices that had to run freely through the ship's tackle. It was an exacting task which Johnny and the mate carried out, while Roy and I, helping where we could, watched and learned. On a whale hunt, the mainline would be spliced onto the lighter foregoer rope which would be coiled down on the line pan, under the gun, and carried over to the whale by the harpoon discharged from the cannon. Each three thousand foot line was roved through the mast blocks, over the drums of the big winding winch, and led down to the line locker below decks, where, under the critical eye of Finn John, Roy and I attempted to coil it down in flat tiers, laid one above the other till each line locker was full.

Next the bales of lighter ropes were brought aboard. The 1½-inch foregoer rope bales were stowed below decks on top of the whale line in the line lockers, while the lifting falls for anchor, lifeboat, and pram were all rove home and spliced around thimbles and deadeye. Here I was allowed to show my ability at splicing, which, though it got a conditional chuckle and nod of approval from Finn John, caused Johnny to wrinkle his nose critically and give a disdainful laugh I would soon learn to hate.

Next came the stowing of the whaling gear. The 120-pound harpoons were shouldered and carried below to the hold where they were each lashed in their own special rack. Bomb tips, lances, flensing

Whaler Brown, *the author's ship in 1941.*

irons, and other grease-coated, rusty tools of the trade were also stowed below, along with chains, cables, and wires. Blubber spades, piercing irons, and marker buoys were all packed in special wooden boxes lashed to the rigging. Finally, the navigation lights were brought aboard and secured in their respective places, and supplies of kerosene, greases, and soft soap were stowed in port deck locker, which also housed the one and only head aboard the ship.

Lee, the ship's emaciated Chinese cook, arrived to supervise loading of the galley stores in the starboard deck locker, and the barrels of salt pork and beef in the hold. That day we had our first shipboard cup of coffee.

Quite suddenly the ship seemed to come alive. After we had fitted new mooring lines, the engineers turned over the main engines, and our large screw cast water astern from under our flared counter. The clank and scrape of the fireman's shovel and slice bar, the rattle of coal on the steel stokehold plates, and the plume of steam from our whistle and atmospheric pipe, all heightened the statement of purpose which the haze of coal smoke from our funnel announced. I tasted the tang of adventure; it surfaced in our happy chuckles, our grins, and mostly in the last-minute rush to complete our fitting-out of the ship. The brotherhood of seamen was forging its first link.

Though all six ships that whaled that season were similar, being built at the same time, each was also individual. The *Brown* seemed not only a happier ship, but also a better ship than the others—to us, at least. We took pride in her handiness, and she never failed us. She was over ninety feet long between perpendiculars, eighteen feet in beam, and drew almost twelve feet of water to displace her hundred-odd tons.

The crew were housed in an eight-berth forecastle under the main deck, forward of the heavily stayed mast. The master, mate, and engineers berthed aft in small cabins fitted in the fantail. On the fantail deck above these cabins was located the emergency steering gear, with a grating over it where we stowed our mooring lines. On the taffrail was fitted a patent log for recording the sea miles we covered. A wooden boat rack above the engine room skylight held the regulation lifeboat and the whaling pram. Fifteen feet long, the pram had a long shallow forefoot designed for running up against the sides of whales when hand-lancing or harpooning was required. Two small compartments or lockers built on deck on either side of the engine room skylight supported this boat rack. The starboard locker was used for galley supplies, while the port one housed our head. To flush this toilet after use, a bucket with rope lanyard was dipped over the side for sea water. Understandably it took a degree of dexterity and caution to accomplish this when travelling in rough weather with the ship at full speed. Though I'd never heard of a user being pulled over the side by the bucket, it was a possibility that was always present in my mind when it was my turn.

Forward of the engine room, and above the three-furnace Scotch marine boiler, was the fidley, a low, steel, trunk housing with openings to the stokehold and safety valves. The *Brown*'s tall, lean funnel and ventilator rose from here. Forward of this, the galley and messroom were housed in a stout steel structure built on deck above the coal bunkers. The wooden bridge, with its steam steering engine and double steering wheel, was located above this area. Forward of the galley and bridge, and bolted firmly to the deck, were the enormous whaling winches with massive grooved drums around which the whale lines were laid to supply a friction drive.

A small hatch fitted between the winches and the mast led down to the hold, which filled the area inside the hull from forecastle to coal bunker, and held our supplies of whaling equipment and whale lines. Below the planked floor of the hold, two huge springs were fitted to the cable easing gear which was carried up the mast where it supported two large blocks below the barrel. The whale line ran

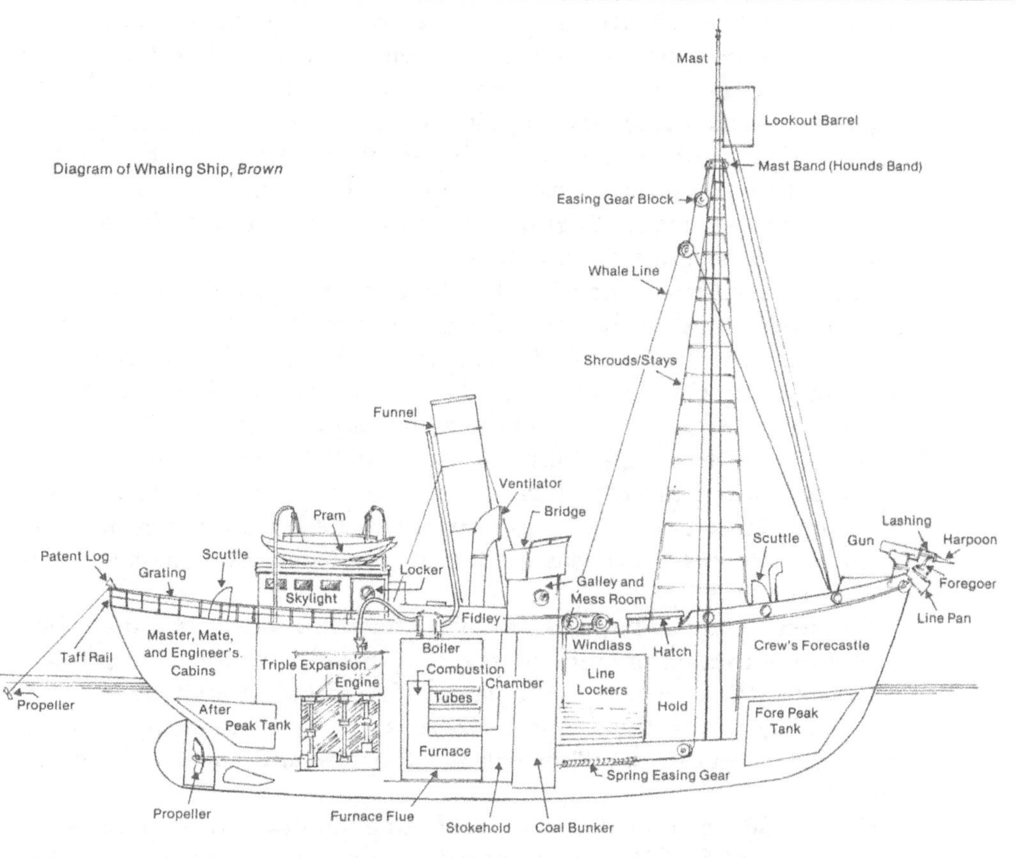

Diagram of Whaling Ship, *Brown*

through these. When the line was stretched by an angry whale, it pulled these blocks downward. This pulled the easing gear which, in turn, stretched the springs under the hold floor. This spring action reduced the sudden shock to gear and rope. The whale line ran from these blocks down to sheaves on the deck, and then forward under the gun platform and outboard over large sheaves on either side of the stem. Here it was spliced onto the lighter foregoer line that was coiled on the pan above these sheaves. Peering over the foregoer pan was the muzzle of our three-inch cannon, and supporting the cannon was a heavy, cast-iron base, secured through doubling plates and carried downwards into the hull to bear on the panting beam above the forefoot.

Roy and I were busy cleaning the *Brown*'s whaling gun of its heavy, time-aged coating of grease, and getting the foregoer pan freed up, when Captain Larsen appeared at the dock edge. He was a tall, lean man, much like my father, but his face was cast in sterner lines, and his eyes, nearly hidden in a permanent squint from a lifetime of peering at distant horizons, noted every detail of the ship and, I felt, the way in which Roy and I applied ourselves to the most important piece of equipment on the ship—his gun. Finn John joined him on the dock and they stood conversing about the ship's readiness, just out of our straining earshot. Silently we prayed this tall master mariner would accept us as members of his crew.

Finn John's first words when he climbed back aboard to join us on the gun deck sent our hopes dashing into our boots. "Vell, boys. The skipper says to pay you two off. You go see Henry up in the office and he'll fix you up till the end of the day. Then come back here and ve'll wash down the quarters and get the mattresses aboard."

Sagging with disappointment, Roy and I nodded dumbly in agreement and started to turn away, when we were surprised to see Finn John's face crack into a jocular grin as he lifted a finger in mock scolding. "Ve sign on articles at 10 a.m. Thursday. Louis says you two can sign on as A.B.s."

Suddenly I was so happy I wanted to hug that walrus of a man, but gave Roy a thumping crack on the back instead, as we both grinned like idiots. "Ve'll be away over six months, so have tomorrow off and get your gear together. But be here at 7 a.m. to load cargo on Thursday. Don't sleep in!" he cautioned before ambling aft to tell the others.

The $2.50 we received for each of our nine days' work netted us a grand total of $22.50, and afforded us a seabag, underwear, socks, some cheap shirts and work pants, but nothing for coat or boots. On hearing our plight, the Salvation Army major at the hostel took us down to the used clothes store they operated at the street entrance, and found us each a sweater, coat, and brown army boots. There was no doubt we were the strangest-dressed whalers that ever went to sea, but we were ready and we were going; that was all that counted. I wrote a letter home explaining vaguely the details of our good fortune, stressing that I would be earning two to three times the pay I had got on the tugboat, and would arrange to have some of it sent home to them. Promising to write more when we reached the Queen Charlottes, I posted it and we took a last evening's walk around the town to complete our day off.

The dew was still wet on the grass next morning as we shouldered our seabags and set off to the ship to claim our berth and load station freight. Last to board was an old seaman named Joe, who, like Lee our cook, had sailed with Finn John when he had been captain of this same ship. At 10 a.m. we were all called up to the office to sign the ship's articles. Both the manager, Alfus Garcin, and the venerable old shipping master looked long and questioningly over their glasses at Roy and I before the latter lowered his gaze and proceeded to read out the conditions of the agreement. Then each man, in order of his importance, signed the articles opposite his position. Roy and I were last, and when it came my turn I blithely put my birthdate two years earlier and my age two years older than it was. Though this bit of deceit was to cause me trouble years later when I was qualifying for my master mariner's certificate, at the moment my only concern was to ensure my opportunity to go to sea, and that fully justified the act.

Though we had drawn our supplies of bedding, soap, and matches after signing on, the arrival of more freight delayed our departure till noon. By late afternoon we had sailed to James Island to take on gun powders and primers, and at three the following morning were alongside the huge gantry dock at Union Bay, taking on a full load of coal.

It rained all the way up there, and Roy and I, standing our watch on the open bridge of the whaler, found our raincoats had been no gift at all, as they absorbed water quicker than cotton sheeting. We had to pad our shoulders with towels and underwear to get any protection from the elements, and this soggy mess became heavily saturated with coal dust as we trimmed the bunkers. Though we survived that first day at sea, the worst was still to come. We departed Union Bay just before going off watch, and, by the end of our next watch on deck, had cleared Christie Pass and were heading for the open sea.

Though well-laden, we still had a lively ship under us, and she plunged her stem into the rolling seas that marched down towards us as we pushed our way up from Scarlett Point to Pine Island and Queen Charlotte Sound. We were to be very grateful for that liveliness during the dark hours ahead, as we faced a storm such as I had never before, or since, encountered.

Besides the freight on deck for Rose Harbour—drums of oil, crates of machinery, and bales of cordage—we had also deck-loaded an extra ten tons of coal. It would almost prove our undoing. Roy and I went off watch at 6 p.m., gulped our supper while holding our plates and cups on the wildly gyrating table in the messroom, then struggled forward to the forecastle and our bunks as Pine Island grew smaller astern of us, and our bows shaped a course for the southern tip of the Queen Charlotte Islands.

Within moments of climbing into our bunks, we realized the problems of finding rest and sleep there. As the ship tossed her head skyward, we were pressed heavily against the mattress, forced relentlessly down against the footboard of the berth as the angle of the ship increased. Breasting the sea, the ship's head plunged downward, and the bunk and mattress would drop out from under us as we and our blankets followed more slowly. Our feeling of weightlessness ended when the ship buried her head into the oncoming sea and shuddered to a stop, while we, with the momentum of free-falling objects, crashed into the headboard.

Willie, the Norwegian fireman, snored heavily in his bunk, his heavy muscular body resting serenely and securely where it should be. Lee climbed down and got into his bunk, and, after smoking a foul-smelling homemade cigarette, soon fell into blissful repose. Roy and I suffered the fate of the damned.

Tired by our long hours of work, unable to find rest or sleep, we literally counted away the minutes of our few precious hours off watch. Even worse than this was the unsettling awareness of nausea and headache that was creeping upon us as the ship's active gyrations stirred her ancient bilges. The odours that assailed our nostrils in that darkened, tightly closed forecastle defy description, and could only be likened to those of an over-used public dry toilet in the heat of midsummer.

Eventually Roy gave a strangled curse, jumped down from his bunk above mine, and struggled into his clothes. As he indicated that he was

Putting her shoulder into it off the Queen Charlottes.

going up on deck, I decided to join him, and struggled even more wildly than he to get my pants and boots on. When all was in readiness, we climbed up the ladder and awaited a favourable moment to unlatch the scuttle door and leap out on the deck. The sound of spray and sea hitting against the mast and scuttle gave us our clue, and as the ship rose quickly under our feet, we jumped through the scuttle, closed and dogged the doors behind us, then, struggling blindly in the blackness, reached out for the mast ropes and hung on tightly as the ship fell into a void that seemed to have no bottom.

Faintly, above the roar of wind and the thunder of breaking seas, the skipper's voice reached my ears out of the darkness that surrounded us, "Hold on there, you damn fools! Hold on!"

As I frantically peered around me, trying to distinguish substance in a blackness alive with sound, motion, and cold sea water that rushed over my boots, shocking my still warm feet, I glimpsed a loom of pale whiteness high above our heads. Shouting at Roy to hold tight, I pulled my head down tightly between my shoulders and closed my eyes, my fingers clenching the rope so hard I cried out in pain.

With the roar of a giant cataract, the cresting sea broke over us, sweeping my feet from under me, and slamming me against the mast so hard that the wind was knocked from my lungs and my fingers relaxed their grip on the rope. I slipped along its length. Unfortunately, I had grabbed the loosely fastened tail of our lifting tackle, and as this was washed aft and out over the port side, I followed. Only the roll of the ship as she fell off to starboard retarded my swift passage overboard, and I slammed down amongst the oil drums that had broken loose from their lashings.

Roy rushed up to me as I painfully struggled to my feet, and together we fled for the doubtful shelter of the deckhouse, stumbling through swirling water and over lumps of coal en route. We found the galley door smashed open, and a foot of water cascading back and forth inside, and were trying to clear the scuppers to let it run away when Johnny came down from the bridge to shout at us, a little wildly, that the skipper wanted the deck cargo relashed, the coal shovelled up, and the scuppers cleared.

Finn John, scowling in ill-humour, appeared at our side and growled at us to follow him. Only when we made our way forward did I realize the engines had been slowed and the ship hove-to. The dull metallic crash of metal on metal guided us to the rolling barrels, and with determination not to fail, we followed the mate, fearful that at any moment a 500-pound drum would come charging out of the blackness to crush us.

Within an hour the job was behind us, and while Finn John and Johnny returned to the bridge to relieve the skipper and Joe, Roy and I relit the stove and put on a fresh pot of coffee. By the time it was boiling, the coal, ash, and pots and pans had been separated from each other, the floor mopped nearly dry, and the ship was again making easy weather of it. With everything looking so normal, it was difficult to recall the chaos of less than two hours earlier, but as near-normalcy returned, so did our nausea, and Roy and I stumbled outside, hoping the freshness of the wind would blow away our complaint.

Now we had time to look around. Miserable as I was, the sight still stirred up a thrill in me. The horizon was ringed in ominous blackness, and seas of six to eight feet hissed and crashed by us as our ship came back up to full speed, but overhead the stars sparkled with a brilliancy I had not seen before. Within moments of seating ourselves on the warm fidley with our backs against the funnel, the heat had driven away the cold clamminess of our wet clothing, and the moon appeared from behind the clouds on the horizon, casting a bright glow over the seas so that each cresting black wave had a long lacy ruffle of silver.

Coming up to call Willie for his watch below, Harold spotted our misery and, with a certain fatherly concern, offered us each a cigarette as a guaranteed cure for seasickness. It was my first cigarette, and the punishment of it was greater than my nausea. I was grateful to toss it overboard and go up to the bridge to take over the wheel when the watch changed.

Though the wind continued to drop till the gusts were less than thirty knots, Louis remained stoically on the bridge, his whole being suspiciously alert for a change in the weather. The ship steadied up docilely under my hand, and the bows lifted and fell to the seas in a comforting rhythm that allayed my earlier concern. Roy came up to take the wheel an hour later, and, after checking the lamps and taking some coffee up for the skipper and mate, I settled myself on the messroom settee with a hard tack biscuit and a fresh cup of coffee. The food seemed to settle my stomach, and the warmth of the galley stove, combined with the gentle motion of the ship, created a restful repose. Without awareness, I broke a cardinal rule of watchkeeping and dozed off.

It was a brief respite. I was shocked awake as everything loose, including myself, was thrown with a crash into the low side of the galley. Struggling to my feet, and peering out over the lower half of the galley door, I saw water rushing aboard higher than the gunwales.

Frantically hauling myself up onto the galley counter, I put a foot on the top of the half door, reached up for the bridge ladder railing above my head, and clawed my way up to the bridge.

The skipper, wedged between the telegraph and the binnacle, was shouting at Roy to get her head up into the weather, and Finn John was fighting his way up towards the steering wheel to give Roy a hand. Out of the corner of my eye I saw the crest of a giant wave high above the bridge, growing larger and closer as the ship held her heel of over thirty degrees and fell into the chasm before it. Putting my foot up on the bridge rail for leverage, I dove towards the steering engine above me, knocking Roy against the wheel as I sprawled on top of him. Grabbing the spokes of the steering wheel from his startled grasp, I swung her hard-a-port before throwing my right arm over Roy and grabbing a secure hold on the steering engine behind him. With one hand holding the wheel and the other wrapped around the oiled frame of the engine, I buried my head in Roy's shoulders, certain we were about to die as the sea crashed down over the ship.

That few seconds of left rudder had been enough to bring her port bow around under the sea, but not enough to lift her clear. Solid water drove down on the sharply heeled bridge, smashing everything before it, but it provided a lee for the boiler room and engine room. Then the ship flipped upright as the crest, passing beneath us, tried to roll her over to starboard. The bridge was like a bucket full of water, and our roll to starboard trapped much of it till we rolled back to port and it poured down the ladder to the deck.

As the water receded, Roy came into view beneath me, sputtering and choking, and the skipper and Finn John, in the jumble of upturned deck grating over on the port side, struggled to regain their footing. Desperately I untangled myself and began swinging the wheel back over to hard-a-starboard as the ship veered to port and plunged down into another chasm of darkness. Arresting her wild sheer to port, I brought the wheel back amidships, then put a full turn of port rudder on her. Miraculously, she held her bows up into the advancing crest, and rose so swiftly the foredeck alone took on water.

I became conscious of the skipper's voice. The telegraph had been swung up to half ahead, and his words eased my fear that the ship was going to be overwhelmed again. "Good work, lad. Hold her shoulder up to it. Don't let her fall off. Don't use too much wheel!"

In that instant the moon disappeared behind the rushing clouds, and I realized the compass lamp had been washed out and called to Finn John for a light. I searched frantically for something to steer by and found a lone star, up near the foremast truck, that still shone, though weakly, through the flying fingers of advancing storm clouds. For a moment or so it gave me a bearing, then the storm shrieked in on us and all was blackness. Only the blur of the light grey bridge railing was visible, and the salt water streaming down from my hair stung my eyes so everything took on an unreal vagueness.

Flying spray hit my face like an icy whip. I shook my head to clear my eyes, fearful to let either hand go from the wheel and the solidness it represented. I held the steering wheel and our fates in my hands, and I was as good as blind, groping to find a heading to steer by that would ease the ship's wild gyrations, using my body to sense the motion and direction of the ship under me, straining my ears to find the direction of each crashing, hissing wave that roared up out of the blackness around us to thunder against the ship.

Never had I cried for my father, but I did that night. Not out loud, I don't think, but certainly in my heart. Never had I felt so alone. I couldn't let go of the steering wheel, nor could I hear a human voice or see a glimmer of light. The noise around me rose to the awesome thunder of a hundred giant waterfalls, of which even the spray seemed dense enough to drown me.

Somewhere inside my head a voice counselled, "Relax, roll with her. Don't let her fool you with that little swing to port. Catch her before she lunges to starboard! Give her more port wheel. Starboard now, not too much!" The words kept repeating till I began to feel every move the ship made under my feet, and understood when she was going to make each lunge. As confidence returned, so did a feeling of glowing warmness to my freezing fingers on the wet wooden spokes of the steering wheel. It was a comforting feeling only I could appreciate.

Moments later my eyes were blinded by a brilliant light, and I almost lost contact with the ship again. Finn John had found the bridge flashlight, and that tiny 1½ volt lamp had shattered my straining night vision. Pulling off the binnacle lamp, and unscrewing the flashlight lens, he shoved it down into the opening and stuffed his handkerchief around it to hold it in the brass tube, subduing its glare into a faint warm glow that illuminated the still-flooded binnacle, so I could see the wildly swinging compass rose.

The rain came then. Carried by the wind in horizontal sheets, it beat upon my bare head like a drummer playing taps. It washed the salt from my eyes and ran off my nose and chin in rivulets. It ran down my neck, back, and on down through my clothing till it ran down my legs and filled my boots. It revived Roy, and he immediately attempted to help me on the steering wheel, but I called to him to stand clear as I swung the wheel over against a sea that lifted our bows up into the storm.

Finn John motioned to him to help with the tangle of gratings, and together they got them back in place before he clumped off the bridge to check the deck cargo. Johnny and Joe, alerted by the commotion, had jumped out of the forecastle to lend a hand. The bright beam of Finn John's five-cell flashlight expôsed the cargo still securely held by its lashings, and they moved aft where the beam of light shone over the fidley and engine room skylight, and up to the boat rack. A quick glance over my shoulder gave me a view of the damage the sea had done. Our lifeboat had been lifted right out of its chocks and smashed against the davits. The whaling pram had been thrown over the side, left hanging by just the forward falls. The chief came up to report water over the stokehold plates, but assured us the fires were bright and steam still up, and the pumps would quickly lift the water out of her.

Other than the galley being flooded for the second time in six hours, and a bit more coal loose on the deck, we seemed to have survived our second boarding with little more than a badly damaged lifeboat to show for it.

The heavy rain smothered the wind, easing it down till the crests of the seas were flattened into a dirty froth on the back of the long rollers that lifted the ship gently as they ran under us. We came back up to full speed and shaped a course to correct for our weatherly one, leaving the storm behind.

Lighting up the pot-bellied coal bogey in the forecastle, Roy and I hung up our clothes to dry at the end of our watch, and fell into our bunks to sleep like true seamen. Rested, and with Lee's hot stew in our stomachs, we took over the watch at noon, and set lookouts to seek a landfall.

An hour later, as Louis and Finn John scanned the foggy horizon through their binoculars, I glanced up from the compass just in time to see a rounded rocky islet that disappeared back into the fog as quickly as it had appeared.

"I see land!" I called, pointing off to the horizon.

"Where away?" demanded the skipper, his glasses never leaving his eyes as he swept the horizon slowly, but his voice smarted my pride with its displeasure at my unnautical report.

"Two points on the port bow," I amended.

"Gray Rock," grunted Finn John after a few minutes, as the fog lifted and we could all see the seas breaking against the solid sentinel, a few miles offshore of Cape St. James.

We set a course to take us up past the Cape towards Houston-Stewart channel, and again my young, keen eyes found the landmark before their binocular-assisted eyes.

"Light, three points on the port bow," I sang out. Louis gave me a quizzical glance, much as my father had done several times when I had gained his approval. The skipper never called me lad or boy after that, it was always Bill, and once, when he was very drunk, he called me Billy, just like my dad.

Chapter Two

Whale Ho!

We entered Rose Harbour through a light fog that was partly natural production of the atmosphere on this extreme southerly end of the Charlottes, and partly the result of evaporation from the whaling station's retorts and cookers. The latter had a complex aroma that assaulted the nostrils and remained in our clothing and hair for hours after our departure. This aroma was composed of three distinct scents.

The first, and probably foremost, was the sweet smell of cooked or burnt flesh. Underlying that was the scent of freshly butchered animal, of warm innards exposed to the air, a smell that conjured up the memory of my pet bantam hens being butchered for our soup pot, or the skinning and cleaning of a black bear my father shot on our back porch in Lynn Valley. The third smell was more revolting. It oozed up from the slime and mud under the station, and out of the old timbers holding the station above the muskeg that covered much of the rockbound island. It was overpowering. The only relief came when the tide covered it, but we arrived on an extremely low tide, with an offshore breeze to carry it out to greet us.

The *W. Grant* backed away from the dock as we slowly stood in to go alongside. As she slipped by us, her captain, Bill Heater, raised his arm in slight token of salute, a gesture returned vigorously by Finn John, but only by a nod from Louis Larsen. The visible members of her crew stared silently over at us, or turned their backs to carry out their task without enthusiasm. Not a happy lot, I recall thinking from my vantage point at the wheel. The truth of that first impression would be confirmed thirty years later, when Graig Fergusson, who sailed on her that season, recounted the sad events of Captain Heater's last voyage, and Lilly Heater read his painfully written letters home, describing his sufferings.

Our stay at Rose was brief. With the freight off-loaded, and word that both the *Green* and *Black* at Naden had already got ten or twelve whales each, we backed away from the dock, anxious to join them and earn our whale bonus. The *Blue*, just in from the west coast with a whale, was tying it off at the float as we moved slowly out. Roy and I took off our hats and waved as we passed close by. The mate, busy with the deck gear, gave us just a quick glance, but the skipper, spotting Roy's curly auburn hair and my lean height, recalled our Mutt and Jeff appearance instantly and, pointing towards us, roared good naturedly, "Good going boys. Good Luck!"

In the first faint light of morning we rounded Rose Spit through a tumultuous weather tide, and settled on a heading to reach Naden Harbour, picking up Knob Hill before going off watch to our breakfast. Our watches of six hours on and six hours off set our meals at the changing of the watches. Thus, at 6:30 in the morning, fed and at our leisure, Roy and I sat on the gun deck and watched the headlands of Naden Harbour come into view. We closed the tricky entrance as Finn John piloted us in over the outer bar with a derring-do that caused Louis Larsen, new to this coast, to suck in his breath as we charged towards George Point. His pent-up breath of relief was clearly heard to exhale when Finn John finally gave the order to haul, and our ship slipped by the rocky beach, less than a boat's length off, at all of her 10½ knots.

Smiling with amusement, Finn John guided us into the harbour, which appeared glassy smooth and miles long before us. A kind breeze blew onshore, driving the smoke and odour of our new home away from us. We stood-down well east of the station on a southerly heading, so the bright morning sunlight highlighted the distant buildings, and their blistered, seagull-splattered, weathered exteriors appeared innocently white and pure to our unknowing eyes. As the engines were slowed, we hauled round to a heading slightly south of the station and began sounding our way across the inner bar, stopping the engines as the bottom rose to within a couple fathoms of our keel, then resuming speed as it fell away and we left the bar behind us.

It was a thrilling arrival to our home base, but one which, through the days and months ahead, was to become so familiar and commonplace we could carry it out with impunity whether daylight or dark, in weather fair or foul, and lugging up to three whales at a time along with us. On this occasion there was no time to look around; the station's freight had to be unloaded, the coal on deck shovelled into our bunkers, and the ship got ready for whaling. Finn John had us working the moment the lines were made fast, and by noon the hold was empty of freight, and the decks cleared of coal and washed down. Under the eagle eye of the mate, Joe and Johnny spliced the foregoer into our number one line and coiled it down on the line pan under the muzzle of our whaling gun. Roy and I, as novices, were given less demanding jobs that allowed us the opportunity to watch this procedure, one that was to become second nature to us as we became proficient as whalers.

Finally the moment came to load the gun, and Johnny brought up a charge of powder from the kegs lashed in the hold. All other work stopped as Finn John took over the job, explaining to all of us the dos and don'ts, illustrating the don'ts in graphic language that shook me to the core and created a determination never to take my job, especially this one, lightly.

First, he ran the swab in the full length of the bore to prove it clear and, if on a quick reload, free of any spark or ember which could pre-ignite the powder charge. Then, as we tipped up the muzzle, he poured in the powder and inserted an oakum plug which he rammed firmly home by using the wooden handle of the swab. From the harpoon rack in the hold, Roy and I unlashed a barbless lance and lugged it up to the gun platform. This was a standard harpoon, complete with bomb tip, that had its flukes or barbs removed so that it would not make fast to the whale and could be withdrawn for a second shot, if necessary. It was actually just a bomb carrier for killing a stubborn whale.

Sliding the wire shackle up the slot in the harpoon's long shaft, he shoved the shaft all the way down into the gun's bore and lashed the harpoon head in place with rope yarn around the front sight. Then, greasing the threads on the forward end of the knuckle, he screwed on

Gun on whaler Brown. *Note rubber block shock absorbers.*

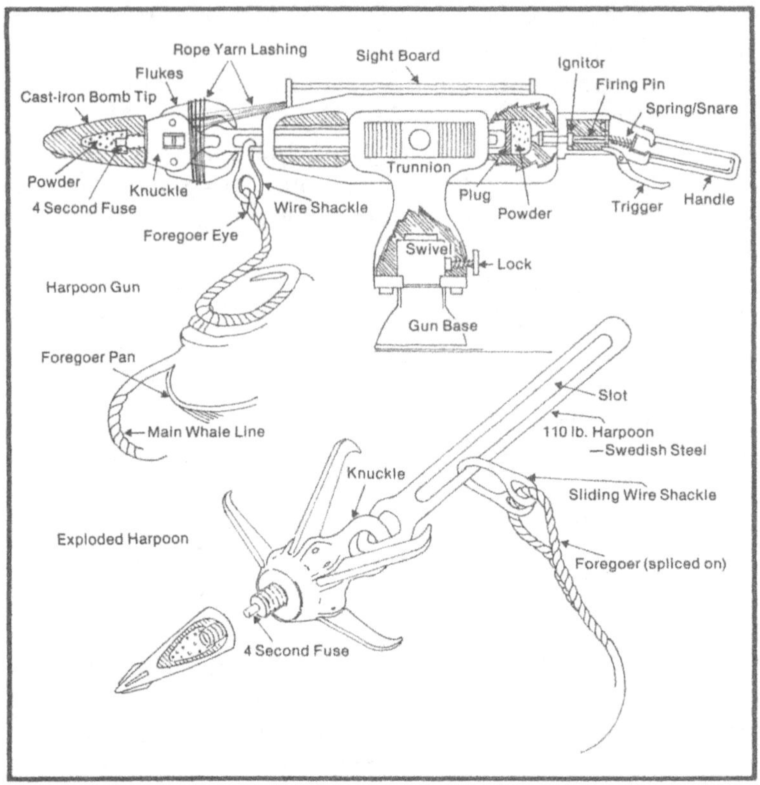

an unarmed and empty bomb tip. The foregoer line was spliced through the eye of the wire shackle, and the gun, with the harpoon poking menacingly out of its muzzle, was swung round to face forward. When all was in readiness, Roy and I, who had been told to fetch the watchman's small skiff, were given a wooden butter box and directed to take it out in the harbour a quarter of a cable or so.

We rowed out, conscious of the loaded gun and its deadly missile aimed our way, and, on signal from the captain, dropped the box in the water and quickly rowed towards the ship. Once we were clear of the gun's discharge, Louis took a brass igniter cartridge from his coat pocket, inserted it in the breech firing block, swung the muzzle towards the bobbing butter box, and elevated the snout to carry the flight of the harpoon onto the target. While he carefully checked and double-checked his range and the sights of the gun, we waited with

Captain Larsen at the harpoon gun on the St. Lawrence. *Photo taken in the Gulf of Georgia in 1908.*

bated breath to see the actual effect of cannon and harpoon—a whale's eye view of what a whaling ship looked like.

A flash of fire and black smoke, followed instantly by the solid thump of an explosion, ruffled the water's surface ahead of the gun. A second later the harpoon appeared out of the black smoke with its foregoer trailing behind it. Like a massive spear it arched up to the crest of its trajectory before curving downwards to the bobbing, innocent box. It landed dead centre, throwing splinters of waxed wood outward, almost reaching us in our little boat.

A cheer went up from the onlookers, and Louis gave a rare grin, slapping the breech affectionately as he spoke unheard words of approval to Finn John, who was standing below him on the foredeck. The fun over, we retrieved the harpoon, swabbed out the bore, and reloaded the gun for real. Roy and I were told off to carry out the whole procedure. This time a fluked harpoon was loaded, and the bomb tip filled with powder and fused. This harpoon would take our first whale, and Finn John made sure we did everything perfectly, including smearing the threads and sealing the bomb joint with grease to make it waterproof. We were severely criticized for our uncertain fumbles. It took us about fifteen minutes to make the short eye-splice in the foregoer. In the days ahead we would learn to do the whole reload, including the splicing and lashing, in less than ten minutes. We readied the number two line, proved out the winding windlass, and laid out and sharpened the whaling tools before supper, and in the evening we made up more wire shackles, cut rope yarns for lashing, and laid out our whale-towing gear of chains, wire, and sliphooks.

Advised we would sail at 3 a.m., Roy and I slipped into our bunks for the first rest since the evening before, agreeing to split our three-hour dock watch so we each got an extra hour and a half's rest. This was standard procedure aboard the whalers; there was always a deck watch kept at sea, at anchor, or tied up in port, but only one seaman was required to stand it unless we were under way, so we would split the hours of duty and use the balance of the watch for make and mend, or for rest.

I stood the last trick of our dock watch, and shortly after 2 a.m., with fresh coffee simmering on the stove, I gave Willie a shake. This shaking had to be carried out with caution, for Willie was a heavy sleeper who invariably threw out his huge arms from the bunk, seeking to grasp his tormentor and stifle him. Shrugging into pants and boots, he came stumbling back with me, took the lantern I had filled, trimmed, and lit, and descended like a grumpy bear into the blackness of the stokehold. Soon the sound of the slice bar breaking up the banked fires, and the shovel scraping up coal off the steel plates to brighten the thin layer of hot coals in the furnaces, echoed through the silent steel ship.

Smoke rose from our tall funnel, and steam began to hiss through the pipes as Willie opened the boiler stop valves, for only alongside the dock were these valves ever closed. After lighting and hoisting our mast light, I gave Roy a shake, then went aft to light our stern lantern and call the second engineer and mate. While I lit the port and starboard side lights and the binnacle lamp, Paddy Egan came forward through the engine room, opening the drains on the main engine and cracking live steam into the cylinders to warm them up. Checking the boiler water level, he paused to see how Willie was making out in the stokehold.

By the time I reentered the galley, they were all there grabbing a cup of coffee and a slice of Lee's fresh bread. Refilling his coffee cup, Paddy returned to the engine room where he cracked the main throttle and rocked the engine back and forth, clearing the cylinders of condensate, before letting her roll slowly over. Roy and I followed Finn John, with his trusty five-cell flashlight, for a quick inspection of the deck, battening down the hatch cover and checking the gun lock en route. He ordered me up on the dock to let go our lines, then ascended the bridge ladder and rang down "Stand-by" on the telegraph.

From the elevation of the dock, the harbour looked serenely calm, its ebony surface mirroring the stars, but I had little time to reflect on its beauty as, skirting the huge pile of coal that reached to the bullrail, I let go our stern and bow lines. Breaking the stern away from the shoaling water that stretched out to the south of the dock by steaming slow ahead on the spring line, Finn John ordered this line taken in, and rang for "Slow astern" as he put the helm hard-a-starboard.

Quickly dropping the eye of the line to Roy, I flung myself over the edge of the dock onto the old, bent, steel ladder that led down to the bumper log, and hung there as the ship slipped by me. Gauging the distance across to her, I leaped for the gunwale, my long arms stretching out to bridge the gap as my fingers clawed at the ratlines for a secure grip, for I was determined not to be left behind.

As we cleared the harbour, Roy brought up coffee to the bridge for each of us, and Finn John, chuckling at our youthful impatient enthusiasm to reach the whaling grounds, spoke of catching whales in the waters through which we passed, and of other interesting sights his old eyes had seen. It was a memorable moment, the sea so calm and serene that even the fresh night air seemed to taste of that tang of adventure. Seagulls, ducks, and sea parrots took noisily to wing as we

Bridge of whaler Brown *in 1941. Left to right: Finn John, Roy Gustavson, Louis Larsen.*

approached, and as morning light exposed the headland and horizons, numerous white salmon trollers, glistening wetly, came into view. By the time North (Langara) Island had opened up to give us a heading into Parry Passage, Lee had prepared breakfast, and the watch had been called.

Roy and I ate our breakfast quickly and were back on deck as we cleared the passage and stood out to sea. Johnny took the first trick aloft in the barrel, and the excitement of officially being on the hunt deterred us from our bunks for another hour, till Louis gruffly ordered us to get our rest. He said if whales were sighted we'd have lots of time to get on deck, and we'd be glad, by the time it was over, that we got the rest we should be getting now. It is a lesson every seaman must follow to survive the rigors of his life: make and mend, or rest, should never be neglected. Emergencies are better met if you and the ship are in good order.

Nothing happened to break the tranquillity of the ship's easy passage through the morning watch, and at noon I made my way up the rigging to take my first turn in the barrel. The climb up the ratlines as the ship gently rolled can only be appreciated by one who has experienced the increasing arc of the mast's swing the higher one goes. I was sweating profusely from the strain of holding on as the ship rolled outboard, and tumbled gratefully, head foremost, into the barrel. I didn't give a damn how silly it looked to those on the bridge, but in the back of my mind, as I gazed timidly over the edge, was the worrisome thought—how was I to get down?

Soon I was climbing up there single-handed, holding a cup of coffee in my free hand and a sea biscuit in my teeth, but that was still a few weeks away, and now my eyes grew bleary from searching the horizon for the elusive blow of a whale. The hours dragged by with a dreariness that sapped my keenness, and I tried to keep alert by going over and over Finn John's instructions about our job when a whale was caught. The long suspense eroded my confidence. I prayed for an early baptism so I could settle these terrible unknowns ahead of me.

Finn John's hail to come down and take over the wheel broke into my thoughts, and I quickly cast one last searching glance around. My heart gave a leap, and I rubbed my suddenly watering eyes, to concentrate more intently on a spot far out on the ocean, where a white puff was rapidly evaporating from sight amongst the afternoon whitecaps. After what seemed a hundred heart beats, a tall cloud of vapour rose from between the waves. I checked the ship's wake to make sure we were holding a steady course, then figured the angle on the bow and approximate distance to the blow, all the time counting off the seconds till it would blow again. I wanted to scream out my sighting, but I also wanted to identify the whale and the direction it was headed. My nails dug into the weathered top of the wooden barrel as I strained to wait just a little longer. Then my gamble paid off; there was no doubt the tall, narrow blow belonged to a large Finback whale—this time the long, low back of the whale rose into sight.

"Whale, ho! Four points on the starboard bow!" my voice screeched off-key as I flung my arm outwards to indicate the bearing. "About fifteen to twenty cables. A Finback, I think," I called down, answering Finn John's hail for more information as he raised his binoculars to check my sighting.

As the whale blew again, Finn John reached behind him and gave a double ring on the telegraph, and, without removing the glass from his eyes, told Roy to bring her four points to starboard. As we came up to full hunting speed, and the ship rolled as Roy heeled her quickly onto the new heading, everyone came tumbling out on deck. Black smoke billowed from our funnel as Willie shovelled coal on the fires, and the ship began to vibrate and pound as she drove into the light northwest swell. The skipper climbed up to the bridge, scanned the horizon with his binoculars, then called up to me to keep a sharp lookout and report any change in the whale's apparent course.

Alerted by our threshing propeller and pounding forefoot, the whale changed its course and began to run. Our spooked whale made frantic shallow dives, trying to evade and outrun our ever-closing fearful presence, and it took over half an hour to get into a firing position.

Following the swirls that rose to the surface as the broad flukes of his tail moved up and down, I could, from my vantage point high above the gun platform, keep the skipper informed of his progress, while he, with his years of whaling experience, plotted the probable point for the whale to surface for his next blow to charge his exhausted lungs. Louis Larsen had an uncanny ability to outwit any whale's plan to escape, and we never lost a whale once he was sighted. This first time was a good example of his talent, and we arrived at the exact point as the whale surfaced to blow.

That moment is etched forever on my memory, for it was both terrifying and majestic. It filled me with awe for the great creature we had hunted, and mortified me with humiliation when I witnessed the horror of our killing ways for the first time. Later, as our skills became more keen and I hardened to the job of hunting and dispatching whales, these feelings could be submerged and ignored in the necessary routines of the job which was earning me a living.

As we followed our first whale (and, ironically, the largest whale caught that season), I could see the swirls getting closer together, the whale's line of progress slightly divergent from ours. On report of this, Louis ordered the engines stopped and the helm altered to bring us in on a converging course, while calling back for no noise aboard the ship. We held our breath as the ship ghosted ahead, and the unsuspecting whale rose towards the surface.

Quite suddenly, through the murky dark green of the water, I saw a vague shape materializing. I called down a bearing and watched, almost hypnotized, as the vagueness took on solid outline, and the vast size of the creature became apparent. It was nearly as big as our ship! I suddenly became conscious of the puniness of man and his tools. Louis Larsen and the fearful gun he now turned on the whale as it pushed towards the surface looked incapable of either taking or holding that whale. The size and power of the beast was such that he could have easily rammed and sunk us, if of a mind to.

The whale's snout broke the surface, and he blew a tall spout of vapour. As his head cleared the water and he inhaled noisily through his blow hole, Louis called back for full speed ahead. The sudden noise as we got underway startled the whale, and he gave a frantic spurt forward, arching his back above the water as he plunged his head downwards to dive.

That was the reaction the skipper had been waiting for. The gun roared black smoke and flame, and our harpoon arched out of it to land with a wet smack on the exposed flank of the whale, right below his dorsal fin and just at his waterline. Hardly had the shaft of the harpoon buried itself in the whale's side when it was blown backwards by the bombtip explosion, and the outward sprung flukes of the harpoon anchored themselves firmly in the whale.

The whole side of the whale was bulged outwards by the force of that terrible internal explosion, and for a split second the whale froze in shock, his recent breath literally knocked out of him in a gigantic spout that terminated with a pink froth foaming from the blowhole. This was usually the death knell of any whale, for we had hit his lungs and he would drown in his own blood. In the weeks and months to come I would see many whales, hit as this one was, die without taking any mainline out of the locker.

This large Finback, almost the size of a full-grown Blue, was not an ordinary whale, and was certainly not ready to give up yet. His flukes lashed the water to a foam as, recovering from his shock, he swam his most desperate race for freedom. His sudden acceleration stretched the foregoer out taut, and as the mainline began to run out, the mast and barrel in which I crouched began to vibrate in a most alarming manner. Our twelve-knot vessel was outrun by our harpooned whale, and the drag of the whale line began to burn the brake blocks on the drums of the screaming windlass.

Finn John dashed down to release the brake, Johnny was ordered up to the bridge to take over from Roy, and I was ordered down from the barrel. To this day I can not remember how I got down to the deck; all I recall is that, when I got there, Roy was just getting there from the bridge, and Joe had started to get our number two line's foregoer coiled down on the pan. Under the urgent direction of the skipper, Roy and I loaded the gun with lance and bomb, then spliced in the foregoer, as Joe lashed the coils down on the pan with rope yarn. As this was going on, Johnny was following the skipper's commands to steer for a position to starboard of the widely veering wake of our whale, and Finn John, gauging the strain on our mast and gear, was snubbing the run-out of mainline.

It was a tense game of attrition, not unlike that played by the sports fisherman who suddenly snags the giant fish of his dreams on his light tackle. Our problem was to hold onto a seventy-eight ton whale that was dragging our hundred ton vessel behind it on a manila rope that had a breaking strain of less than twelve tons.

Fifteen minutes later, his blows dark pink with foaming blood, our whale slowed his pace across the surface of the choppy seas, and our own way carried us forward into the slack of the whale line. Joe opened the throttle of the steam windlass as Finn John, at his elbow, relayed the skipper's order to "heave in the slack." Roy and I were ordered below to coil in the line. This was the most fearful and dangerous part of whaling.

We were in the dark line locker, coiling the rope, as it came down, into layers of kink-free and loop-free tiers, continuing until the whale was heaved in close enough for our second harpoon. If the whale tried to free itself with a frantic run away from the ship, the call to clear the line locker would be shouted down the hausepipe and the mate would engage the brake to slow the run of rope, while we ducked the flying loops of heavy wet rope and jumped clear of the locker. Finn John had already cautioned us of the hazards, with graphic accounts of men who had lost limb or life when legs or heads had been suddenly embraced by a flying loop of rope moving at a speed that often exceeded 1500 feet per minute. It all lent a certain youthful alacrity to my long legs, and an equal amount to Roy's shorter ones.

Both line lockers were approximately nine feet square, constructed of heavy timber, and fitted with slots between them to assist

Depressing for a kill shot with the whale up short on Number 2 line.

circulation and drying of the whale line between usages. Placed side by side, athwartships on the planked floor of the hold, they backed against the forward bulkhead of the coal bunker. When the lockers were filled with over four feet of rope, tiered one layer above the other to accommodate our 3000 foot whale line, there was only crouching room left for us. Steam and water poured down the hausepipe upon us, and the thunder of the big-engined windlass, inches away on the steel deck above our heads, gave the place the look, feel, and smell of Dante's inferno.

Though there was no way for us to tell what was happening outside, our nervous fear and anxious ears caused us to scramble for the narrow exit several times before the gruff hail of the mate warned us to jump clear. Three times we hauled in the line, and twice our whale pulled much of it out again. Then, finally, the call to come on deck brought us up to watch the end of our valiant whale.

The Finback was close ahead of the ship, just the length of the foregoer, when Roy and I, perspiring freely from our efforts, sprang into the ratlines to better view the gory end. At near full speed we sheered to starboard across the whale's tail, pulling him over on his side, then, just as swiftly, we veered back across his tail again, running the slack of the line. Louis Larsen called for "Stop" on the engines, and swung the gun towards the exposed side of the spent whale.

The tremendous explosion and discharge of the gun hid the final moments from our eyes, but when the smoke cleared, the whale lay

The Brown's *first whale of the 1941 season, a 70-foot female Finback.*

dead, the waters around it red with blood. Only then, as we looked sheepishly around at each other, did we notice the blood and foam that had blown back over the forepart of the ship and over us. I think I would have been sick then, but Finn John's voice roared in my ears, and we concentrated on the job of bringing the whale alongside.

Hauling in the foregoer, we brought the ship close to the whale. After throwing a weighted heaving line over its tail, and retrieving it from the underside with a pikepole, we were able to pass a long heavy wire around the tail, and this, when led to the nigger head, pulled a heavy chain around after it. This was drawn up snug, the foregoer line was cut from the harpoon with the long wooden-handled spade iron, and Louis came slow ahead on the engines while turning the ship to starboard. This caused the whale to roll over and slip alongside, and heaving in again on the chain lifted the tail up out of the water and brought it tight against the fairlead in the gunwale.

Under Finn John's guidance, Roy and I plunged the air lance down into the exposed abdomen, and held it there while the engine room compressor pumped air into the cavity to give buoyancy to the carcass. Taking the sharp spade iron, Joe chiselled off the tail flukes, then, changing to a piercing iron, he neatly cut a hole in the stub through which the tie-up line at the whale float could be fastened. To complete the job, he carefully cut our mark of three notches in the stub so we would be credited with this kill and entitled to our first whale bonus—a whole four dollars a man!

After reversing the windlass to back out the length of foregoer to be coiled down on the pan and spliced, Joe went to supper and Finn John took over the bridge so the skipper could do likewise. While he and Johnny swung the ship back towards North Island and Naden Harbour, Roy and I set about the tasks of loading the gun and making the ship ready to take whale again. Should a whale be sighted, even at this late hour, we'd mark our whale with buoy and lantern, drop it, and be off after the blow in less than five minutes.

Chapter Three

The Way It Was

For Roy and I, the taking of our first whale meant the end of our unsure suspense. We had been tried and were not found wanting in our new role of whalers. Tired, but justly proud of this fact, we fished up the tie-up line during the middle of our night watch, as Finn John manoeuvered the *Brown* carefully alongside the whale float at Naden Harbour. Tying the line through the hole Joe had cut in the stub of the whale's tail, we knocked back the link on the chain's slip-ring, and our whale splashed its tail in the water for the last time as we backed away.

When we were tied up at the wharf a few minutes later, the mate walked up to the general store to enter the ship's kill in the watchman's ledger and get the cook's shopping list filled, and we began taking on bunkers. Willie joined us for a few minutes after the chute was in place and manhole covers removed, yet in those few moments of generosity he shovelled as much coal, if not more, than Roy and I did in total.

He was like a ballet dancer, his brawny body dipped and swung in flowing, seemingly effortless motion, while his huge feet remained solidly planted between the coal pile and the coal chute at the dock edge. There was not a wasted effort nor pause in his motion, the shovel was heaping full each swing, and the cascade of coal down the chute was almost continuous. It was a metered motion without flaw, an example by a master stoker, and he grinned happily after giving us our lesson, then hurried back aboard to fire his boiler.

The few tons required were soon aboard, and that distasteful job behind us, but it was a job that had to be carried out every trip into the station. No matter the weather or the haste, coal and water, supplemented by groceries and supplies, were always taken aboard at the station.

Before daylight we were on our way again, and my afternoon watch was spent, in part, up in the barrel, looking for whales. We stayed at sea most of the time, hunting whales through the daylight hours, and laying-to with banked fires during the darkened ones. We stood our watches, then rested during the hours of our off-watch, a routine that was only broken by bad weather, the catching of a whale, or a call at the station for coal and supplies. If the weather turned extremely bad, we might run for shelter to Port Louis on the west coast of Graham Island, or lay-to at Egeria Bay in the lee of North Island. If the weather gave indication of settling in for awhile, Roy and I would sometimes be allowed to go ashore and shoot a deer or bear for fresh meat. Roy was a very good shot with the mate's 30-30, and our quickest kill took ten minutes from the time we stepped ashore till we lugged a dressed deer back to the pram—a lovely, small four-pointer at that.

Food was always uppermost in our minds. The meat, when it did arrive and we finally got it aboard ship, was often blue or purple with age, and even large lacings of Lee's garlic could not hide the signs that it was turning bad. To replace it, we hunted game, bartered coal for fresh halibut and cod from the fishermen, and fished for flounder and sole whenever at anchor. We used heavy cod line and a jig we fashioned by pouring melted lead into a boxwood mould in which we had fixed a large treble hook and a soft wire eye.

Fruits and vegetables, when they arrived—and this was not only subject to the distance they had to be freighted by vessels without benefit of refrigeration, but also by the delays that adverse weather could cause—were often dried and wizened by the time Lee reached the bottom of the fresh vegetable locker that stood out on the weather quarter. Staples such as salt beef and pork were stored in wooden barrels in the hold, and canned goods were kept in the small starboard locker.

Lee's fresh bread and buns, when weather and supplies allowed, were our only luxuries; pies, cakes, or cookies were unheard of. Roy and I satisfied our sweet tooth by going in debt at the company store for candy—Pep-Chew toffee bars mostly, because the sweet chewiness lasted so long and gave such comfort during our cold watches aloft or on the bridge.

Other than the galley and messroom, there was no shelter on deck, and there were few comforts below deck except for our bunks. We bathed our bodies and washed our clothes on the open deck. A small steam jet was fitted at the fidley, and fresh water was only allowed for soaping up; salt water had to be used for rinsing ourselves or our clothes. Often we preferred to sit out on the hatch or fidley to sew and mend our gear, for the only source of light aboard these ships were coal oil lamps, and even in bright sunlight it was gloomy below decks.

The *Brown* had taken a dozen whales that late spring of 1941—mostly Fins and Humps, as the Sperm had not yet arrived in our area—when one of my teeth began to throb with infection. They were notoriously poor teeth, and my supplement of Pep-Chew toffee bars hadn't done them any good. My face became so swollen that my lips could no longer close. Medical facilities were very limited on the islands, even in those days, so at the first opportunity I was ferried over to the small fishing village of Masset to see the local doctor.

By 10:00 that morning I was sitting tensely on a hardwood chair in his dining room while he probed my mouth with a stubby, nicotine-flavoured finger, pawed through a faded canvas folder of extractors and chisels, and selected a tarnished, wicked-looking pair to perform the surgery. I opened my mouth and he clamped on the tooth, no form of pain reliever had been offered, and pinwheels of flame exploded behind my eyes as he twisted and grunted to loosen the roots of that damn tooth. Bone cracked and blood spurted from my mouth as he dragged me and the chair across the highly polished floor.

Finally, when I knew I could take no more of that torture, I grabbed his hands and, with a vile curse, jerked back my head. He fell down on the floor on one side of the chair, and I fell over onto the other side. Wiping my hands with a large soiled pocket handkerchief, and stuffing much of it in my mouth to stay the bleeding, I helped him back up so he could examine my wound. He said there was no infection in the gum and that it would all heal up in time, then charged me a dollar for his services and led me to his kitchen door, where he bid me farewell.

I wandered around the streets and pathways of Masset, spitting blood and pieces of bone out every few feet of the way, while pain throbbed in my head and my stomach churned. Unaware of when the ship would call for me, and unable to eat anything, I realized I could not stay on my feet much longer and booked a room at the small hotel, where I threw myself down on the bed in a faint.

When I awoke it was dark and not a sound could be heard. I knew I was very weak; my heart was beating with a skipping, fluttering sensation, and lifting my head caused bursts of light to explode behind my eyes. I explored a sticky pool of fluid that lay in the hollow of the bed against my body. Even in the dark I knew it was blood and realized I had to get back to that old doctor and stop the bleeding before I closed my eyes again. I didn't turn on the lights; I'm not sure if I knew where one was. I just rolled off the bed, crawled till I found the door, and, pulling myself to my feet, slipped out into the hallway where a dim nightlight burned.

The sight of my clothes and arms soaked in blood gave desperate strength to my sagging limbs, and I stumbled down the stairs and out into the dark to find the pathway to the doctor's house. It took him a few minutes to answer my pounding on his kitchen door, and when he finally opened it, I fell inside onto the cool floor. I'll say this for him; he knew who I was and what he had to do, and wasted no words as he got about it. Within seconds he was back with his medical bag and, kneeling beside me, packed cotton into the spurting hole in my jawbone. Then he brought a basin of water and a cloth, and bathed my face and hands, saying very little. I said less, while the coolness of the floor calmed my fluttering heart and the doctor came into proper focus in my gaze.

After about fifteen minutes, he shoved a roll of blanket behind my shoulders and head so I could lie on my side, then offered me a small glass of liquid that smelt like medicine but burnt like liquor. Soon I was feeling much better, so he offered me one of his hand-rolled cigarettes. While we smoked, he told of how long he had been the only doctor here on the islands, and how his son had followed him into the medical profession. He apologized then for the discomfort I had suffered, explaining that a proper dentist now visited the islands on regular occasions, so few people ever called on him to remove teeth anymore.

For over an hour I lay there, gathering back my strength, while he told stories of the area, including one about a whaler who had been shot. A steam whistle wailed, faintly at first, then again more loudly as the ship drew near, and I knew it was the *Brown*. The old doctor walked me to the street and saw me on the right way down to the dock. I don't recall getting aboard the whaler, but I do remember trying to drink a cup of coffee after reaching the galley, only to have it run down my face and drip into my lap. But I was young, and, after a couple hours of rest, was back up standing my watch as though nothing had ever happened.

During those first few weeks the weather was foul, and the whales few. We ran north along the coast of Alaska, laying-to some nights so close to the capes that we could hear the wolves howling onshore. When storms drove us to anchor, and slashing rains made deck work miserable, we would retreat to the hold to mend gear, season harpoons, or splice lines. Often during these quiet moments, Finn John would entertain us with stories about whaling or sailing, for he had come off a big, four-masted, square rigger to join the whaling company.

I recall two incidents he enjoyed telling. One was the story of the *Black*'s harpoon, which ricocheted back off a whale's tail and struck the ship's mast below the hounds band, dropping it and the man in the barrel into the sea. The other was of the *Orion*, whose gunner, after a long unsuccessful chase of a whale, had left his primed gun insecurely locked while he returned to the bridge with a hot cup of coffee to look for more whales. The weather turned extremely rough, and they hauled round to run before it. In doing so, the ship rolled violently in the trough, and the heavy gun slipped its lock and swung round till it faced the men on the bridge. At that precise moment, the foregoer line brushed the trigger lever and the gun discharged, throwing the harpoon aft, just clear of the mast. The men on her bridge were appalled to see the live harpoon hurl through the bridge railing between them, clear the steering wheel, bounce off the railing, and crash through the funnel, before the tangled foregoer halted its flight directly above the engine room skylight, where the bomb tip exploded, showering the ship with shrapnel. The only man injured in that melee was the engineer who, according to Finn John, tried to duck behind the main steam pipe to avoid a ricocheting piece of bomb iron that had shot down into the engine room, breaking the boiler gauge glass. The steam and boiling water, escaping up through the gratings where the engineer crouched, burnt his legs.

Roy and I, in that spring of 1941, were, of course, completely ignorant of any of the history of the whaling company we had suddenly become part of, and of the people we would come to know. Because of this, we didn't understand many of the things we saw and many of the stories we heard. In fact, it was years later before my studies and research for these notes brought appreciation of the events of that summer. I will get back to our own experiences, and many more of the oldtimers' stories, but in order that they can be best comprehended, it would be well to investigate some of that historical background.

The first whalers on the west coast were the Indians of Vancouver Island and Cape Flattery. Stalking the huge mammals in frail wooden dugouts, they used techniques remarkably similar to those of the white men who followed. Spears, thrown by hand at close quarters, lodged detachable heads in the whale's flesh. Attached to the spearheads were floats made of inflated sealskins which dragged behind the fleeing beast, slowing his progress. As the whale became exhausted, more floats would be added until it could go no further, whereupon it would be killed with a lance and towed to shore for butchering. Although the natives pursued the hunt steadily during the migration season, their toll on the stocks was minimal. A good hunter might take fewer than a dozen in his entire career.

American whalers rounded the Horn in 1792 and found Sperm

Archie Seymour, native of Alert Bay, BC, age 25 years. He was a member of the Indian whaling crew which caught this Sei whale in 1905.

whales abounding in the Pacific ocean. British whalers, when they finally arrived in the Pacific, concentrated their efforts on the Southern Right whale of the Antipodes. By 1809 the whalers of New Bedford and Nantucket were hunting Sperm whales in west coast waters, stretching their supply lines to the limit. By 1834 there were so many of Captain Ahab's tribe prowling the waters off Vancouver Island that Hudson's Bay Company governor Sir George Simpson began laying plans to establish a profitable provisioning trade, but it never transpired.

The establishment of the first shore-based station on the west coast is credited to Captain J.P. Davenport, who began taking Gray whales on the lower California coast in 1854. The Gray whale, a tough little kelp crawler, returned from his arctic feeding grounds each fall, fat with blubber, to breed and calve in the warm water bays and lagoons of lower California before returning to northern waters in the spring.

Captain Melville Scammon had discovered these breeding grounds in the Baja area of the California peninsula a few years before, but

Carmel Bay whaling station, California, from 1861 to 1884 at Point Lobos, the site of a present-day abalone cannery.

managed to keep the exact location a secret for a score of years. Unable to follow Scammon into this remote and difficult area, pelagic whalers were forced by declining Sperm whaling to concentrate on the lower migratory route. Their activities attracted those farming ashore to set up lookout towers to alert them to the passing of whales.

The success of Captain Davenport's company of shore-based whalers caused many others to follow suit, and within a few years over a dozen of these stations dotted the rugged coast line. The operation of these early shore-based stations is interesting. From April to September, while the majority of the crews engaged in farming, a lookout was posted for whales. On signal of a whale being sighted, the whalers would drop their tools and launch their boats to give chase. From October to March, while Gray whales were in these southerly waters, whalers spent all the daylight hours, weather permitting, in whaleboats at a distance of eight to ten miles offshore. The lookout tower and flag pole were located on a prominent headland, and messages were conveyed to the whaling crews at sea by positioning the flag in a prearranged code. The whaleboat crew would raise or lower the sail, or slowly turn the boat, to convey a message back to shore.

Powered by sail and oars, these boats carried a crew of six to eight men. The crew's method of whaling was to make fast to the whale with a harpoon fitted with a special long, light line that was coiled down in tubs within the boat. Snubbing the line around a towing post in the boat, they created a drag that eventually tired the whale so they could pull themselves close to it again. Then they would pierce the lungs or heart with a long, slender, steel-tipped lance. The whale often managed one more desperate dash for freedom, and the whaleboat would be towed along behind, the crew soaked by the blood-stained foam and spray blowing back over it. Eventually the weakened and tired whale would be given the coup-de-grace by the boat captain, and would then be towed back to the shore, to the flensing deck, rendering pots, and settling tanks.

This new method of hunting, coupled with the discovery of Scammon's Baja lagoons, so decimated the Gray whale herds that most shore operations simply folded up. Captain Thomas Welcome Roys' discovery of the Arctic Bowhead attracted the reduced American Sperm whaling fleet, and signalled the end of Gray whaling.

Meanwhile, Captain Abel Douglass had come north to the gold capital of British Columbia, where in 1869 he joined forces with James Dawson of Victoria to take whales in Saanich Inlet, using the schooner *Kate*. Captain Roys appeared on the scene, determined to invest the fortune he had amassed from Bowhead whaling in perfecting a harpoon gun for taking the larger Rorquals, the Finback and Blue whales. He planned to practise on the smaller and more easily stalked Humpback whale, which was known to abound in the confined tidal waters. The failure of his weapon drained Roys' fortunes and his health, and he died of yellow fever less than ten years later, a broken and dispirited man in the Mexican sea port of Mazatlan.

The fortunes of Douglass and Dawson fared hardly better. After creating a station at Whaletown on Cortez Island, and later moving it to Whaling Station Bay on Hornby Island, they joined forces with the Lipsett Whaling Company, which had equipment and housing at Pasley Island and Tunstall Bay respectively, to form the British Columbia Whaling Company. By this time, four whaling ventures were at work in the area of Yellow Rock at the south end of Denman Island. They depleted the Humpback stock and, shortly thereafter, all these ventures failed, as did Captain E.J. Fader's operation at Blubber Bay fifteen years later.

The vagaries of the Humpback's migratory route to this coast, after leaving its breeding and nursing grounds around the Sandwich Islands, was subject to many whims of nature, and the large numbers of Humpbacks that had been observed in these sheltered waters were families of whales which remained in the area for only a few years, and so could not sustain any concentrated effort in reducing their numbers. It was a lesson that Dr. Ludvic Rissmuller should have noted before he proposed the building of a whaling station at Page's Lagoon, just north of Nanaimo, thirty years later.

When the Norwegian inventor Sven Foyn (who had examined Roys' experimental gun) finally perfected a harpoon gun and a fast, steam-powered whaling ship for taking the larger and swifter Finback and Blue whales, he opened up a new, almost surefire method of harvesting the large group of migrating whales that had been noted for years off the west coast of Vancouver Island by the sealing men of the area. Ironically, on this coast at least, it was the familiar small coast-crawler, the cavorting and playful Humpback whale, which felt the first sting of these new craft, and it wasn't till Kyuquot station was built near Cape Cook that the Blue whale's migratory routes came within cruising range of our shore-based steam whaling vessels.

With the inventions of Dr. Rissmuller and others, shore-based processing plants could render and process the complete whale into oils and meal, which were easily transported by ship to the markets of the world. The isolation of this remote western area, a difficulty that had plagued the development of its whaling industry, was overcome, and set in motion what might be called the golden age of whaling in the northwest.

It was the tail end of this second-to-last phase of Canadian whaling that I was privileged to see first hand. It began back in 1904, when Captains Sprott Balcom and William Grant, who owned a number of large sealing schooners and the Victoria Sealing Company, created the Canadian Pacific Whaling Company, and laid plans to build a station on the west coast of Vancouver Island. Of all the colourful sealing masters and shipowners in Victoria, these two were acknowledged to be without peer. Their derring-do had been noted by the Victoria *Colonist* for years, and they had good sound connections with both the seafaring people and those in business and marine commerce.

Sprott's brother Ruben was sent to Norway to oversee the building of their whaling steamer *Orion*. Charles Smith, S.C. Ruck, and Bill Scaplen were brought out from Newfoundland, where over fourteen whaling stations using Sven Foyn's harpoon cannon and equipment had already been built, to construct a whaling station on Pipestem Inlet in Barkley Sound. This station soon became known as Sechart.

In 1905 Sechart began operations, processing over three hundred whales supplied by the *Orion* under command of Ruben's son Willis, who had sailed her out from Norway that spring. While whale landings had been highly successful, the processing of them was not, and Dr. Ludvic Rissmuller, inventor and supplier of much of the processing equipment, was invited out to rectify the problem.

His observations of the whaling prospects on this coast prompted him to join forces with the fledgling Canadian Pacific Whaling Company. One of his better decisions was to form the American Pacific Whaling Company, an affiliate of CPW, in Washington state. The APW eventually became the largest whaling company on the Pacific coast, swallowing up its parent company in the process.

This was much later, however, and the results of the 1906 season were so encouraging that more whaling ships were sought by the Canadian Pacific Whaling Company, and two new stations planned. One was near Departure Bay, which Dr. Rissmuller proposed; the other at Kyuquot sound, north of the Sechart station, proposed by Sprott Balcom. This one became known as Cachalot, and during its short, fifteen-year lifetime it landed the most whales and witnessed the most interesting experiences of any whaling stations on this coast, a rewarding tribute to the insight of Captain Sprott Balcom.

To supply these stations with whales, three older-type steamers were purchased from the declining whalery in Newfoundland. First to arrive was the *St. Lawrence*, which opened the winter season in the Georgia Straits by lugging three large Humpback whales into Page's Lagoon. In the spring, the *Germania* and *Sebastian*, the latter destined to become the oldest active whaling ship on the coast, sailed with the *Orion* for Sechart and Kyuquot stations.

With the continued decline in sealing, and the hardships caused the Canadian schooners by sealing agreements between Russia, Japan, and the United States, it wasn't difficult to entice sealing masters to leave their wind ships for command of these whaling steamers. Their share of the catch earned them princely returns, far above that enjoyed by the lordly masters of the new fleet of luxury passenger steamers, then beginning to ply the coast.

During the next two years, whaling profits grew to such magnificent proportions that expansion of Canadian Pacific Whaling was planned to spread further north, and even south of the border, into Washington. Sprott Balcom's view lay northward and, forming the Queen Charlotte Whaling Company, he sailed with Captain G.A. Huff of Alberni to these northern offshore islands to select a station site. On Kunghit Island, north of Cape St. James, they secured a grant of land for a station that was to be named—of all things—Rose Harbour! The name had nothing to do with whaling or the station

Sechart, in Barkley Sound, BC, about 1930. The first whaling station on BC coast (1905–1917); converted to herring reduction plant before being abandoned.

Cachalot whaling station at Kyuquot, BC. CPR steamer Tees *is loading barrels of whale oil, 1910.*

built there, but referred to the 18th century British MP George Rose, who had supported the voyage of discovery to this coast, undertaken by the snow *Queen Charlotte*, for whom the islands had been named. The whalemen also included a visit to the placid sheltered bay of Naden Harbour, and made tentative plans for a second station to be built there at a later date.

Dr. Rissmuller, meanwhile, pursued his dream of an American whaling company by securing, through a holding company in Seattle, a site at Westport in Grays Harbor. Tentative orders were placed in Norway for six more whaling steamers to service the Canadian stations, and to the Moran yards in Seattle for four steamers, on the lines and displacement of the *Orion*, for the new American station.

All these grand plans came to a grinding halt in late 1909 as disaster loomed over the Canadian west coast sealing fleet, in which both Sprott Balcom and William Grant still owned a large equity. Eighteen months later, Canada signed a treaty which saw American, Japanese, and Russian sealing ships sharing small portions of the Pribilof Island seal catch, while pelagic sealing was outlawed. Victoria's fleet of schooners rotted on the beaches.

Forced to solicit capital to meet its commitments, the whaling company offered shares to the public, but found little interest in the profit potential of whaling when assured profits could be had for the taking in land sales. The Canadian Northern Railway was building towards Vancouver, and the Grand Trunk towards the new seaport of Prince Rupert, and land prices were spiralling upwards as people turned their eyes from the sea to the interior of the province.

It was not until early 1910 when Mackenzie and Mann, who were building the Canadian Northern Railway and developing coal exports from the Nanaimo area, offered the Canadian Pacific Whaling Company one million dollars for its assets and agreements. At the same time, the principals, Balcom and Grant, were offered shares in the reorganized whaling company. The ink had hardly dried on this agreement before the first whaling steamer arrived from Norway. She was delivered in prefabricated sections to the Victoria Machinery Depot, and, as Rose Harbour was rushed to completion, so was the *W. Grant* assembled and launched, and by late June both were busy taking and processing whales.

Mackenzie and Mann went to England to raise capital to realize plans more grandiose than those envisioned by the whaling company's former directors. In the spring of 1911, the remaining five steamers from Norway arrived in Victoria, with the *Brown* and *Blue* entering port on March 23. At the same time, they incorporated the American

The Belvedere, *a steam barkentine whaler of the Seattle area from 1880 to 1920, with Captain Charles Foley, master.*

Pacific Whaling Company, and work started on the Westport station in Grays Harbor. In June the Moran shipyards in Seattle launched the steamers *Moran* and *Paterson*, and during the short season off Cape Flattery they managed to supply the new Westport station with forty whales, losing an equal number of dead or dying whales through faulty equipment and inexperience.

All this activity, and the earlier launching of the twin-screwed whaling steamer *Tyee Jr.* for a successful whaling venture out of Sitka, Alaska, caused many American investors to take sudden interest in this modern flowering of a business they had been world leaders in during the heyday of sail.

Property was quickly secured on Akutan Island in the Aleutians by the newly formed Alaska Whaling Company, and Duthie's yard in

Point Ellice dock of the Pacific Whaling Company at Victoria, 1912. All ten whalers are in this picture—tenth one is hidden behind rigging of whaler in foreground. They are Orion, St. Lawrence, Germania, Sebastian, W. Grant, Brown, Blue, Black, Green, *and* White.

Seattle was commissioned to build the *Kodiak* and *Unimak*. The equally newly formed United States Whaling Company gave orders to Moran's yard to build the steamers *Star I*, *Star II*, and *Star III*, as construction of a whaling station at Port Armstrong on Baranof Island in the Alaskan panhandle area was rushed to completion.

All these vessels, plus the American Pacific Whaling Company's *Aberdeen* and *Westport*, were delivered by their builders and joined the whaling hunt in 1912. Over four thousand whales were landed and processed between 1911 and 1913, and by the end of 1913, the glut of whale products, including the highly prized whale oils, depressed the available markets. These markets were further overloaded by lower-priced petroleum oil products, as many new oil wells were drilled and put in production.

The Canadian North Pacific Fisheries, with a slight name change since incorporation, had more bad news to digest. Its parent company, Mackenzie and Mann, was in trouble with both its railway venture and its coal mining and export business. The land speculation boom had busted, and the country was slipping quickly into a full depression. Race riots flared between the cheap East Indian and Chinese labour forces employed by Mackenzie and Mann, and the angry White population that was losing jobs.

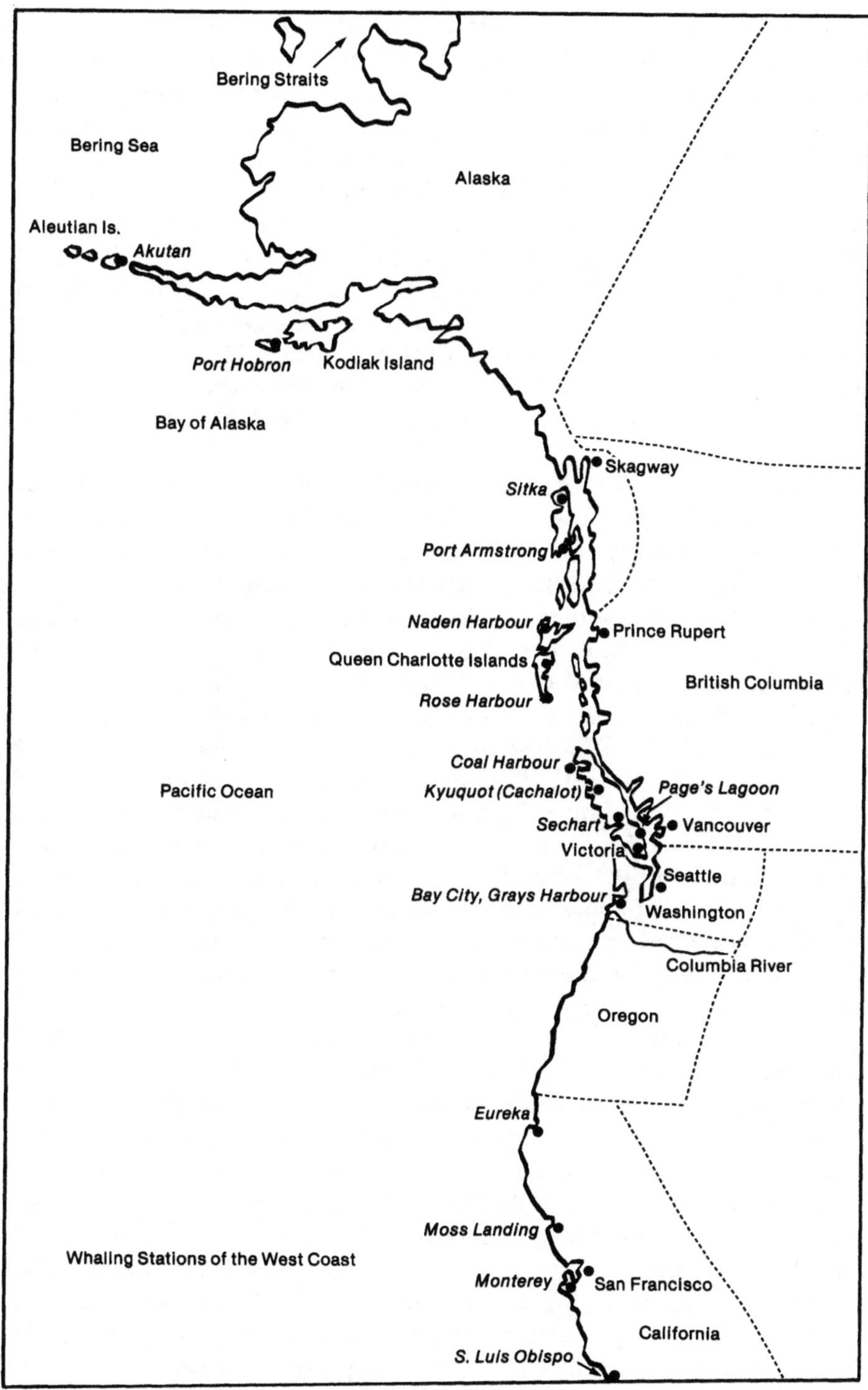
Bering Straits
Bering Sea
Alaska
Aleutian Is.
Akutan
Port Hobron
Kodiak Island
Bay of Alaska
Skagway
Sitka
Port Armstrong
Naden Harbour
Prince Rupert
Queen Charlotte Islands
British Columbia
Rose Harbour
Coal Harbour
Pacific Ocean
Kyuquot (Cachalot)
Page's Lagoon
Sechart
Vancouver
Victoria
Seattle
Bay City, Grays Harbour
Washington
Columbia River
Oregon
Eureka
Moss Landing
Whaling Stations of the West Coast
Monterey
San Francisco
California
S. Luis Obispo

Cries of foul echoed through the land and into the provincial legislature, where Sir Richard McBride's government, trying to launch the Pacific Great Eastern Railway, tottered visibly. Then, during the hot summer of 1914, World War I broke upon an almost bankrupt country, and business ground to a halt.

Dr. Ludvic Rissmuller, finding himself an enemy alien, ducked across into the neutral United States, and Canada clamped a tight embargo on all whale oil shipments out of the country. The distress of the whaling company was total. When the McBride government fell in early 1915, the British Empire Trust called in Canadian North Pacific Fisheries' bonds and placed the Yorkshire Securities Corporation of Vancouver as trustees of all the whaling company's assets. These assets drew no tangible inquiries when offered by Yorkshire to satisfy the debt.

Sprott Balcom may have considered making an offer, but his fortunes had dissipated with the failures of the trust companies and the whaling company, and he could only look with bitter rancour at the silent ships tied up at the former Victoria Sealing Company's dock, beside the Point Ellice bridge. However one man waited in the wings for the opportune time to make an offer, and only a few scraps of paper still remain to show how well his waiting rewarded him.

William Schupp was a self-made man of finance who had the knowledge and the stamina to gain the advantages that wartime restrictions had to offer. He had been involved in the reorganization of the Alaska Whaling Company two years earlier, when it became the North Pacific Sea Product Co., and his connections with the whale product markets in the United States, along with his understanding of the motivation of people in government, gained him export licenses for the whale products still stored in the company's warehouses, and also secured, with the Canadian munitions board, a market for all the whale oil he could supply during the war.

First he had to wait for the right moment to buy the whaling company, and then he had to put into force a plan of action that would shape the whaling business into an efficient and viable industry. In June 1915 Schupp made his move, and before the season was over, Kyuquot and Naden Harbour stations had processed just over two hundred whales. American Pacific Whaling Company, now managed by Captain LeMarquand and unaffected by the embargo, processed over three hundred, to supply a suddenly hungry wartime market. By the fall, Schupp was able to present Yorkshire Trust with its final payment, and incorporated his new business as the Victoria Whaling Company, appointing C.Rogers Brown as general manager.

A large Rorqual, undoubtedly a Blue whale, on the slip at Port Armstrong, Alaska, in 1915.

Remaining well in the background, William Schupp dictated a form of austerity never before experienced by the whalers, yet in less than eighteen months all his employees, who had been working at half pay, had a healthy bonus in their hands and a full pay check in their pockets. In the last two years of the war, Schupp's whaling venture annually grossed over a million dollars, more than five times the price he had paid Yorkshire Securities.

Never again, however, would the whalers experience the free and easy style of those earlier years. Schupp tolerated no waste, and every penny, until it absolutely had to be spent to satisfy a creditor, was invested to earn interest. Through the next two decades, the depressed years seemed to come more often and last longer, while the good years were shorter and more lean. Yet by putting back into the business only that which had to be put back, he kept the whalers at sea and the people employed, one of only a few businesses that did so. Thus, a job with the whaling company was highly prized, proudly worked at, and a credit to the man who few whaling people ever knew.

Schupp bought the station at Akutan, and the two steamers *Kodiak* and *Unimak*, when North Pacific Sea Products failed, and purchased the *Tyee Jr* when Tyee Whaling Company closed its doors, amalgamating his four companies as Consolidated Whaling Corpora-

Crew of the whaler Kodiak *at Akutan, Alaska, in 1935.*

tion of Seattle. A few years later he again reorganized, forming two companies: Consolidated Whaling of Victoria and American Pacific Whaling (the parent company) in Seattle. Though he considered it seriously, he finally declined the offer to buy up the *Star I*, *Star II*, and *Star III* when the United States Whaling Company closed Port Armstrong. Those ships formed the fleet that Captain Anton Larsen sailed into the Antarctic when he discovered the feeding grounds of the Blue whale and nearly bankrupted American Pacific and Consolidated by supplying a glut of whale products to world markets.

Through most of the Great Depression during the 1930s, Schupp managed to keep the large station tender *Gray* working at a modest profit, and those whaling stations that operated, in repair. By 1941 it was a very marginal operation. Only the flames of war offered it any hope, yet those flames would indirectly destroy it.

Three months after we left the North Pacific, the Japanese invaded the Aleutians. Attu and Kiska fell; Dutch Harbour and Akutan were strafed and bombed. Shipping west of the Charlottes was curtailed and guarded by naval vessels. All lights and aids to navigation were either removed or extinguished. Estevan lighthouse, on the west coast of Vancouver Island, was bombarded in the spring, and the people of the west coast, fearing an imminent Japanese invasion, interned all aliens and hurriedly stationed guns and naval vessels at all entrances to our inland waterways. After a brief season at Rose Harbour in 1942, whaling off the coast ceased, and the ships were again laid up.

The demands of wartime left nothing for their up-keep, and their gear perished through the long years of war. The stations were used by

Auctioning off the whaling vessels of Consolidated Whaling Corporation at Point Ellice wharf, Victoria, BC, 1947.

the armed forces, and the equipment that was not forged into war machines was removed by looters. There was little left at war's end, and very few funds to replace it. The market for whale products was also down, due to the new technologies and sciences generated under the pressure of war, and there appeared to be few whales about anyway.

In 1947 Consolidated tried to place three steamers back in service for a season of whaling. The *Blue*, *White*, and *Brown* were selected as best suited, but they failed to come up to the steamships inspection standards. An attempt to bring over American Pacific Whaling's *Kodiak*, *Unimak*, and *Paterson* also failed, as did a public offering of the ships, stations, and whaling licenses. No one, it appeared, was interested in whaling. The Roosevelt-initiated Reconstruction Finance Corporations loan of $100,000, carried over from the early 1930s, was called, and all assets of American Pacific Whaling and Consolidated Whaling were seized and auctioned off to satisfy the debt. William Schupp died in 1948, less than a year after his empire tottered and fell in a pile of dust.

Chapter Four

The Balcom and Grant Story

The whaling industry through its glory years was mainly a story of the men who made it: the full-time gunners and pilots and the entrepreneurs who provided the crucial management that kept the whole thing going. It is the story of these men that illuminates the history of west coast whaling, and it is their story I have seen as my principal task to record. Throughout this next section I will deal with some of the stalwarts of the business.

"My father brought his sealing schooner round the Horn in 1892. Mother, my sister, and I came overland by train the following year," Lawrence H. Balcom, eldest son of G.W. Sprott Balcom, stated quite matter-of-factly, as though it had just happened yesterday rather than over eighty years before. "Of course, I was still in diapers, so I can only repeat what I was told," he chuckled. For a man in his middle eighties, he was both spry and alert, with a catching type of dry humour that could be more realized in his turn of phrase than in any outward expression.

We were in the large kitchen of his Victoria home on Faithful Street, the late afternoon shadows of winter slowly darkening the room. He sat in an old, hard, high-back wooden chair near the window, his face partly in the shadows, and I was at the wooden table near the stove, asking questions and trying to record with pen and paper his clear, unhesitating recall of those years.

"My father's schooner was seized that same year, and he and his crew were thrown in jail in Vladivostok for sealing inside the Kuril Islands. I think you'll find Kipling wrote a story about it." Laurie's voice rumbled loudly in the quiet house, as he replied to my question of how the Balcoms came to be in Victoria. "When they got back here—and they had to sell everything they had, including their gumboots and dad's watch, just to afford steerage passage back—they found two Victoria schooners, the *Florence M. Munsie* and *E.B. Marvin*, had just returned from the Falkland Islands with over two thousand seal skins each. So my father wired his brother Ruben,

Sprott Balcom, founder of the whaling industry on the BC coast.

whom he had appointed commodore of the Balcom fleet of schooners on the Labrador coast, to sail down to Cape Horn, take what seals they could, and then join him in Victoria.

"Uncle Ruben was quite a man! You know, he spent two years up in the Klondike looking for gold after he arrived back in Victoria. I guess that would be about 1897 or so; I was only about four at the time, so I can really only go on the stories I've been told. But after Dad got the whaling company going, I'd guess that'd be about 1908 or so, Uncle Ruben had the *Agnes L. Donahue* over in the Indian Ocean, sealing, and he rescued seventy-five men from a wrecked Norwegian ship. I think her name was *Solglent*, or something like that. He went into retirement just after that, and I seen quite a lot of him for a few years. But after I came back from the war, I guess about 1919 it was, he sailed the *Isabel May* down to Christmas Island and the South Seas for some treasure hunters.

"Dad was the practical one. Uncle Ruben was rather a romantic, always chasing rainbows I guess you'd say. But I enjoyed him. Best uncle a young man could have. He died just a few years after Dad, shortly after the stock market crash. That was really the start of hard times for us."

Lawrence Balcom was a big man with broad shoulders and long arms, a man who had worked hard most of his life, and now, in his eighties, his heavy, high-topped trousers hung loosely from the wide suspenders draped over his snow-white dress shirt, hinting at a recent loss of weight. Easy to talk with, he was honest, gracious, and willing to help untangle the many puzzles I'd encountered in constructing a set of notes on the men of the earlier whaling company. Though he was quick to tell me that he himself had never sailed as a whaler, with prompting from information I'd gleaned from the archives, he was able to offer some helpful comments. Later I talked to his nephew, Graeme S. Balcom, who had a keen interest in the family's history, and custodianship of much of its memorabilia, and he generously agreed to read over these notes.

"There were four or five schooners that went down to the Falklands. The *Ola M. Balcom*, named after my sister, was one. My half brother Harry was master of her. I think he was twenty-one at the time, and Willis, Uncle Ruben's son, sailed with him as mate. Two others Dad was having built in Lunenburg followed soon after. They were the *Edith R. Balcom* and the *Agnes G. Donahue*, named after my cousin. If I recall correctly, the *Florence M. Munsie* left from here to join them, and they all did pretty good, too. But Harry and Willis paused to rescue some shipwrecked Chileans, so were late getting to the grounds and didn't get as many skins. Willis was presented with a pair of binoculars by the government of Chile for his part in the rescue."

When I voiced my wonder at what it must have been like here in this big house when all the Balcoms got together, Lawrence laughed good-naturedly and shook his head. "No, no. We didn't live here then.

Home of Captain William Grant at 304 Bay Street, Victoria—locally known as the "Point Ellice House." This photo was taken in 1953, a few years before the house was torn down.

We all lived down near the Gorge, at 2838 Douglas Street. Captain Grant, may that old pirate's soul rest in peace, lived right across from the company dock, just on the other side of where the Bay bridge is now. There was a trestle bridge for buggies and streetcars called the Point Ellice bridge. It fell down once—killed a lot of people. I was just a lad. Did you know that?" he cocked his head, and hurried on when I nodded. "Well, we all lived up the road a ways from there. The Heaters, Andersons, Rucks, Garcins, and ourselves. Even Rissmuller lived there at first. After that we moved over to Howe Street, and in the thirties, we moved here."

I asked him about the old Pacific Whaling Company that his father and William Grant had created, and what part he had played in it. "I wasn't a whaler, nor a sailor, you understand, though I did make a trip out with Bill Heater in the *W. Grant* once. But I drove the company cars, a big Packard and a Chalmers, during the off-seasons, and worked during the season at Kyuquot as a scale man before going in the army. Sweeney Cooperage had a shed out at the outer wharf, and the *Gray* would go out there and load barrels for the stations. During the off-seasons I'd often drive my father and other people from the office out there to talk business. That's how Sweeney started up his barrel business. And during the season at the station, I'd fill those same barrels with whale oil and weigh them, ready for the *Otter* or *Gray* to pick up and bring down to Victoria.

"I built a boat, about a sixteen footer, out of lumber I picked up around Sweeney's. It was all good, clear, edge-grain stuff, cost about $15 a thousand in those days, which was select grade, not this junk they sell today for $150 a thousand board feet!

"It was a nice little boat, and Captain McPherson of the *Otter* took it up to Kyuquot for me. Well, the Japanese foreman up there liked it so well he persuaded me to sell it to him before I left for eighty dollars and a box of choice cigars. That was a lot of money in those days, over a month's wages. Captain McPherson was quite sore when he found out; he'd offered to buy it from me on the way up to the station, and I'd refused. He was a great old sailor, been with both the Pacific Navigation Company and their successors, the Canadian Pacific Steamships. The whaling company always sent him a big box of choice cigars each Christmas. He later became the Commissioner of Wrecks for this coast."

I asked him about Dr. Ludvic Rissmuller, inventor and patent holder of a number of specialized pieces of equipment used by the whaling company. (William Schupp's Victoria Whaling Company acquired his patent rights by default, after Canada went to war with Germany, and Rissmuller became an enemy alien.) "Dr. Rissmuller?!" Laurie snorted without humour. "He was the biggest blowhard of all, had more wild ideas. Always trying to promote something. My father believed in him, though I don't know why. They lost a lot of money on his wild speculations, land deals and such, that didn't materialize. Page's Lagoon was Rissmuller's idea. He had the construction crews working all summer on overtime to complete it. Cost over a hundred thousand dollars, even in those days, but it never worked out. It was supposed to be a winter whaling station, so the company could work all year round and that way hold the crews together.

"They brought the *St. Lawrence* out from Newfoundland, and in the fall of 1907 she worked out of Page's Lagoon. Larsen was gunner on her. They got mostly small Humpbacks, but not enough to keep the station working profitably. In the spring my Dad sent him up to Kyuquot, and he landed over three hundred whales—one boat! Hard to believe, eh? I remember because everyone was saying how smart my father had been to push for building a station away up there—everyone, that is, except Rissmuller. It was right after that they bought the *Germania* and *Sebastian*, and they worked out of Sechart, while Willis with the *Orion*, and Larsen with the *St. Lawrence* worked out of Kyuquot. That was the best station we had."

Whaler St. Lawrence *at the whaling company's Point Ellice dock, Victoria, 1912.*

My next questions brought to the surface an old bitterness that had obviously rankled Lawrence Balcom most of his life. Showing him some pictures of the *Gray* and the old catcher boats, *Germania* and *Sebastian*, I innocently mentioned the colour boats.

"The colour boats? Oh, yes, I remember them well. Best boats ever built. My brother Harry had the *Green*—he died of a burst appendix while I was away in the army. Fool doctor up there at Rose Harbour said he just had a bellyache. Harry died at sea in utter agony, he was only thirty-eight at the time."

Laurie switched on some lights to look at my pictures, then continued, "Yes, the colour boats I recall quite well. You know they had quite a fight over what names to give those little ships. Old Rissmuller blowing off steam about naming them after rivers in his fatherland. I believe his brother in Germany had invested money in the company. Then one of those Mackenzie and Mann guys from Vancouver got into the act, wanting to name them after rivers in Scotland. Well, there was quite a to-do about it, even the newspapers got into the act. My Dad ordered the first one sent over here in parts, just like a meccano set. She arrived aboard the CPR's *Titan*, and Spratt at Victoria Machinery Depot put her together. They named her the *W. Grant* after the old pirate. Dad didn't really care what they named the others, but the builders in Norway were ready to launch them, so he threatened to put numbers on them if the board couldn't make up their mind. Dad was still manager of the company at that time, and I guess you could say it was his idea to use colour names,

Whaler Green. ***Originally Harry Balcom's ship, she was bought at scrap price in 1947 by Max Lohbrunner and survived until the late 1960s, when she sank at her dock. Gun and crow's nest salvaged for Victoria Maritime Museum.***

because he got sore at their meeting and pounded the table and roared, 'I don't give a tinker's damn what you call them! Call them Black and Blue, or Red, White, and Blue! But if you don't settle on a name, I'll launch them with numbers painted on their hulls!'

"After the Mackenzie-Mann gang took over the company, it wasn't the same anymore. They had so many big plans, no one really knew just what the devil was going on. Both my Dad and Grant slowly got the heck out of it. Rissmuller went to the States to operate the new company they had formed there, American Pacific Whaling. He'd come up and visit us once in a while, but when the war started he couldn't cross the line or they'd throw him in jail as an enemy alien. I don't know what finally happened to him. When I got back from the war, old Grant was gone, my brother had died, and the whaling company was owned by some eastern guy named Schupp. Dad probably knew him well enough, but I never met the man."

Laurie nodded agreement to my statement that whaling had been big business during this time. "They all earned good money in those earlier years, and most of them spent a lot of it, too. Whether anyone actually made much money out of the whaling company, I don't know. A lot of sealing men lost money over the sealing treaty, my Dad and Grant included. Why, you couldn't sell a sealing schooner here, after that. They were leaving them up on the beaches to rot. Without the equity in their sealing schooners, the whaling company couldn't raise the money they needed, so they had to sell out to that Vancouver bunch."

Whaler Orion, *the first steam whaler on the BC coast. Photo was taken in 1907, when Willis Balcom was master.*

I asked if his father had realized a profit from his long involvement in the whaling business, and Laurie gave a derisive snort, "The money he and Grant got for their shares of Pacific Whaling was good. I know he invested a lot of that in property and buildings around here, but the shares they accepted in [Mackenzie and Mann's] Canadian North Pacific Fisheries were worthless. Empire Trust took everything and sold it for just a few cents on the dollar. That was criminal, but I wasn't here then. I was away in the war like a lot of young fellows from here, so what could we do about it? Dad had lost a lot of money in that Dominion Trust failure just the year before, so even if the company had been offered back to him at ten cents on the dollar, he wouldn't have been able to raise enough money to buy it."

We discussed those difficult years that surrounded the beginning of World War I, and Laurie commented, "McBride was premier then, and he had sunk millions of dollars into the railroad development to open up this province, and a lot of people had got rich in the process, but the cheap labour force they imported into the country caused race riots all over when things got tough. They had to send the army up to Nanaimo, where Mackenzie and Mann had a large coal development, to stop the bloodshed and keep the mines from being flooded. It was bad, believe me, it was really very bad around here then."

Laurie Balcom's description of William Grant as an "old pirate" compared very poorly with the impression I had received from my research of this seaman, so I asked another old sailor his thoughts on the man. Captain Jim Goodwin hails from a seafaring family that goes back as far, at least on this coast, as do the Balcoms. The Goodwins built and ran the steamer *Dominion* between the Gorge and Victoria until an electric street railway, which had been built out to Esquimalt, built a branch line to serve the summer homes and residences along the Gorge. Marine traffic was no longer profitable, so the Goodwins cut the old *Dominion* down into a tugboat. It joined the *Ping Pong*, one of the first gas-engine boats on the coast, used for towing sealing schooners out past Brotchie Ledge, and a small steamtug, the *Dong*, in the Goodwin Towing Company. They later added the steam tugs *Beatrice*, a former sealing schooner, and *Saanich*, a former whaler. Jim and his brothers, Cal and Charlie, all had long successful careers as towboat masters on this coast, so Jim Goodwin's opinion is highly valued.

"When I was a lad working for my Dad, we often tied the *Dominion* up at Grant's wharf. That was the base for the Victoria Sealing Company, and later, the Pacific Whaling Company, both of which Bill Grant was senior shareholder of," Jim said, rolling himself a cigarette, and brushing the multitude of tobacco crumbs absentmindedly off his vest before lighting the limp cigarette with a bullet lighter. "Sure I remember Captain Grant well. He was a small spry old man. Hard as nails. I've heard he sailed out of Frisco a few times, leaving some of his drunk sealers behind on the beach without a penny, but that was only hearsay, and well before my time. My father got along fine with both him and Sprott Balcom, and I never heard him say a bad word against either man, and for my Dad, that was praise enough.

"I've heard that most people liked Sprott Balcom better than old Grant, but really they was as different as night is to day. Did you know Grant hailed from Grantville, Cape Breton. I believe his family founded the place years before. He was a blockade runner during the American Civil War, did you know that?" When I nodded, Jim continued on with hardly a pause. "Guess you knew they caught him, eh? Burnt his ship and threw him on a penal island. He escaped though, and took over command of the *Olive Jordon*, the biggest sailing ship built in Nova Scotia. He was only twenty-two at the time, and he took along his young wife and their son. They lost her with a full load of grain on her maiden voyage to Europe. They all got off OK. Then he went down to the River Plate in South America with three brigs, and ran them through the blockage. You know he was attacked by pirates in the China Sea after his crew had mutinied and left him short-handed. When he fell ill with yellow fever, and was near death, his wife Helen sailed that large ship all the way back to Montreal by herself and a couple of loyal hands. They was so close to Krakatoa when she let go that volcanic ash and rock fell on their decks. Bet you didn't know Helen Grant was the first woman in Canada to ever hold a school trusteeship? She served on the Victoria school board, and she was very active for women's rights. Their son Harold was older than me. He became a mining engineer. He'd been with them in the China Sea mutiny, and became a hero rescuing people off the Point Ellice bridge collapse. I seen him a few times at the dock."

When I again nodded and repeated my question about Captain Grant, Jim chuckled and crushed out his cigarette. "Oh, he was tough all right. Tough as they come and feared no man. I've seen him many times go across the street and round up the whalers from the Rock Bay Hotel, herd them down to the ship, then stand on the edge of the dock with a belaying pin in his hand and literally threaten to lay it on their thick skulls if any of those big bruisers tried to get off that ship before she sailed!"

Captain Goodwin opened an old notebook stuffed with clippings and pictures, and leafed through it, looking for something, as he continued to speak. "Grant died about the middle of the first war, I think he was over eighty, and his wife Helen died during the second war. But I remember something that was in here about Sprott Balcom. I think he died during the mid-twenties. Ah! Here it is. A note, copied from something I'd guess, but I don't know if it's my Dad's writing or not. It's dated December 22, 1925. 'Captain Sprott Balcom—A big upstanding man of sterling integrity, tolerant and kindly in manner he was warmly esteemed by a very large circle of acquaintance by whom his death will be deeply regretted.' "

CHAPTER FIVE

FEAST TO FAMINE

William S. Lagen's grandfather, William Schupp, owned and operated all the whaling vessels and stations on this coast from 1915 to 1947. His father, Marc Lagen, was manager of the Port Hobron whaling station in Alaska, and, in later years, became the general manager of American Pacific Whaling Corporation, which controlled the Consolidated Whaling Corporation in Victoria, where I had signed on the *Brown*.

I had corresponded with Bill Lagen for over a year before driving down to Seattle to visit him at his home in Bellevue on the eastern shore of Lake Washington. I had been bothered by hundreds of questions about the whaling company and the people involved in it, but mostly I wanted to know who William Schupp really was, for his involvement in the whaling story had only recently been revealed to me. Few people seemed to know of him, and of those that did, few knew anything about him.

Lagen graciously spent considerable time with me, explaining the mysterious man who was his grandfather. He opened the doors to much more information when he allowed me to examine the company's ledgers and correspondence files stored at the University of Washington. As when Leonard McCann made the Victoria Whaling Company's 1915 correspondence file available earlier in my search, it gave many answers, but it also created more perplexing questions.

"My grandfather was an enigma to most people. Barrel-chested, short-legged, and sternly aloof, he stumped heavily and bellowed loudly. I guess you could say he was a self-made man who hadn't forgotten the harsh lesson learned getting to be one," Bill Lagen smiled at me. A well-built man a year older than I, he shared my desire to see the whaling story properly told, and I listened with rapt attention as he recalled events that William Schupp had directed from this house for over a quarter of a century.

"My great-grandfather owned the Bank of Saginaw, but my grandfather ran away from all that at the age of thirteen. His father was one of those harsh, Teutonic Germans who made him work most

William Schupp and William Schupp Lagen (R) sitting on main forward hatch of the Gray *circa 1933, en route to Naden and Rose Harbour.*

of his waking hours in the bank, tolerating no frivolities and demanding a continued dedication to God and dollar. No doubt in those few precious years he remained under his father's roof, he had learned how wisely invested money makes money." Bill, himself a successful business man, chuckled ruefully at his understatement.

"He went west, that would be about 1877, working in lumber camps for a dollar and a quarter a day. But he saved and invested much of his money, and by the time he was forty-five, was in the position to arrange bonding for the Canadian Northern Railway, who, in turn, bought out the Pacific Whaling Company. My grandmother was a large shareholder in Proctor and Gamble, which may have been one of the reasons my grandfather bought up the whaling company from Canadian North Pacific Fisheries when Mackenzie and Mann were having all their trouble."

Bill Lagen grinned when I recounted stories I'd heard about William Schupp being a bit of a tyrant. "Everything my grandfather did was given a great deal of consideration before the orders were given to carry it out. If he wanted a boiler moved out of one whaler and into another by tomorrow, and he told you to see that it was done, then God help you if it was not done by that time. The problems you encountered were your business. He had faith and knowledge that you were capable of overcoming them, or he wouldn't have given the job to you. He wasn't interested in excuses, only results. If someone argued that the job was impossible, he'd swell up with indignation, roll up his sleeves, do the impossible job, then fire the man. Believe me, it was an object lesson that didn't have to be repeated often to get the message around. He was quite opposite to my father, who always made time to listen to people, and enjoyed his friendship with the whalers."

Bill Lagen was a member of the volunteer search-and-rescue team that had just returned from a four wheel drive up into the mountains, looking for a downed plane. He swirled the contents of his coffee cup reflectively as we sat in the large living room of his grandfather's house. The big picture window looked out over Lake Washington and down to the water's edge where the home base of the American Pacific Whaling Company once stood.

"My grandfather loved hunting and fishing, and often took us along to rough it out at a mountainous campsite. He doted on my mother, Emily, and treated me more like a pal than a grandson," Bill said. "He loved cars. Large powerful cars. He had this big Pierce Arrow, and soon after he got it, he took me out for a Sunday drive without saying a word to my mother. Before it ended we had boarded the S.S.

Gray and gone on a trip to the whaling stations in the Queen Charlottes."

Bill got up and went over to the wall of the living room. Lifting down a slender fishing rod with a polished wooden reel, he gave it a gentle flick to show the limber of the obviously well-cared-for silk-bound, split-cane rod. "My grandfather bought me this and some clothes in Victoria, so I could do some fly fishing when we reached the Charlottes."

While I examined the rod, Bill chuckled as he recalled a humourous incident of that trip. "We had to go through customs on our return, and my grandfather became quite indignant as we were forced to wait while the customs officer methodically examined everyone's luggage. Finally, when he got to my grandfather's luggage, he unwittingly made some remark about its contents. Grandfather blew up with Teutonic rage and roared affronts at the poor guy till he was quaking in his shoes!"

Replacing the rod in its rack, he returned to his seat and smiled ruefully over at me. "If we were to try that, they'd probably have us cooling our butts in the customs office for quite some time, but grandfather could get away with it. He had that air of authority and knew the customs regulations, probably better than the guy he told off."

We discussed the frugal policy of William Schupp. "During the Depression, American Pacific Whaling lost a lot of money. It got so bad grandfather couldn't even send out the whalers." Bill sighed, for, like myself, he had been too young to feel the full impact of those

William Schupp visiting Port Alberni.

hopeless years. "He lent money to many of the whalers who found themselves in dire straits. I don't think he ever expected to get it back, but he'd tell them not to worry about it, and pay it back when they could. The men felt better about getting a loan than a free handout; it allowed them to keep face. Neither my father or my grandfather received a salary during those years. After they got the RFC [Reconstruction Finance Corporation] loan they went back whaling, but at half pay, and there were hundreds lined up for the jobs. APW never recovered from those years. When whale product prices started to go up again, so did the costs. Profits were so marginal they were just able to manage a payment on the interest charged by the loan; nothing could be repaid back against the principal of the loan."

There is no doubt the conditions aboard the old whalers were tough, even for those of us who had been seasoned by ten years of depression-created austerities, but they were not so different from those on many other ships sailing during those days. It was the uncertainty, if not the delay, of our supplies that accentuated the real harshness, and this was more true for the Alaskan whalers of American Pacific. Bill Lagen's recall of those days illustrates what they accepted as the norm in their trade.

The Grays Harbor whaling station at Westport in Bay City had closed down in 1924. Before the winter storms halted shipping into Alaskan waters the following year, a new station on Sitkalidak Island, Port Hobron, had been completed, and the American Pacific Whaling Company was put under the management of Captain George LeMarquand. Marc A. Lagen, Bill's father, managed Port Hobron, with Harold Onset commanding the *Moran*, Gus Wester the *Aberdeen*, and Chris Olsen the *Tanginak*. American Pacific was quoting whale meat, salted and packed in barrels, at ten cents a pound, FOB Port Hobron, and one cent more a pound shipped to San Francisco.

Bill Lagen was coming into his teens when he first sailed north to Alaska with his father and mother, and his memory of those events was still crystal clear. The entire American Pacific fleet, and all the workmen, would set sail from Seattle to the Bay of Alaska on the same day in the spring. Bill said, "The majority of the whalers, both the men in the ships and the crews in the stations, had worked for the company for many years, some as far back as the turn of the century in the old plant at Westport [Grays Harbor]. The oldtimers were, by and large, pretty solid citizens, but there were a number who, as near as I could figure out, spent most of the winter down in the skid road.

"About two weeks before we were due to sail, my Dad would make arrangements with the police to start rounding up the whalers and keep them in the tank at the old city jail on Yesler St. Then, on sailing day, which as I recall was from Pier 42, and by chance we always sailed on the S.S. *Alaska*, Dad and I would go down to the jail in my grandfather's Pierce Arrow, or in Dad's old Packard, and take the men directly from the jail to the ship.

"They went steerage, we went first class, and nobody really thought much about it, because that's the way things were in those days. In any event, after we had delivered a load to the S.S. *Alaska* we would then go back down into the skid road. Dad would double park out in the street, and I would go into the bars, looking for the sailors. I was a kid of about 12 at the time. I must confess the whalers generally recognized me before I recognized them. There would be a whoop, and a 'Hello, Bill,' and we would go out to the car, and collect another load in various stages of sobriety, which we would deliver to the ship, and then away we would go for Alaska."

They travelled northward to Cordova or Seward in the *Alaska*, then transferred to the *Curacao* or *Cordova* for the trip to Port Hobron, Bill recalled.

"I can't remember much about the *Cordova*, other than that my Dad was on board her when she caught fire in the Straits of Georgia, around 1937 or 1938. The *Curacao*, though, I remember vividly. She was small, I guess about 1000 tons, a whaleback, or at least a partial whaleback, and I was told had been sunk during the Spanish-American war. This was made more believable by the worm holes in the bannister leading down into the main salon. She also had a peculiar smell about her, not altogether unpleasant, compounded, I suppose, of varnish, age, old wood and mildew. Mostly varnish, I would gather. But I remember the smell vividly. She had a Scotch marine boiler and, of course, a triple expansion engine which, like all of the triple expansions of Alaska Steamships, squeaked on each revolution. She turned up, I suppose, about 70 rpm, and the squeak could be heard throughout the ship. As I remember, her speed was around 7 knots, at least it seemed that way to me.

"Our Australian sheltie, Bola, who weighed no more than 45 pounds, had fought with every dog in every port on our way north. At Seward, where we transferred station freight to the *Curacao*, our stay in port was long enough for many of the dogs there, that had been beaten up by Bola, to gang into a nasty pack and challenge our passage back to the ship.

"My god, there was such a dogfight! We climbed up on a nearby pile of lumber to get away from them, and the whalers and some of the crew had to run across the dock and rescue us," Bill chuckled. He continued more soberly, "The *Curacao* had loaded a large iron chink—a huge iron wheel, suitably fitted into an iron frame, that cleaned and prepared salmon for canning—on the forward well deck. It sat to the left of the main hatch, and gave the old ship a slight list to port as we steamed out of Seward at a modest seven knots to cross the gulf of Alaska. Halfway across we picked up a gale that threatened to send us to the bottom. There was no way the captain could keep the ship's head up into the seas; her heavy lading and slight list caught the full force of the storm, and her power was inadequate to keep her from falling off into the trough. She rolled over to her beam ends, and would hang there for what seemed an endless time, before slowly working herself back up to a stable position, before being pushed back over on her side again.

"My mother and I shared a cabin on the weather side, right below the bridge, and for three days we could not leave the cabin, nor could anyone get to us. We had only the food my mother had carried into the cabin for late snacks. Water poured in under the cabin door, and trying to stay in our bunks was a real effort. Later I was told the captain thought the ship was a goner. I can't vouch for what he thought, but I certainly thought she was, and all of us along with her." Bill paused, then chuckled and added, "You know, that was forty years ago, and a lot of my memory may be somewhat hazy, but I'll never forget that gale in the old *Curacao*."

I asked him what he, as a young lad, did at a remote Alaskan whaling station while his school chums were probably lolling around in the warm southern reaches of Puget Sound.

"We usually arrived at Port Hobron a few days before the whalers, and this seemed time enough to get most of the equipment ready, for the whalers began hunting for whales within a day of their arrival. One of my jobs was to catch fresh fish every day for the cookhouse, and I used the company dory to carry this out. I set gear out overnight, and at first light I was up to check the state of hooks. Halibut was prime fish for the table, with salmon taking a modest second place, so often I baited my hooks with hunks of salmon. I think those mornings out on the bay, by myself, were the finest moments of my life. You've travelled on those northern waters during the first light of morning. I'll bet you've felt it." Recalling those short summer nights, and the virgin freshness of the dawn, I nodded agreement.

"Alaska Steam usually had a vessel in to the station at least once a month with mail, food, and supplies, and would load out with whale oil for the States. You know the smell of the station, so I don't have to tell you about that. Living there, we never really noticed it, but the people on the ships coming in looked pretty green sometimes, when the wind was offshore and we were cutting up a big whale or two." Bill gave a wry grin and continued, "But sometimes those vessels were late, especially in the fall when storms would spring up quickly, and sometimes the ships got wrecked and we'd have to wait two to six weeks for a second vessel to come. When that happened, my dad would arrange for a large dory, loaded with three or four men and myself, to

Whale bone pile behind the station at Port Hobron, Alaska, about 1935.

Five whales on slip at Akutan station about 1935. Note small Humpback whale in front of large Rorqual.

go down to the head of the bay and shoot ducks. It's hard to believe now, but we'd fill that boat with ducks, several hundred of them. A few days later, if no supplies had arrived, we'd go out again and shoot more. Fish and ducks were the only fresh food we could get.

"Another interesting phenomenon at Port Hobron was the way the grass would grow. When fertilizer was made at the station, it was dried in a big rotary kiln, and a certain amount would escape up the stack and blow over the surrounding landscape. No matter what was being processed, either bone meal or blood and meat, it was excellent fertilizer, and the grass grew beyond belief. It was over six feet tall, and the stems were probably as big as pencils. It was almost impossible to walk through, it was so thick. Then, as summer went by, it would dry out—a real fire hazard if a spark ever dropped in it. One summer we had an awful long dry spell and the grass was like tinder. Suddenly it caught fire. What a spectacular sight it was. Fortunately the wind was onshore, or we might have lost the station. As it was, it worked its way quickly up the mountain side and beyond the range of the fertilized growth, and burned itself out."

Other men remember William Schupp's whaling companies from a different perspective. Harry Osselton was one of those men who joined Consolidated Whaling in Victoria during the Great Depression of the thirties. A former Blue Funnel engineer, Harry was happy with the offer of an engineer's berth aboard the *Gray*, which was being recommissioned after a two year lay-up. "We were signed on at half pay and damn glad to get it," he chuckled. A spry man, his eyes sparkled as he relived for me some of the highlights of his years with the whaling company.

"Why, you know, captains were sailing as deckhands, and a good many engineers I knew were on the beach. There were thousands of men just looking for a job. Any job! Half pay was certainly better than no pay." Harry shook his head sadly as he recalled those difficult times, but he smiled when he found out I was an engineer, schooled in triple and compound steam engines with Scotch marine boilers. As two former nut splitters we had much to discuss, and coal, the fuel that breathed life into those glorious, ever-reliable old machines, was foremost on our list of topics.

"Why the coal that old *Gray* used when I first joined her was atrocious!" he exclaimed in answer to my query, after a lengthy discourse on an engine repair he had carried out. "I had them go into Union Bay and load up with some of that good hard Comox coal, and we steamed so long without taking on more fuel that old Alfus Garcin [the general manager] accused me of stealing coal off the docks at Naden and Rose Harbour! Why, we was burning less than twelve ton a day, and her averaging a good nine and a half knots at a steady 78 revs. Jim Hunter was skipper of her then, and Archie Bell was mate, and they kept coming down below and asking me when would I want to take on bunkers, and I kept telling them we didn't need any." Harry paused to sip some tea and draw on his pipe before continuing. "You know that when I first joined her, the firemen were dumping fifteen to twenty buckets of ash and clinkers each watch. Why, they took on coal at Ladysmith or Nanaimo going north, took a bit off the dock at Naden before coming south, then took on more coal at Nanaimo before going on to Tacoma and back to Victoria. After we loaded up with that Comox hard, we ran up to the Charlottes, down to Tacoma, then Victoria, before going to Union Bay, and we had over ten ton of coal still in the bunkers! Nanaimo wanted to know why we didn't get our coal from them, but when I showed old Garcin the savings, he even smiled. Why, they had been paying three dollars a ton for that stuff; I got Comox hard for two-eighty a ton, and we did three times the distance on it! You know, that's the best coal you can get. Gives off a little white ash, no cinders, and burns slow and hot. Boy, did the firemen like it. A lot less work!"

Leslie Hampten, the chief engineer, left at this time, and Harry Osselton was offered the chief's job, and at full pay, too. "They offered me a hundred and eighty-five dollars a month," Harry grunted as he puffed his pipe alight. "After the sixty dollars I had been getting, I could hardly believe my ears, so I was still nodding yes, and grinning like a kid being given candy, when Garcin added that I would be expected to look after the spring refit of the whalers as well."

This had been the responsibility of the engineering superintendent, but George Harvey, who had taken over from Bill Scaplen in the late twenties, had left when the whalers didn't sail in the early thirties. Harry became both engineering super and chief engineer, a role he carried out till the *Gray* was sold to the Frank Waterhouse Company, and he returned to the Salvage Company.

When I asked him about William Schupp, he had this to say, "Why, I never really spoke to the man myself, but I do recall him well enough. A silent heavy-set man who seldom smiled or talked to anyone. He wouldn't even come aboard the ship when we arrived at Seattle or Tacoma. But he'd be waiting for us each time we tied up. Hunter would go ashore, and they'd walk up and down the wharf while he reported our voyage and got his orders from Mister Schupp."

I asked if Schupp had ever sailed on the *Gray* while he was there, recalling Bill Lagen's trip to the Charlottes, and Harry chuckled a little knowingly. "Yes, once Mister Schupp and his party came on board at Victoria. I recall he had a young Swedish girl with him, his secretary I understood." Harry's eyes twinkled and he gave a little wink. "I'm not one for gossip, but there was some speculation on the side; after all, Schupp must have been in his late sixties and she in her mid-twenties. We knew he had been divorced for some time, and it was none of our business anyway. He paid us good, and I never heard anyone really speak badly of him. Jim Hunter and Garcin were the only ones who dealt directly with Schupp, and old Garcin would almost go off the deep end each spring, waiting for word on which stations or ships would operate that season."

He continued talking about Captain Hunter, and Captain Boss Allen, who took over from Hunter as skipper of the *Gray*, "Well, you know, Jim Hunter was over seventy-six years of age when I joined the *Gray*, a former government skipper. He was very closed mouth about the company's business to the rest of us. He was bonded to the company, and Boss Allen was just the same. He went with her to Waterhouse, and later became the super over there."

His mention of "old Garcin" brought up the subject of Schupp's austerity. Harry clicked his tongue and shook his head in mock despair. "Oh, they were cheap! My god, they were cheap, cheap, cheap. You'll never believe how cheap old Garcin was. Why, you know, for note pads or logsheets we had to use the other side of old company ledgers and tally sheets. Moses Keil, their general all-round dock man was just as bad. He saved everything that had not been thrown overboard, and stored it away in that wharf shed of theirs. It was so full of junk you could hardly walk around inside of it, and couldn't find anything if you did."

Recalling an incident to illustrate his premise, he took a swig of cold tea and hurried on. "You know, Nickerson was purchasing agent and Jack Lawson, I think it was, was accountant. Well, the *White* needed her boiler retubed, so Archie MacIntyre, her chief, and I went up to see Garcin and his gang. Usually the ships were just taken over to Victoria Machinery Depot and the job would be done. Those guys thought it would cost too much—I think they were quoted about a thousand dollars—and claimed the company couldn't afford it, and were deciding to lay the ship up. Well, we all needed the work, and Archie and the others didn't want to be without a ship, so I suggested to Garcin that we'd do the job ourselves if they'd get us some boiler tubes." Having put in a few tube stoppers in my time, and recently helped remove and retube part of the boiler for the old steam tug

Alfus Garcin, General Manager of Consolidated Whaling until 1947.

Master, I knew the job well enough to appreciate Harry's story. "Garcin did some quick arithmetic on an old piece of paper before asking, 'You sure you can do it, boy?' It tickled him when I replied, 'Well, we always did our own, deep water.' Well, we started cutting out the old tubes right away, but they were very dirty and scaled up, and we used more gas with the cutting outfit than I had figured on, so I had to go back up to Garcin to get him to OK more gas to finish the job.

" 'Another bottle of oxygen, boy?' he thundered, as though I must be out of my mind. This rankled me a bit. We were saving them almost a thousand dollars on the job and he was quibbling over a mere bottle of gas.

" 'We've not used a full cylinder yet!' I thundered back just as loud as he. 'It was less than three-quarters full when we started!' and marched over to the door. Then I turned back to him, and asked him real quiet-like, 'By the way, Mister Garcin, just how much does a cylinder of oxygen cost?'

" 'Four dollars and fifty cents, boy!' he choked.

"Well I was so mad I shouted back, 'Four dollars and fifty cents! My god, the way you was sounding I thought they must be at least forty bucks!'

"You know, maybe I wouldn't have got so mad, but we were working like dogs to get those tubes out and were dirty as coal monkeys, just to save them money. I'd even borrowed the rolling and swagging tools from VMD for free, to complete the job. Oh, they were cheap. I had to go up there and fight with that gang two or three times a year for things the men were entitled to, but the company or Garcin wasn't going to give them."

I asked Harry Osselton what he did through the winter months, after the whalers were laid up, and he replied, "A lot of us used to get work with the Pacific Salvage Company during the winter. That's when they'd get a lot of work. Why, you know, every time there was a big blow or gale, I'd pack my bag and put it there, right at the door. Often the phone would ring in the middle of the night to tell me a taxi would be picking me up in five minutes. They always kept the *Salvage King* steamed up and ready to go in those days. A dozen taxis would suddenly converge on the salvage dock when the call went out, and guys with their clothes just thrown on, and a bag in their hands, would run for the old ship. I've seen us under way from the dock within an hour of a distress call coming in."

"I recall quite vividly how hectic it would be around home, and down at the dock, when the whalers were getting ready to sail!" chuckled Win Garcin, son of the long-time general manager of Consolidated Whaling Corporation, Alfus Garcin, the man who had peered out at Roy and me that day Finn John decided to give us a chance. "Father never knew till the last possible moment how many ships were to sail or what stations were to operate. Mr. Schupp allowed him very little working capital, and demanded almost daily accounting of all expenses, so nothing could be done till his wire or phone call came. My father would be almost a nervous wreck, trying to keep officers and men available to man the ships and stations, to make tentative orders for supplies, yet with little or no funds to secure them.

"You've undoubtedly heard all kinds of stories of how tight-fisted and cheap my father was supposed to be. But that was the way Mr. Schupp forced him to run the business. If he hadn't run it that way, Mr. Schupp would have got someone who would, and my father would have been out of a job. That was the way Schupp was. He was a real tyrant. They say he was very fair, even my father vouched for that, but whenever Mr. Schupp came up from the States to look over the company, my father shook in his shoes!"

CHAPTER SIX

THE HEATER STORY

Few names crop up in the history of whaling out west as often as the name Heater. The Heaters of Victoria have a long history of seafaring in their family. They settled in Newfoundland's Harbour Grace during the early eighteenth century to become fishermen, and arrived in BC before the turn of this century. Allan R. Heater is a sixth-generation master mariner, and his story is all the more interesting because he entered the whaling scene under the tutelage of his grandfather, Captain William Heater, a long-respected sealing and whaling master.

Though Allan's father had often sailed up the west coast of Vancouver Island in the family sealing schooner, accompanying his father when he picked up his crew of Indian seal hunters, Ronald Heater ventured no farther to sea than this, content to stay ashore and pursue a career in retail business. No doubt he hoped Allan would follow in his footsteps, but the call of the sea was in his son's blood, and, recognizing this, his grandfather agreed to take him aboard the *W. Grant* as seaman for a season of whaling.

The old captain's offer to take Allan to sea was not greeted with joy by the boy's parents. In fact, their initial refusal to hear any more about it was only won round to a reluctant agreement to consider it by a great deal of persuasion and pleading by Allan. They finally agreed to the plan, if Allan could meet one condition—and for a lad just turned sixteen it was a difficult one. He would have to complete his schooling each year with passing marks.

"We left for the whaling mid-April and didn't return till mid-October," he remembered, "so I had to write my exams early to get away. I did extra studies during the winter to get ahead of my class, and then I had to do extra studies when I returned in the fall to catch up with them. Our principal was a pretty good guy, and knowing why I wanted to get away early, arranged that I got the extra studies and time to write my exams."

Captain Allan Heater is a man of imposing stature, weathered by years of keeping watch on the large vessels of the BC Ferry System.

Allan Heater, age 17, and his grandfather Captain Bill Heater, 1936.

"My grandfather and I were real pals before I went to sea with him, and even during the winter months, when I was back at school, we got along fine. But out on the whaler, he was the captain, and I was just a lowly seaman. He was a tough old bird, and he didn't let family relations interfere with the running of his ship. I was treated the same as all the others in the forecastle, and maybe at times a little more harshly.

"You remember Pete Bromson?" he asked, casting a sidelong glance my way, and when I nodded, continued, "Well, that guy once knocked me out cold, just for coiling down a worn foregoer the wrong way. He clouted me right on the temple, and I dropped like a sack of spuds. It knocked me out for a few minutes. I remember opening my eyes and seeing my grandfather looking down at me from the bridge, but he didn't say or do anything, just looked down at me, and as soon as I got up, he walked away. That's the way those guys were. Hard as nails. They were so tough they could almost use their fingers for marlin spikes!

"They treated me fair. I might be the skipper's grandson, but they never let me take any advantage from that. Sometimes it almost seemed to me they were extra tough on me, and it wasn't all my imagination either, because several of the older crew members tried to

Whaler W. Grant, *the first steam whaler ever built in BC. Note Captain William Grant's home behind bridge span.*

shield me from my grandfather and the mate's rather harsh discipline. In all fairness, they themselves had come up through some pretty harsh disciplines, and really, they knew no other way. Those little ships, like the sealing schooners they had left, just couldn't tolerate carelessness. Every piece of gear and rope had an important job to perform, and if it wasn't capable of doing the job when it was needed, the ship itself could easily be lost.

"There just wasn't room for mistakes, so the skipper and mate were always watchful to see each man did his job properly. There was no excuse if you didn't. You did it their way, or they'd kick your ass right off the ship. Fortunately I was quick to learn, and soon carried my weight. I was paid the same as the rest of the seamen, $22 a month, and a buck and a half whale bonus. It was damn good money in those days! But I earned every penny of it.

"We stood watches of four hours on and four hours off, and the only break away from that routine was when we were at anchor or tied up at the station for some reason other than to load coal or grub. I never got enough rest with those hours. Later I know they went to six hours on watch and six hours off, but during my time I recall being often very tired and hungry.

"Often I was called out from my watch below because of weather at our anchorage, a whale to heave in, or, worse, twenty tons of coal to shovel aboard. Many times during that first season at sea, if given half a chance, I would have gladly quit. But I toughed it out, and by the time we got back to Victoria and I got my hands on all that money I'd earned during the season, the hardships, hunger, and the lack of sleep would be forgotten. By the following spring, I was all excited and ready to go again!"

Allan Heater snorted derisively when I told him about our short rations on the *Brown*, and what I had considered hardships of those days. "Hell, Bill. We couldn't eat in the galley messroom. That was for the captain and officers. We had to line up outside at the galley door with our tin plate and cup in hand, and wait for Mac Wong to dish out each man's portion onto his plate. It was up to us to get it back safely to the forecastle, where we had a table to mess at. It wasn't as good as the officers' grub, and by the time we got to eat it, it was less than lukewarm and usually well-doused with rain or sea water. When the weather was fine, we'd often just sit right out there on the boiler fidley and eat our grub as fast as we could, before it could get cold. But in rough weather we'd often lose some, if not all of it, just trying to get it to the forecastle to eat. Mac Wong would often refuse a refill when this happened. Maybe he thought we were trying to get seconds, or maybe he didn't have enough for the rest of the crew. At any rate, he'd shake his head and close the galley door, and we'd go hungry till the next mealtime."

Allan chuckled softly as he recounted an almost-forgotten anecdote. "The second engineer's fireman got so riled up at Mac Wong once for not replacing his lost supper that he went after the cook with murder in his eyes and a large heavy slice bar in his hands! Quick as a wink, Mac Wong grabbed up one of his razor sharp knives, and after a few desperate minutes struggle along the deck, he had that big Norskie fireman pinned against the engine room skylight with the knife drawing blood at the fireman's adam's apple every time he swallowed.

"Mac Wong had been cook with my grandfather for years, and favoured him a great deal with special baking or cooking, and if we ever dared to ask about it, or for some of it, Mac Wong would sputter indignantly and chase us away with a knife or a ladle. 'You no touch! For Captain Heater, he likee very special my cooking. You get your food, by and by.' "

Allan Heater put down his tea cup and leaned back reflectively in his chair as his mind returned to those years. "I guess food was always uppermost in my mind while I was a whaler, mostly because I never got enough of it, and what you got was the plainest of fare. The CNR's *Prince John* used to bring up most of our food and mail, while the *Gray* brought up coal and whaling supplies, and took away oil and meal. We did a lot of fishing whenever we were anchored up for weather, or sometimes shot ducks, geese, or deer to supplement our meat supply. When all that failed, we always had a barrel or two of salt pork or beef to fall back on. Mac Wong baked bread in the oven of the galley stove, and sometimes, maybe, buns, but I don't recall any cakes or pies—though others may have got them. Over all, we got, at best, just enough to live on, and certainly nothing to spare. I guess we were all guilty of charging up a bit to the company store for candy or smokes, and sometimes those canned cookies or fruit, to enjoy during the off-watch comfort of our bunks."

Graig Fergusson also sailed with Bill Heater, and the story he tells is interesting because it describes not one, but two occasions when the crew dictated terms the master was forced to submit to: to allow equal privileges to his crew, and to step down from the highest office aboard a whaling ship, that of gunner.

Fergusson sailed with Heater on the *W. Grant* the same season I whaled out of Naden on the *Brown*. Recalling Allan Heater's comments about eating conditions, and some of the gossip I'd overheard between the older whalers at the time, I asked him how they had managed to get messroom privileges. "Oh, we suffered it out for over a month, carrying our grub forward from the galley to eat in the forecastle, before we asked him to accede to modern times and let us eat our meals in the messroom." Graig was another of those outspoken, fearless characters who had been a whaler, and he clapped his large hands together with a dry chuckle as he described the events. "Old Cap was a fine man in many ways, and a damn stubborn one in many other ways. It took two of us to push and hoist him up the ladder to the bridge, and then he'd stay up there, often eating his meals there, till he was so weary he was nearly falling over. Then we'd help him down the ladder to the deck, and get him to the messroom or his cabin to rest. He suffered badly with arthritis, and could move only very slowly, leaning on his stick for support.

"Well, we had some fairly young fellows up forward. Three of us were under twenty-three, and another guy had whaled out of South Georgia, so when Cap refused to allow us to eat in the messroom, we made an even stronger presentation of our case, actually demanded the right to eat where he ate. He didn't like it, but he needed us more than ever, so finally he agreed.

"He certainly had a bit of the William Bligh in him, but he was of the old school, tough as nails, and still the best seaman aboard the ship. It was uncanny the way he could bring us right back to shore in a heavy fog, and he'd name the rock or spot we should see first in making our landfall, and you know, he was right every time. It was like he had built-in radar. We had a lot of fog that year; you'd notice it more when coming back in for a landfall. He'd just sniff and listen, and bring us right in where we should be. Not once, you understand, but many times! I'll bet we could have put a blindfold over his eyes and he'd have done it."

Graig Fergusson was a retired oil company manager when I met him to make these notes, and was more than willing to talk about his days as a whaler. Born on Pender Island in what is locally termed the Gulf Islands, Graig had spent much of his earlier years fishing, and was salmon trolling with Fernie Hough's brother out of Bull Harbour, at the north end of Vancouver Island, when he learned from other ex-whalers fishing there that the whalers were going to sail again. So he travelled down to Victoria and signed aboard the *W. Grant* as seaman.

Graig offered this story to better illustrate the turn-of-the-century thinking that still persisted within the whaling fleet, especially on Bill Heater's ship. "There was seldom a light taken down into the hold where the powder and barrels of salt beef and pork were stowed; we relied on the light from the open hatch, so it was usually quite gloomy down there, even on a bright day. But when Mac Wong would duck quickly below for a piece of meat, he'd only lift a couple hatch boards and toss back the corner of the hatch tarp, so he had to sort of feel around till his eyes got used to the gloom. He was seldom there more than a few minutes, just long enough to roll up his sleeve, push the lid aside, and feel around in the brine for a likely sized piece of meat. This he'd catch up in his apron, pull the lid back, and get the hell out of there.

"Well, I was down there one day, putting lashings on harpoons, when I got a whiff of this really rotten odour. Grant you, those old boats had a real throat-grabbing stink in their bilges, especially when they did a bit of rolling around, but this was different. It was really wicked. I finally lifted the lid of the salt beef barrel, and my god, it almost gagged me! So I cautiously lit a match and had a look. I damn near heaved up my supper when I saw this big, bloated, rotten rat floating belly-up in the brine. We'd just had a big hunk of salt meat for supper from that same barrel. I quickly got the guys and we lugged the barrel up and threw the whole damn thing over the side, but somehow the cook found out about it and told the skipper. He called the whole crew on deck and dressed down us young fellows severely, stating we had no right to waste company stores unnecessarily, and said he strongly considered deducting it from our pay. He said if it ever happened again, we should never waste the whole barrel of meat, but just dump the rat over the side. Believe me, he was not joking. Waste not, want not, was a fact of life on the whalers."

"Another thing I can recall," Graig said as we discussed old Bill Heater, "was the skipper setting up the detonators ready for the next day's shoot. He only set up one day's supply at a time, and these he would often prepare while sitting out on the warm boiler fidley, during the quiet of the evening. We often gathered there for an evening's chin wag while we did our washing, or carved whale's teeth or bone. Sometimes it was around someone getting a shipboard haircut while sitting on an upturned bucket, or we might make up rope yarns or wire shackles for the harpoons. If we were at anchor or laying-to, we'd discuss the news passed on over the radio-telephone, or change a foregoer, or even turn a mainline end for end. There was no end of little jobs to do to fill in a quiet afternoon or evening.

Graig brought up the name of Mac Wong, Captain Heater's long-time cook on the *Grant*. "He was supposed to be a confirmed Christian, at least, he had sailed on the coastal mission ship *Columbia* years before, and claimed he believed in God. I think it was a bit of play-acting or leg-pulling, but each evening he'd pray before going to bed. He had a shoe box, one of those white cardboard boxes, all decorated up into a tiny alter complete with cross, which he'd place on the forecastle ladder step and knelt before it.

"I can't remember his exact words, but it always included a passage something like this: 'Please mister God, look after and protect us all, and please give Captain Heater a good straight aim for the next whale.' He was a good cook, and had also served his time as both fireman and seaman, but he had a sharp temper and brooked little nonsense from us younger guys before he'd blow his top and sputter out, 'You know bugger all! I was whaling before you were born, god dammit!' "

Graig chuckled when I mentioned the infected tooth I had had removed at Masset the season we both whaled with William Schupp's Consolidated Whaling of Victoria. "Hell, it was just such an abscessed tooth that broke Cap Heater's long career as gunner with the company," he reflected. "Old Cap was from the era of wooden ships and iron men, and ran a very tight ship. He had no intentions of moving ahead with the times, and the crew were given no privileges beyond the letter of our article of agreement. You know, so many ounces of meat and vegetables per week, a sweat rag and a bar of soap per month. We had that showdown to get messroom privileges, and we finally had a real showdown to get him to relinquish his position of gunner to our mate, Oscar Luddvicksen.

"His arthritis was so bad he could only move very slowly along the deck with the aid of a stick. Once we hoisted him up to the bridge, he had to stay there till we helped him down again. Getting him up onto the gun platform, and then keeping an eye on him to see he did not fall overboard, was a trying experience, but the whales he missed because he could not handle the gun fast enough cost all of us the loss of our whale bonus. Everyone was quite upset and unhappy with the circumstances, and really did not want to be party to breaking such a fine seaman's heart. Yet old Cap refused to acknowledge the fact that his days of being a whaling gunner, at least, were over.

"We put a proposal to him. Oscar had stated he did not want the gunner's bonus, which was much larger than that which he received as mate, but was quite willing to do the shooting and have Bill Heater claim the credit and bonus for himself. Actually, we were saying that no one else but us would ever know that old Cap wasn't doing the actual shooting!

"The ship was loaded and almost ready to leave Rose Harbour when we made this formal approach to him. He was on the bridge and we had all gathered on deck around the bridge ladder. Cap leaned over the railing, glaring down at us as though we were a bunch of mutineers, while we tried to talk up to him. When we finished, he just snorted as though it was all rubbish, and turned away. Well, we demanded an answer, and he just as determinedly refused to hear anymore about it and ordered us to get the ship ready to sail immediately.

"That's when we had to tell him we would not sail the ship till he acceded to our demands. He flushed angrily then, his face swelling up and his eyes squinting down to inspect each one of us, as though we were marked men. 'Avast that talk, or I'll have all you troublemakers ashore! Now stand by your lines, we're leaving,' he roared, limping over to the telegraph and ringing it noisily back and forth till he placed it on 'Stand-by.'

" 'We'll quit before you do if you don't agree to give up the shooting,' we shouted up in a chorus of discontent.

"The skipper limped back to the rail and snorted scornfully down at us before turning away again in a show of dismissal. This caused an irate fireman to shout, 'Then the hell with this ship!' and he climbed up on the dock and walked to the manager's office and quit.

"We all began to growl amongst ourselves, trying to decide whether to follow suit, when my watch mate, Les Painter, who came from one of the old and well-established families in Victoria known to Captain Heater, jumped up and went up to the manager's office. I knew he had been suffering with a badly abscessed tooth, but the skipper didn't. Les went up to arrange for a month's leave to return to Victoria to have his tooth fixed properly.

"But old Cap believed he had gone up there like our fireman, to quit, and would carry back to Victoria a story of how Bill Heater's crew had lost faith in him. Admitting defeat, Cap slowly lowered himself down the ladder, brushing away any help. Part way down, he stopped and glared at us, 'It's a miserable Italian trick!' he snarled, referring, I suppose, to the back-stabbing Mussolini had given poor little Ethiopia. Then, swinging his stick to drive us out of his way, he slowly dragged himself aft to his cabin, and stayed there, out of sight, as we got underway.

"Short crewed as we were, with a seaman and fireman gone, Oscar still managed to get quite a few whales, and everyone's spirits began to pick up. A day or so later the old man got over his sulking and came back on deck. I guess he knew that, if we had quit, he'd have been through too, so it was better this way. Before the season was over, he was again speaking to most of us, which made some of us feel much better about the part we had played in removing some of old Cap's laurels from his crown."

Captain William Heater was born at Harbour Grace in 1865, and died at Victoria in 1947 at the age of eighty-one. His son Ronald died in July 1977, and shortly after, when I visited Allan and Lilly Heater at their north Victoria home, they brought out the letters written by Allan's grandfather to his son during those difficult years. Graig Fergusson's mutiny story was but one of the many torments suffered by this ancient mariner. As these letters reveal a family rift that developed over the years into a tragedy, I've asked Allan Heater to sketch in the background.

"My grandfather and his brother George had a falling-out about the time I was born. I think that was why my great-uncle left the whaling business and went back to fishing. It had something to do with a woman he was involved with in those years after his wife died, and my grandfather thought it indecent and demanded he get rid of her. They never talked to each other again. Mind you, I don't think the families ever were what you'd call close, but after that they spread completely apart," Allan chuckled, settling back in a large chair, before asking me if I had read much about the Heaters previous to our meeting. When I shook my head, he quickly sketched in the events that brought the Heaters to this coast before the turn of the century.

"My grandfather was mate of a large sealing schooner called the *Ainoko*, which was commanded by his brother George. After a series of wild gales in the Bering Sea, they found themselves well within the Russian-Japanese restricted sealing grounds, and hurried to get her clear of the area before being discovered. Hardly had they got all sail on the ship when they were overtaken by a big Russian man-of-war and ordered to heave-to. The ship's papers and navigational instruments were seized, and the *Ainoko* was put under arrest and ordered to proceed to Japan.

"Well, besides the master, mate, two white seamen, and a Chinese cook, the *Ainoko* carried twenty-three not-so-very-civilized west coast Indians as seal hunters, and when these suspicious fellows realized the ship was not heading east towards their native home, but west, away from it, they threatened mutiny, ready to take over the ship themselves.

"Mutiny in those days usually meant the dumping overside of the losers by the winners, and with the threat of five to one odds facing them precariously across the wet narrow decks of the schooner, and the Russian naval vessel already hull down on the western horizon, it didn't take my grandfather or his brother long to decide to prudently turn their ship about and square away for Victoria, three thousand miles to the sou-east."

Allan Heater slapped his large hands and gave a couple of heavy belly chuckles as he tried to relive the circumstances these fifth-generation Heater masters had found themselves in. "Of course the Russians had already sent some tersely worded protests to Victoria before the arrival of the *Ainoko* caused both ship and cargo to be promptly confiscated. There was also some consideration given to placing both my grandfather and great-uncle in jail, but that didn't come to pass. Though in Sprott Balcom's case around about the same time, the ship and all their possessions were seized and they were all interned in a jail in Vladivostok. However, the Balcoms had actually been sealing in restricted waters; the Heaters had not, and this was quickly realized after verification of the ship's position and the weather they had experienced. The point there were no fresh skins discovered by the Russian boarding party, and that the ship was under all sail out of the area, helped prove the case in their favour."

There was still a bit more to tell to set the stage for his grandfather's story, and Allan Heater struggled to simplify the tangled web. "My grandfather took command of the family schooner *Libby* shortly after this, and continued sealing till about 1908 or 09, when Sprott Balcom offered him a berth with Pacific Whaling. When the *W. Grant* was launched at Victoria Machinery Depot, he was given command of her, a position he held till she was sold to become a towboat in the mid-forties.

"His older brother George finally left sealing when the treaty was enforced, and took command of the *Orion*, and Willis Balcom, who had been in command of her, took over the new ship S.S. *Black*. When William Schupp took over in 1915, he sent George out with the *Orion* during the off-season to try halibut fishing, and she actually made money at it. Not enough to satisfy Schupp, but it interested George, and a few years later he went into the fishing business, setting up a large fishing camp out on the west coast. It was during this period he lost his wife and took up with the young lady that caused my grandfather to refuse to talk to him till he broke up the association with her. Unfortunately, Uncle George passed away before they could reconcile their differences.

"But my father had a falling-out with my grandfather over much the same type of issue," admitted Allan, taking a packet of letters and flicking them like a deck of cards before passing them over to his wife.

The ex-whaler Orion *as a yacht before becoming Vancouver's fireboat.*

"I was about fourteen when my grandmother passed away, and for a couple years after, my grandfather batched alone in the old family home. Then suddenly, and to the embarrassment of my dad and his sister, my Aunt May, he took in a young woman as housekeeper, supposedly to look after the house and make his meals. But one thing led to another, and soon gossip began to fly, and my father asked him to discharge the young woman and put an end to the gossip. When my grandfather stubbornly refused, my father swore to have nothing to do with him till he did. Sort of an echo of the past, eh?"

"Allan's grandfather pretended not to be upset by this, but we now know from reading these letters that he was very lonely and brokenhearted, but too stubborn to admit he had made a mistake," Lilly Heater added, pausing in her perusal of the letters.

"To everyone's surprise, he up and married this gal, and she took him for everything he had!" continued Allan. "We now know from his letters why he did it, but she must have thought him so old and feeble he'd die any day, or at least fall over the side and drown so she'd collect his whole estate.

"But it was not that easy. Grandfather hung in there till he was eighty-one. God, how she must have ate her heart out! She was so spiteful, she burned and destroyed all which she could not sell. Not a single family heirloom was even offered to us. Like a wolverine, what she didn't want or couldn't sell, she either gave away or destroyed, just so we couldn't get our hands on it." Having witnessed two similar instances, I nodded knowingly, understanding the heartbreak this must have caused.

"In a sense, this jane, as he referred to her, didn't have the last laugh. It turned out she was what you might call a professional widow. After my grandfather passed away, she promptly married a man she met on a train trip, but he turned out to be a bigamist and she got nothing from his estate. Then she came back to Victoria and married a retired banker. He died suddenly, and in the will she was named sole heir to the estate. Suspecting foul play, his son came up from California to investigate. He found she had married numerous old men and collected their estates. He visited my Dad to enquire if Captain Heater had also succumbed quickly after marrying her. When my Dad told him just how long that old whaler had made her wait to get her greedy hands on his estate, they both had to chuckle. I don't know what finally happened to her, but I don't think they could prove she did much more than make some old men's lives more miserable than they were."

"He goes from gossip to copper paint without pause," chortled Lilly Heater, as Allan refilled our cups with tea. "This letter is dated Blue Bay, July 15, 1937, aboard the S.S. *W. Grant*. Shall I read it?" I checked the recorder and nodded, and Lilly cleared her throat like a soprano and spoke the words the old whaler had written to his son over forty years before.

> Dear Ron, the weather here is on the bum, fog and wind, and no whales. I have only got one whale in the last ten days. The other two boats have not got one for over two weeks. Well, the catches are, three for the S.S. White, 44 for S.S. Grant and 43 for the S.S. Blue. I hope to make fifty. There were eleven aeroplanes passed me by to-day, going north.

"Now, here's a little bit of gossip he puts in," laughed Lilly, skimming through the rest of the letter. " 'I hear that Fernie Hough has stolen Harry Anderson's wife. He's all cut up about it. Well now, I'll put on some copper paint. . . .' " She gave an incredulous laugh and shook her head. "He goes from stealing wives to putting copper paint on the boat without pause! Oh, look here Allan. Here's a newspaper story of when you went whaling." A touch of excitement added a lilt to her voice as she lifted up a faded clipping from the Victoria *Colonist*. "Skipper takes grandson whaling with him," she read, then laughed, "Oh, look. There's a picture of the *Grant*. It's dated April 15, 1936."

The whalers of the W. Grant *in 1936. Left to right: Astor Johnson, Tommy Hill, Oscar, Allan Heater, Louis Heglund.*

"Well, that proves the date. I thought it was thirty-five that I started," Allan mused, and we discussed this significant moment in his life for a few moments, till Lilly selected a letter that she felt was interesting enough for my notes, and began to read it aloud for us. "Now here's a letter from 1938, put in an envelope from 1941."

Dear Ron, just a line to let you know what you might already know by this time. News goes to wing fast. I'm being talked about by everyone for the last three years and watched every move I make, and some persons keep you informed of every move I make, so I've come to the conclusion to get married and put an end to all that talk. I could not possibly live alone and batch at this time of life. You may think hard of me and say I'm foolish, but you or May could not put me up, and I could not think of being in the way. Now put yourself in my position. Do you think you could live alone? The woman is wife in name only. I was forced in doing what I have done, to keep people from talking. If there was no talking going on, I'd still be single. It was no happy adventure, I can tell you. I will regret it.

My time is short. I am all in. I shouldn't have come whaling this year. I never expect to see you any more, so don't think too hard of me, Ron. I have never altered my will in any shape or way, and never intend to. Everything is between you and May, you have the lion's share, and the boat is yours. In the event of me not coming back, Taten Howe has the will. If she thinks she's got it all, she'll be badly fooled.

Allan Heater sat back quietly in his chair, his large hands folded across his belt. I suspected the reading of these letters was causing him some sad reflections, and only the hum of the recorder could be heard as Lilly opened another letter and quickly scanned its contents. This exploration into the elder Heater's private thoughts, as confided to his son, caused me to be a little awed; for Lilly Heater it was a part of her family history which, I suspect, Allan had spoken very little of, and which she now found an exciting revelation.

Rose Harbour, July 13, 1941—aboard the Wm. Grant.

Dear Ron: Your letter received and contents noted. Well now, I'm very happy to hear from you and know you are well, and remember me on father's day. Well now, I'm still on deck, but badly bent. My legs are bad, I can just get along with my trusty stick. My feet and leg swell and give me pain night and day. I thought I was finished last night. Had to get out and rub for all I was worth. Anyway, I only come out here to go over the bow. I've been close to it a good many times. I have no command of my legs. Anyway, it's out one end, or the other.

I'm proud of Allan. He's going to keep up the title. Good for me, good for him. I'm glad I started him on the way. He's very

> likely to get one of those new corvettes. Too bad Gordon got knocked out on the Nora.
>
> Well son, I can still knock a whale over, but I have been working with half a crew most of the time, so that puts us behind. I have forty-six now and lost three, fisherman's luck. The weather last week was fine, I got eight sperms and one humpback. Lost a fin yesterday. Winch broke down, stud in main bearing broke. Harpoon pulled out of the whale, it was a rough sea. Say I will never go to sea again, if I live to get ashore. Do you know that I have not been off the Grant since I left Victoria. No pleasure. I am sick of it. May was telling me that the jane sold my car and bought Victory bonds. If she did, there will be a victory fight when I get back. I never thought I'd be whaling at my age, seventy-six. Not many do it that long.
>
> Well now, I'd like to see Allan in his uniform, all brass bound. Remember me to him. Well now my boy, I hope you are having a pleasant summer. They say they are going to whale till September, I can't see it. We have nothing to work with only scrap iron. Well, we'll be seeing you, if I don't go overboard. Good-by and good-luck. Yours sincerely, Father.

This letter touched us all. The brevity of his sentences and the variety of his subjects—especially his pride in his captain grandson, and his anger at the jane for considering him good as gone—spoke eloquently of a man alone, reaching out to set things right as he felt his time near. His reference to half a crew supports Graig Fergusson's account of life aboard the *Grant* at that time. Allan Heater's comments about his grandfather are equally valid to describe others in positions of command. "Everyone saw him as a hard crusty old man, without worry or concern for anyone. He never told anyone his troubles, so everyone just thought he had none." Allan clenched his thick fingers, and looked from his wife to me as he tried to unburden his own feelings. "When you're the Captain, everyone treats you as though you shouldn't have feelings, or fears, or misgivings. But these letters prove that even tough old whalers like my grandfather still suffer all the same feeling as the rest of us. They just do a better job of keeping it bottled up inside. If it hadn't been because of that woman, he'd have never gone out whaling during his later years. She drove him there, hoping, I suspect, that he'd fall over the side or die at sea, and she took everything he had as payment in full for looking after him in those final years."

Lilly Heater reached over and patted her husband's hands

comfortingly, then picked up the last letter and began to read, "August 1941—this is to Allan's mother!—'Dear Myrtle.' "

> Your welcome letter to hand and glad to hear from you. Well now, here we are still killing whales. I got ten this month, sixty-four to date. Weather has been very fine since August came in, but it has changed now. Blowing a sou-east wind for three days, so we are laying in. I'm not sorry, believe me, as I am all in. I can just walk with my stick forward as far as the gun. I'm getting my hell here while on earth, I hope I don't get another when I leave here. What do you think about it?
>
> Well, I'm glad to hear your son is a skipper now. That boy is climbing, he will get there. I'm delighted he will keep the name up. You'll have to excuse the writing, this stuff is in my hands, they are paining every stroke of the pen.
>
> Please remember me to Captain Bilton and family. Now I hope you'll enjoy your holidays. I'm sorry I could not get an answer off before, the mail boat don't call here going south, now. We had one on the sixteenth and won't get another till September. Remember me to the Loughheeds, I'm not able to write them. This is quite an effort. You'd be sorry if you could see me creeping along. It is an awful job for me to get down to the cabin. Once I'm out, I only go back at nights to sleep.
>
> Well now, I'll say farewell and god bless the whole of you. I remain sincerely, Cap.

Chapter Seven

The Whalers Recall

One of the best storytellers amongst the old whalers was Charlie Watson, a big handsome man full of vim and vitality that belied his seventy-five years of age. He not only sailed with the whalers much earlier than I, but he also returned to sail with the new whalers, years after I left. As chief engineer of the Western Whaling steam whaler *Bouvet III* in the mid 1950s, Charlie's comments on the modern whalers and those of Arnie Borgan are very valuable to our story. His recall spans a period from 1920 to 1955, and he is both observant and articulate.

Discussing how he had come to go whaling, Charlie explained that he had been born and raised in Duncan on Vancouver Island, and had served his machinist's apprenticeship in Victoria during World War I. "Yes, the old Hutchinson Bros. engine works went belly up on a French engine contract near the end of the war, so I finished my time in the CPR shops at the foot of Bellevue Street, under a foreman named Bill Scaplen." He paused to light up a cigarette and knock back a bit of whaler's tea. (On the whaling boats, a pot of very strong cold tea would be kept near the stove. Some of this, poured into a heavy mug and diluted with boiling water, was "whaler's tea.") "I went to sea for the first time on a big four-crank Yankee job as fourth engineer. If I recall rightly, the Americans called that position the third assistant engineer. They paid off in solid gold coin in those days. American sailors would not accept paper money after the currency crash in Europe at the end of the war.

"When I got back to Victoria, the whaling company's steam tender *Gray* was looking for a second engineer, so I signed on. Tom Rankin was chief and old Captain Billington was master. She was a good ship, steamed like a damn, and ran smooth as silk. If I remember correctly I got $145 a month. We carried a lot of freight for the fishing companies, as well as the freight and oil for the whaling company. We had gangs of Chinese coolies unload the coal at each station, and load all the whale oil aboard in wooden or metal drums. Sometimes we'd get the Indians to do this work, but mostly the coolies would do it. The Japanese wouldn't touch this type of work; they kept off by themselves and carried out only the flensing and cutting up of the whales.

"I was on the *Gray* less than a year before they ceased whaling. I think they had too much whale oil on hand and the price was away down, so it wasn't profitable to send the ships out. Yes, that was it. Well, when they did get going again about a year later, old Alf Pepper gave me a call and asked if I'd like to go out as second with him on the whaler *Black*. It paid $135 a month, but jobs were getting pretty scarce, so I took it gladly."

It is a phrase I've heard many times in making these notes, how times were tough and how glad these men were to get a job with the whaling company, even if it was seasonal and very hard work.

"Now Alf Pepper had a wooden leg, but he was a good engineer, yes, a very good engineer," Charlie continued. "Well, we were busy working down below, getting everything ready for the steamship inspector, when who should climb down below but Bill Scaplen. 'Are you following me around,' he laughed, 'or am I following you?' It turned out he had just been made the marine superintendent of the company and, spotting my name on the worksheets, dropped down to say hello.

"You see, it was Bill Scaplen who had pointed out the whaling company to me when I was finishing up my time at the CPR shops and looking around for a job to get sea time. He was a Newfie, one of the good kind, and had worked for the whaling company years before when Balcom and Grant had run it. I think he came out here with old Ruck to build the station at Kyuquot, and also helped build the one just north of Nanaimo. Page's Lagoon, I believe they called it. It was gone long before my time."

Our talk turned to whalers and weather, and Charlie exclaimed, "Ah! Cape St. James! I'll tell you an experience we had out there with the old *Black* that most people won't believe! You know, they get winds up there that often reach a hundred miles an hour or more?!"

He pawed the clutter of papers on the table, searching for a fresh package of cigarettes, as I reflected on some of the weather I'd experienced, and the stories I'd heard of the area where I received my baptism as a seaman. I recalled all-too-vividly the night we were hove-to inside Cape Calvert when the Egg Island lighthouse had been washed away by a huge sea, but I had to strain my imagination to consider the strength of the gale that had swept away buildings at the Triangle Island lightstation years before my time. That light had been built to guide in vessels far out at sea, and its base had been located

Charlie H. Watson, second engineer on Black *in 1924, age 21.*

over 600 feet above high water. Charlie would have to come up with a pretty lively story to beat that one.

"Before I tell you about the *Black*, I should mention that two years before that, on the *Gray*, I guess that would be 1919, we lost the whole deck load of empty drums between Cape Scott and Cape St. James, in seas that buried all the *Gray*'s decks completely underwater. You know, there were hundreds of brand new steel drums drifting around out there for months, but we never recovered a single one of them."

"Ah, yes. Now the *Black*. I guess it was around the end of May, or in the first part of June. We'd been hanging in the lee of Anthony Island for almost three days, while a damn sou-easter whipped the clouds through the tree tops ashore. Well, Willis Balcom watched that weather damn closely, he was a top-notch seaman, and he was ever watchful and usually well-prepared for the worst. Willis had brought out the *Orion* from Norway in 1904 and had been whaling ever since. Yes, he knew the area better than any man on the coast. Well, the minute that sou-east started to back round to the west, Willis picked up the anchor and headed south towards Cape St. James.

"His plan, he told me later, had been to run around the Cape, scouting for whales on the way, and by nightfall be in the lee of Kunghit Island. Or, if the worst did come, and a real nor-wester developed, we'd go up into Heater Harbour, or Calm Bay as we called it in those days. But no matter whether we lay there or farther south at Luxana Bay, we'd have to be prepared for the Willies, and set both anchors with steaming watches.

"Well, by midday we were about fifteen miles south of the Cape, and carefully hauling up towards the Straits, when it happened. I hadn't been on watch very long when all of a sudden the telegraph rang quickly over to 'Stand-by' and our whistle gave out a couple of watery warning gurgles. I made a grab for the throttle and hung on for dear life as the ship tossed her head swiftly upwards. She threw her head up so high the coal in the bunkers shifted aft. I could hear it thunder against the bulkhead forward of the boiler. Then she rolled away over to port. She fell so far over that everything went flying. I thought I was going to be thrown right across the engine! Before she could right herself, or we could let go to do anything to help her, she was buried by a huge sea and tons of sea water crashed down into the boiler and engine room, through the open skylight and scuttle. Boy, I'll tell you. I thought we were goners!"

Charlie shook his head as he recalled those far-off events which had happened before I was born, but which were more vivid than last week's news to him. "You know the centre fire in the boiler went out in a cloud of steam, and even the wing fires started to fail as the funnel lost its draft. I eased the throttle down to conserve what steam we had and still hold steerage on her. My god! You never seen such a mess! Coal was washed right back into the engine room bilge. Oil, rags, pieces of wood, grease, and oil buckets, mixed with layers of ash, floated back and forth, the cranks of the engine splashed and sloshed around in it, and steam and water fogged up everything below my feet on the gratings.

"I waded around below, and put the main injection suction on the engine room bilge, and the general service pump and bilge pump on the stokehold bilge line. It took over half an hour to pump her out, and a lot longer to get everything back into shipshape again." Nodding his head, Charlie pointed at me as he took a quick puff on his cigarette. "You know, if that had happened at night, we'd never have known what hit us. She would have foundered for sure. Believe me, there were a lot of shocked people aboard that ship that day. The accommodations were flooded, both our lifeboat and pram had been lifted out of their chocks and stoved in, and Willis Balcom and the man on the wheel had both been nearly washed overboard. Only the guy in the barrel was dry. Badly bruised and scared after being thrown about, but dry," Charlie chuckled.

I told him briefly of our modest experience within fifty miles of the story he had told. He nodded understandingly and sucked on his teeth as I told about the moment on the bridge when I looked up and saw that giant wave cresting high above us. "Exactly sir. Exactly the way Willis Balcom described it later to me," Charlie nodded. "According to Willis, that wave appeared suddenly, towering thirty or more feet in the air, while another of almost equal size converged like a triangle upon the ship in the centre, as she was carried forward by the following sea.

"Later, when we got back to Rose Harbour, I heard him tell Bill Rolls, the manager, that he'd never in his whole life seen such a jumbled maelstrom of seas all in one place at the same time as he did that day. And you know, I think, for once in his life, he didn't know what to do about it but hold on!" Charlie chortled, wiping a tear from his eye.

"Willis Balcom was a bridegroom that season. He had married Alfus Garcin's sister and she came up to visit him at Rose Harbour. The company lent them a small house while she was there. Willis wasn't a young man when I knew him, but he never spent a moment aboard the ship once we got tied up at Rose! She was a registered nurse, a very nice lady. I can't remember the cause, but there was an accident that left her crippled. She was confined to a wheelchair and you know, that man literally waited on her hand and foot, doted on her every wish for the rest of his life. Yes, now all you've heard about Willis is correct. Not only was he the senior whaling captain, but he was the best gunner by far of any of them, at least while I was there. I've seen him many times shoot a whale so far off that the whole foregoer would be straightened right out by the time the harpoon hit the whale. Sounds impossible, eh? But he really was that good. He's the only man I know who shot three whales at the same time."

Charlie waited as I changed tapes on the recorder so I could get this story. "Now about those three whales he shot, well that was a little before my time, but old Captain Billington on the *Gray* told me the story once, so after I'd worked with Willis for awhile I asked him about it, and here is the story he told me. Look here, I've even got some notes on it here in my log book for 1924.

"Willis told me that they had been out all that day off Kyuquot, chasing whales but never getting close enough for a good shot. There was a good sea running, a cross sea with a heavy sou-east swell under it, and he was hanging on with all his might to the gun as they tried to get closer to a big sulphur bottom that had no intentions of pausing in those waters. Willis was getting colder and hungrier up there on the exposed gun platform, and the blows of the Blue whale were getting farther away each time he surfaced, when all of a sudden the lookout called down that there was a whale just coming up to blow close on the starboard bow.

"Well, not only was the ship rolling like a log, but she was heaving up to each swell and bowling down the other side so as to make aiming damn near impossible, but Willis swung the gun around and took quick aim just as the whale breached, and jerked on the trigger. Willis claimed he never did see what really happened; that smoke and all, as he shot to windward, blew back in his face. Only the lookout up in the barrel had a clear view, and here is how he explained it to Willis. Just as Willis fired, two more whales surfaced outside the first whale. The harpoon, tossed high by the heaving of the ship, hit the first whale, a small Bottlenose, just back of the head and passed right on through, striking the second whale near the tail, where it ricocheted upwards off the backbone and struck a third whale just as its head broke the surface. Willis said there was a little excitement around the ship till they could get the whales heaved in under the bows and dispatched. My god, he was modest! Can you imagine what it must have been like? He had a dead whale on the harpoon, and between it and the ship was a whale caught by the tail and another threaded on the whale line like a piece of popcorn, each of them well over thirty tons and fighting mad!"

Charlie Watson was in his element talking with me once he knew I had also served time as a marine engineer of a steam ship. "You know, it took over a month to refit all the machinery and get that boiler ready when I first joined the *Black*. Old Alf Pepper and I worked like monkeys. They'd laid up over two years, and even the fibre discs in the air pump's valves had perished. But once we completed the job she ran like a top. They were fine little ships. God, they were lovely ships!

"Let's see now, those triple-expansion engines were built in Norway with a form of Marshal valve gear that was quick and easy to throw across into astern, even at full speed. They turned a hundred and forty revs with a hundred and eighty pounds of steam on the gauge. Very lively engines. Yes, indeed. We'd cruise at ten knots normally, but if the old man gave us a double ring on the telegraph, we could open them up to better than twelve knots. Yes, now the auxiliaries. We had a Westinghouse-type simplex steam pump for supplying air to blow up the whales, and a general service duplex pump that was used mostly for boiler feeding when laying-too, but could be used for pumping bilges also. The main pumps—bilge, circulating, air, and boiler feed—were all carried off the rocker arm beam from the high pressure crosshead. The boiler was about an eighteen-ton, three-furnace Scotch marine type, which burnt about 3½ tons of coal a day, less if we laid-to at sea at nights. We got a good grade of soft bituminous coal from Ladysmith for about three dollars a ton, which steamed well and required tube-punching only about once a week.

"But I guess you really want to hear more about whaling than marine engineering for your story," he grunted, as I tried to explain, without hurting his feelings, that selling a book required popular interest content, such as man against beast. "Yes, yes. The sight of massive pieces of well-built machinery all turning, or sliding and nodding, being pushed and pulled through their cycles by a force created with such simple materials as water and fire, no longer creates awe and respect for man's handiwork. I guess that's the price of progress. But by god, I'm forever grateful that I was born at a time when this type of craftsmanship could be seen and respected. I really love engineering; it's been my life!" Charlie shook his head a little sadly, then, like the great guy he is, rebounded to flash me an impish grin and chuckle, "You know, Willis Balcom shot a big Blue whale that took every foot of line out of our locker. God, was she a big creature!

"I was below in the engine room when he let fly, and it wasn't a good shot. Not by a damn sight. Willis claimed afterwards that it was the worst shot he had ever placed in a whale. I guess it was just an off-day for him, but he never should have tried it, not with a Blue whale. Well, we were running ahead at half speed when I heard the gun go off, and soon after that felt the winches rolling the line out and the brake being snubbed down. Then I got a ring down for half speed astern, so I knew Willis was going to try and drag on the whale line in hope of tiring the whale.

"Well, sir. I didn't even close the throttle, no need to with those engines, just pulled the reverse links under the valves, and was astonished to see the whole engine come to a complete stop! Even when I opened up the throttle a bit more, the engine just sat there and sort of quivered. Finally, when I had the throttle fully open and she still did not move, I hit her with live steam on the intermediate and finally the low-pressure piston. All that did was to lift the relief valves, and I began to lose my vacuum on the condenser, so I had to stop that. I had just closed the throttle down when the telegraph rang over to full speed ahead. Of course, I wasn't aware of it at the time, but that whale had pulled out almost all our line, and Willis had decided he had better chase that whale and try and get some of it back.

"I pulled the forward links under her again and my god, you should have seen that engine turn over. The cranks were just a blur, I was afraid she would throw a bottom end or burn her guides, so I gave her just enough steam to keep the pistons loaded. That whale was pulling us through the water so fast, it actually was causing the propeller to windmill in the wash! Like a tail wagging a dog.

"That whale was still going faster than the ship, and showing no signs of slowing down. The line was almost all out of the locker and we were being towed towards China, hanging on the bitter end. Willis was trying to decide whether to hang on a bit longer in hope the whale would tire before we broke some of our gear, or cut it loose and kiss three thousand feet of good six-inch manila line good-bye, when our whale swung over towards the *Brown*, who was chasing a whale off on the horizon.

"Well, sir. That whale charged across the *Brown*'s bows so close, she reared to a stop. I think old Canute thought it was going to ram them, but he didn't lose his cool, as they say nowadays. He just dropped the gun sights down from the whale he was going to shoot, and shot ours instead, just as it surfaced on the other side of the ship. We finally came to a frantic halt less than half a cable off Canute and his boys, and hauled the whale back to us. God, were they mad at that, till they realized it was our whale they had shot!"

Charlie slapped his leg as he concluded this story, then fished out a photo from the box and handed it over to me, "Here, see there's a picture of me standing on that same whale's belly as we began to tow it back to Rose. You can see it's damn near as long as the ship!"

Charlie Watson standing on the belly of a large Blue whale, en route to Rose Harbour.

Another source of whaler stories was Captain D.B. (Dode) MacPherson, seventy-eight years old when I first met him, and more than eager to talk about the old days and the way it was when he went to sea with the whalers. He had started with the Victoria Whaling Company the year William Schupp first sent his whalers to sea, and his observations and recollections were very interesting to me. Not only did he have a good clear recall of those far-off days, but he had notes, records, and pictures to authenticate his statements. A man of average height and build, he spoke with a strong, fearless voice and a friendly twinkle in his eye as he flattered me by assuming I was as knowing a sailor as himself.

"My father had a master mariner's certificate signed by Wilfrid Laurier," Captain MacPherson stated, then paused for my reaction. The name conjured up a memory from my school days of a history book picture of Sir Wilfrid Laurier, Prime Minister of Canada.

Dode laughed as I shot him a glance of amazement. "Yes, he was Minister of Marine at the time, and my father's certificate was for steam passenger tugboats. Those were small steamers that carried loggers, miners, and fishermen up the coast, and towed logs, scows, or sailing vessels south on their return trip."

Knowing he had had a long career as towboat master and skipper of several large sternwheelers in the BC Interior, I asked him how he had happened to go whaling. "My dad was a towboat skipper when I was young, so it was only natural I should try my hand at the same thing. After two years of that I thought I was a pretty salty young fellow and began acting the part, till one of my dad's friends joked about my smooth water sailing. When I failed to see any humour in his remark and got angry, he suggested, not unkindly, that if I really wanted to become a sailor worthy of the name, I should go for a season or two with one of the old boys of the whaling fleet.

"Well, I'd heard that Captain Anderson of the *Blue* was top gunner of the fleet, and, green as grass, I marched down and seen him. I just told him I wanted to become a good seaman, and would work hard as hell to become one." Dode smiled, remembering it as though it were yesterday. "Oh, he just smiled and nodded good-naturedly. I was sure he was going to tell me to go and see someone else, but would you believe it, he said he'd give me a chance. God, was I ever surprised!

"Well, it didn't take me long to get ready to go. I don't need to tell you how excited I was. But, my god! I didn't know what it was really going to be like till we reached the west coast. That boat rolled and tossed till my stomach was sore from being sick and my body was sore from being thrown around. Believe me, it was only my greater fear of

D.B. MacPherson at the wheel of the Blue, *1920.*

our tough old mate that prevented me dying of sea sickness that trip. I've never kidded anyone who ever got seasick since, I know what it was like. But, like all things in life, I eventually got used to it, and it has never bothered me since."

I asked Captain MacPherson about the first whale they took, and whether they hand-lanced a whale that had not been killed by the first harpoon, or used a harpoon lance bomb like we did. He chuckled knowingly and nodded, "We always hand-lanced any that we had not killed outright with the harpoon. Those old boys would never dream of wasting powder and time to shoot a whale a second time. Sometimes there'd be six of us, all up on the gun platform, pushing

Lancing a whale to finish him off.

and prodding with our long lances down at the whale threshing around under the bow, while it blew steaming vapour and blood all over us. Usually it took two of us together to plunge a lance down into the whale and twist it around till it broke a vital organ or got into the lungs. Believe me, it took a lot of getting used to. And, I'll admit, I never did really get used to that."

Dode pressed his lips together as he recalled this distasteful task, but after a moment his face broke into a grin as a humourous aspect of it was brought to mind. "We went out in the pram once and actually lanced a whale to death. Just as a dare, you understand, we didn't have to do it. Captain Anderson said he could do it, and I went with him in the boat. We didn't make fast with a harpoon, you know. At least that way we would have had something to hold onto. No that was too easy for John Anderson. We just rowed up alongside and he struck the whale with an iron that hit the lungs first try. Then he told me to try it. But every time I tried to push the lance into the whale, the fool boat would drift away, and I'd almost fall in the water alongside the whale. It was pretty terrible, trying to stick a lance into an angry whale, and we were doing it under good conditions. I just don't know how the old whalers could do it, especially when the seas were running and the whale was lively."

About his first whale he was a bit hazy till he found his notes. "Let's see now. We went up to Sechart and worked out of there for a while with the *St. Lawrence*. Arversen was skipper of her. I believe they had just opened Sechart after a two-year shut-down, but there were no whales around there. So when Willis Balcom began catching whales at Kyuquot, they told us to go up there."

He thumbed through his old notebook and his eyes brightened as he found what he was looking for. "We got our first whale, a big Sperm, off Cape Cook, April 14. Never got anymore till May 1. That was a big bull Sperm, too. You know, we never got a cow Sperm the whole time I was whaling! Here's a tally of the whales caught by each boat that season. Arversen, on the *St. Lawrence*, got most with 73 whales; Willis on the *Black* got 69; Canute Halvorsen on the *Brown* got 48; Harry Balcom and Bill Heater each got 70 whales on the *Green* and *W. Grant*; and the *Orion*, which had been out on the halibut fishery with George Heater and was late starting, only got 22. We on the *Blue* got 45, and at $3.00 whale bonus for Sperms and $1.50 each for the others, it brought my average pay up from $45 a month to about $57, which was pretty darn good for those days."

I asked if they got many Blues during those earlier years and he nodded. "The last year I whaled we got twenty-four large sulphur bottoms, right in Dixon Entrance. Course, the boats were in top condition in those days, they were only six years old. We didn't worry much about the gear, so went after the Sperms and Blues, just because the whale bonus was higher." He added that most of the Blues in those days ran up to 100 tons or more. His face suddenly broke into a mischievous smile. "Say, Bill. I just remembered something I'm sure you'll want for your story: three whales being harpooned at the same time with the same harpoon!" (No, you're not reading in circles—I've included Dode's version of this incident for comparison.)

"We were up in the Charlottes when the *Gray* came in. She only came once a month with fresh meat and stores, so if you wanted to get yours before all the vegetables and fruit wilted, and the meat went completely bad, you'd try to be near the station when you knew she was coming. Well, this was after I'd been with the company a few years and was mate of the *Blue*, so I was able to get in there and hear the story first hand.

"Hawes was skipper of her then, and he told the wildest tale any of us had ever heard. He claimed as they were leaving Kyuquot, Willis Balcom came in with four Bottlenose whales. Later I heard it was only three, but all shot with the same harpoon. The harpoon had gone right through the first whale, ricocheted up and went through a second whale, and finally struck the one Willis had been aiming at where the bomb exploded and the flukes took hold. It killed that one right on the spot, but the other two were fighting mad and Willis had to heave all three under the bow and lance them. Now that would have been something to have a picture of—three whales strung out on a whale line, like herring on a jig!"

When I asked him about the whalers he sailed with, what they were really like ashore and afloat, and what they did when they weren't whaling, Dode laughed with glee, rocking back in his chair and rubbing his hand through his thinning hair. "Oh, they were a strange group. Yes, a strange group in many ways. Spent all their money on women and booze, and were usually broke two weeks after the season closed. Yet they were all good hard-working men when out at sea.

"The whaling company wouldn't allow liquor of any sort on the ships or at the whaling stations because of the trouble it had caused in the years gone by. Yet, in town, the whalers all met at the pubs; that's where you'd go to find them. You remember, of course, the Rock Bay Hotel across from the whaling office. Actually it was down the street a little, in front of the Victoria Machinery Depot. And then there was the Coach and Horses out on the Esquimalt Road. You could always find some of the whalers in there. When I became mate, that's where I'd go to start rounding up a crew," Dode smiled.

"But others were complete abstainers and religious as nuns. Captain Arversen of the *St. Lawrence* was a great big farmer of a man and very religious, he sang hymns a lot. Sometimes when he was at the gun you could hear him roaring away at the words of a sacred song, while trying to get a big Humpback in his sights," Dode mused, a smile tugging at his bony face. "Bill Heater used to act very religious, but I think he was just pulling everyone's leg."

MacPherson sailed four seasons with the whalers, the last two years as mate, or pilot as they called them then. His keen observations present those silent, stalwart whalers in a more humane light. After showing me his master's certificate, with its endorsement for minor waters, he dug out some of the old service recommendations that had allowed him to qualify to sit for the examinations.

"This is the one I like best," Dode smiled modestly, as I quickly scribbled down the details of a lovely, script-written document:

> To whom it may concern.—This is to certify that Donald MacPherson as served with me for three whaling seasons—one as deck hand, one season as 2nd mate and this present season of 1919 as Mate, and I found him a sober, steady and capable young man and gave me every satisfaction, and I recommend him where ever he may go. (signed) J. Anderson—Master of the Blue—Dec. 1919.

John Anderson hailed from Petites, Nova Scotia, and was sealing master of the schooners *E.B. Marvin* and *Saucy Lass* on the Falkland grounds before joining the local whaling company in 1911. "Did you notice he didn't write 'has served,' but, like the old Newfie he was, he wrote 'as served'?" Dode lit up a pipe to hide his feelings. "He was the best damn man I ever sailed with, and I'm proud he was my tutor! Everyone said he was tough, difficult, and reticent, but he always treated me fine. And everyone aboard the *Blue* thought him tops, too. You know, he'd sometimes walk the decks when we were anchored up, waiting for tide or weather, and recite little bits of poetry. I'll bet you've never heard this one. . . 'She buried low her bosom in the snow, she buried her lee cathead. . .' Trace that one, if you can!" snorted Captain MacPherson, enjoying an audience to hear his tales.

His face became more alive as he recalled those days of his youth, and only the recorder and my heart could capture the thrill he still felt, as he told the stories of how it was. He explained how, in those days, the mate did all the piloting of the ship back and forth between station and whaling grounds, and the skipper did all the hunting and shooting of the whales. Thus, the skipper was often referred to as the gunner, and the mate as the pilot, terminology that became confusing when some of the ships carried a second mate. John Anderson often took over the pilot's watch so Dode could get a little rest on the long run in or out of Naden, so they were able to dispense with a second mate on the *Blue*, and realize a larger share of the whale bonus between them.

"You know, he and Bill Heater used to call each other uncle. Uncle John and Uncle Bill. They were great friends. You remember old Moses Keil? He was sort of a wharfinger for the whaling company, a small little Scotchman who saved everything and hid it away in that warehouse of theirs at the dock. I don't know when Moses Keil started there; everyone spoke as though he'd been there forever. Both Ruck and his ginger-haired assistant, Lawson, treated him like a supercargo. They approved of his saving ways and god knows they were experts at squeezing a nickle. You know they had to go to the bank every month to borrow money, just to run the company. Old Schupp didn't believe in leaving a penny laying around to gather dust.

"Well, Old Moses Keil was really religious. You know how those Norwegians swore. Well, every time Moses heard them say, 'Jesus Christ, God almighty!' he'd wag his finger under their big grinning faces and righteously scold, 'You're speaking of a man you know very little about!' so they nicknamed him John the Baptist," Dode chortled as, for a moment, he recalled a funny moment in a life that must have been as hard as any man's.

Dode MacPherson was born in Victoria in 1899, and attended the old Norfolk School on Douglas Street, so I asked him if he also knew any of the Grants or Balcoms. A few weeks earlier I had met Lawrence Balcom, the last remaining son of Sprott Balcom, who had been instrumental in creating the whaling company we both had worked for.

"Sure I remember the younger Balcom boys, Bert and Art. We went to school together," he nodded to my question. "But Lawrence was older. He and my brother were about the same age. I just remember him because we often saw him driving his father home to lunch in the company's big Chalmers automobile. Used to see Mrs. Helen Grant, Captain Grant's wife, driving around in one of those little Edison electric cars. She'd be all dressed up in her finery, with a huge hat bouncing on her head. They had a beautiful home down on the Gorge, right across from the whaling company offices, complete with a widow's walk on the roof and lots of flowers growing in a garden that stretched right down to the waters of the Gorge.

"You know, when the Point Ellice bridge collapsed, and street cars full with people plunged into the Gorge, it was the Grants and their sealers who rescued many of them. Laid the injured out in the living room and the dead were laid on the lawn. Used the drapes off their windows as shrouds for the dead. I know there's many stories about the Grants, but my dad said Bill and Helen Grant were real good people. I was too young to really know the old man, but Mrs. Grant lived over twenty years after his death, and was an institution of good around Victoria for many of my years."

I asked him about those Balcom men who went whaling, and the men who were managers when he sailed with the company. "Well. Willis Balcom had the *Black* when I was there, and Harry had the *Green*. I think it was Willis who sported a very fine black beard—course I could be mistaken, it might have been Harry, but I recall it was one of the older Balcom boys. One thing for sure, at this late date no one is going to challenge it." Grinning over at me as a thought struck him, Dode changed the subject slightly with hardly a pause. "You know, Harry Balcom was a confirmed bachelor. A big, heavy-set, quiet type of man, he often stayed over the whole winter at the whaling station as sort of a watchman. I think he liked the solitude of the station to the noise and fuss of the town."

When I drew a comparison between Rose and Naden Harbours, Dode nodded in agreement. "I liked Naden, too. The weather was better up there, more steady, and we could spend more time whaling, and there were several good anchorages when we couldn't. Let me see, now. I think Gosney was manager there my first year, after him came

Duckett, then Alfus Garcin. There were a couple of old-time whaling captains that held station manager's jobs when I was there. I think Captain LeMarquand was down at Grays Harbor, but he had been at Naden before I joined the company. He was well-liked, a real man's man. Then there was Captain Gilmore at Kyuquot. He was stone deaf, but a tough old salt."

Pulling off his glasses and leaning back in his chair, his face alight with happy memories, Dode continued, "Talking about LeMarquand reminds me, he had a brother-in-law by the name of Scaplen, and I've known Scaplen's daughter since our teens. She's a year older than I, and getting to that point in life where the separation between memory and imagination may be called suspect. But to hear her tell it, her father practically built the whaling company. They all came out here together from Newfoundland, way back in 1904 or 5—her father, LeMarquand, Smith, and Ruck—to build Sechart, and later Kyuquot and Page's Lagoon.

"According to Olive, her father was in charge of building the Page's Lagoon station, and she and her two sisters lived there during the time it operated. They had a governess to look after them, but the only way to get back to Nanaimo was by boat, and that could be quite awkward because it was a bit exposed to the winter sou-easters. Scaplen left and went to work for the CPR in their shops during the confusion just before Schupp bought the company, but after the war LeMarquand saw to it that he got back with them as marine superintendent. Later, when American Pacific Whaling built the new station, Port Hobron in Alaska, Schupp sent him up there to superintend its building." Dode paused as his wife appeared at the doorway.

Chiding her husband for talking so much, Mrs. MacPherson shooed us out of the den where Dode's memorabilia was kept, to the dining room where she had laid out coffee and cake. This caused the conversation to swing round to the sea-going people they both knew who had visited their home.

"Old Captain Heater used to visit us once in a while—he was all crippled up with arthritis and could hardly walk up to the door. I know he was all broken up—his boy Ronald and him had some sort of a run-in. There was a bit of gossip about Cap around the waterfront. I think he took in a young lady as housekeeper. But, my god! He was an old man then; I'm sure he couldn't have got into trouble if he'd wanted to. Poor old guy, I don't think he died with much. I believe he married that young housekeeper of his to stop the gossip, and she cleaned him out, lock, stock, and barrel!" Dode remembered, with age-tempered humour.

Chapter Eight

Rose and Naden Harbours

As well as the men and ships of the whaling companies, the stations stand out in the memories of the whalers, especially the isolated stations on the Charlottes. The Queen Charlotte Islands are the peaks of an offshore undersea mountain range. Graham Island, to the north, is largely flat, with rolling hills surrounding two large inlets. One is Naden Harbour, fed with fresh water from Naden River. The other is Masset Inlet, a salt water basin with nearly a hundred miles of inland shoreline. This vast watershed drains down to the sea in a tidal channel past the village of Masset. The village is built on a sandy isthmus that terminates, to the east, in Rose Spit. The eroding of this side of the island has gradually filled in portions of Dixon Entrance and Hecate Straits, and it is not uncommon for vessels encountering storms in these unpredictable waters to find sand and seashells carried by the seas onto their decks.

The Pacific Ocean side of Graham Island, and the dozens of islands and islets which form the archipelago south of Skidegate Channel (of which Moresby, and Kunghit Island at the extreme southernmost end, are best known), are weathered outcrops of sheer solid rock. Rose Harbour, situated on the south side of the rock-strewn Houston Stewart Channel on Kunghit Island, has access to the Pacific via Rose Inlet. This put it less than an hour's travel from the whaling grounds—an advantage over Naden Harbour that was paid for dearly in adverse weather. The entire area is a sailor's nightmare, offering unexpected, conditional shelter to the knowing, and anxious, if not disastrous, moments to the ignorant.

Captain Dode MacPherson had vivid memories of Rose Harbour. "We stood watch and watch on deck [a nautical term meaning so many hours on watch and the same number off, six and six, for example, rather than a schedule of four hours on and eight hours off]. If the weather was good, we might lay off and let the boat drift during the night, but we seamen still stood our watch while everyone else could grab some shut-eye. Even the fireman could bank up his fires and bunk down for a few hours. I dreaded the job of coaling up. I swear it always rained when we coaled up. At least, that's how I remember it, and the damn grit would grind into my hands. Then we'd have to go down into the bunkers and trim, so we could get a bit more coal in. It was the worst job of whaling, but it had to be done, for you never knew how long it would be before you got more."

I asked about the weather at Rose, and Dode pursed his lips thoughtfully as he considered the appropriate words to describe it. "The weather up there was atrocious, perhaps I should say abominable, unpredictable, and always adverse, and the currents contrary. But that's where the whales were, so that was where we went!" He nodded his head in agreement with other mariners' recall of the weather at this southernmost tip of the Charlottes. "We had a lot of fog up there, and when it wasn't foggy, the wind would be blowing. Often I swore it blew continually, and only paused to shift around and blow again from a different direction. The damnable thing about Rose was, there wasn't a decent place to anchor and get away from the weather. Even Sperm Bay didn't have good holding ground, unless you went right up to the head end and snuggled in behind the island.

"Those damn Willies would spring up in the middle of the night and shake you loose. Then we'd have to heave up the anchor, stow the chain, and steam around in the pitch blackness of that place to find a place out of the wind in which to try again. Anthony Island, off the west coast, had good holding ground, but it was only a lee for a

Rose Harbour whaling station, Queen Charlotte Islands.

southerly wind; if she backed up to the west, we had to get the hell out of there, too. I didn't like Rose too much. We only went in there when we had whales, or needed grub or coal."

Charlie Watson had an eye for the rugged beauty of the Charlottes. He talked at length about the natural sanctuary for the creatures of the wild, and the many artifacts of the aboriginal history of the area. Not only was he there when Dode was, but he revisited the islands over thirty years later, as chief engineer of the *Bouvet III*.

"We put in at Anthony Island in 1956, and I had a chance to go ashore and look around. I was sort of pointing out the sights to the other guys, but my god, I was shocked to find hardly anything left of the old graveyard. The only totem poles or lodge poles left were those rotting on the ground. There was nothing standing! Why, when I was there last with Willis Balcom, in 1923, there were dozens of totem poles, and more canoes than I cared to count." Charlie reached over and refilled our cups as he continued, "Know how they buried their chiefs? In a canoe, placed high up on posts so the animals can't get them, and their families were laid out in boxes around the base of the clan totem pole. God, they were big. All carved with the legendary symbols that told the family's story. They were very forboding to see, all leaning at various angles, glaring down at you as you entered the woods where they were hidden. The Indians wouldn't set foot on the island; they claimed it was haunted. But someone, probably tourists or fishermen, tore down all those totem poles and carted them away. How they did it, I can't guess. They were tremendous things. But there wasn't even a bleached bone left!"

Charlie lit up a cigarette as we sipped the last of the whaler's tea, then gave a sigh. "Yes, it's all coming back to me as we talk. There was another graveyard by an old Indian village down near the south end of Kunghit Island, but we never put in long enough to go ashore. But many of those old places have since been renamed in honour of the old whalers, like Balcom Inlet, Larsen Point, Orion Point, Germania Rock, and Grant Bank. Heater Harbour was named after Bill Heater, and Garcin Rocks after Alfus. There's a few more, but I can't put my finger on them right now."

When we discussed the small mule deer of the Charlottes, Charlie nodded and chuckled, "You know, I believe it would be impossible for anyone to die of starvation in the Charlottes during the summer months. There were always deer close at hand at the head of those bays, and around Rose there was a special breed of elk that had been imported to the islands years before. They were very good eating, if you were lucky enough to shoot one," he chortled, recalling, I suspect, a happy incident of the past. "Oh, my god, yes. For anyone with the minimum of resources and ability, there was all kinds of berries, fish, fowl, and game available. But during the winter months it could be a pretty lonely and hungry place if you got into trouble. I believe the only hospital even now is at Charlotte City, and for a long time the only road there ran from the City up to Port Clements' beer parlour. It's a great place, if you don't mind being a bit remote."

When Charlie Watson sailed aboard the *Black* under Willis Balcom in the early 1920s, Canute Halvorsen had taken over command of the *Brown* from Finn John, and had with him, as engineers, two colourful characters, even as whalers go. Buster Brown was second engineer, and Fisheye Thompson was chief. Charlie recounted a story involving them to illustrate the plight of whalers drying out in such lonely outposts as Kyuquot, Rose, and Naden Harbours in the days before air travel and nearby beer parlours.

"Fisheye was a bit of an unstable chap at the best of times—a top-notch engineer, yes sir. Indeed he was. He was a man who could keep any bucket of bolts steaming right along, but he required a drink or two to do it and still keep his peace with the world. He had a notorious short fuse whenever his drinking supply ran out, and during one of those occasions, Buster Brown's fireman earned a crack across the head with a wheel spanner, that sent the poor man to hospital. Just because he had knocked a cock open on a tank full of lubricating oil, and it all drained down into the bilge!"

Charlie gave me a grin and a knowing laugh. "Hell, you know how it was around those places. If a man wanted a drink bad enough, there was always someone who would sell it to him, for a price. Why, even Bill Heater on the *Grant* found his standard compass drained of the alcohol, and water substituted. I'll bet someone paid a good price for that poison. Yes, there was always a little squeeze to be found around Rose Harbour when I worked out of there."

Unfamiliar with the term "squeeze," I asked Charlie its origin. "Oh, I guess it came from the fact that anyone daring enough to risk his job to bring booze into the station could squeeze the last penny out of those dried-up drunks that needed it so badly!" Charlie coughed on a throatful of smoke as he tried to chuckle and inhale at the same time. Drying his eyes and blowing his nose, he continued, "God knows, after a month or two of sobriety, those guys would have sold their own mothers for a drink. Of course it was almost worth your job to have it in your possession. The company was death on it. They'd had a lot of trouble from drinking during and after the war.

"Well, poor old Fisheye was desperate. His supply had run out, and no one at Rose had any they would sell him. So, when the *Gray* came in, Fisheye went after the strange little steward they had aboard her in those days, and managed to buy a few bottles of suspicious-looking stuff. God knows where that steward got it, but it must have been nearly poison. Well, Fisheye knocked back a couple of pints of that stuff and began acting like a raving lunatic. They had to ship him off to Essondale for quite a while to get over it."

Charlie shook his head sadly. "Yes, it was too bad. He was really a good engineer otherwise. But if booze was the downfall of some in the whaling game, bad meat had to be the bane we all suffered without recourse. Oh, I remember once, a bunch of the boys showed the company just what they thought about it. My God, it was funny! Bill Rolls was manager at the time, and we and the *Grant* were tied up at the dock, taking on coal and supplies, when the *Gray* arrived with meat and supplies for the station. Well, you know how they carried the meat in those days—hung on hooks out on the open deck. Both the *Gray* and the *Prince John* had their boilers and engines aft, and, of course, that was where they hung the meat. The heat and soot ripened it till it was oozing slime and black with blowflies, hardly appetizing, even for people like us who had been waiting weeks for its delivery. The cooks from both ships had been given permission to take their meat at the pierhead, and got several of the deck crew to give them a hand. But once they saw the state it was in, they told the boys to heave it over the side into the chuck.

"This was the final insult to our crews. They had carried that rotten stinking mess from the slings over to the ship, the ooze dripping down over their clothes and hands. Then they were told to dump it over the side. Realizing the company was going it cheap rather than put in a proper meat locker on the *Gray* or have it shipped by a company with refrigeration, they decided it was time to show their displeasure. Keeping the rotten quarters of beef on their shoulders, they marched all the way up the dock to the station office and stalked inside, where they threw it right through the manager's plate glass door and left it lying right on his carpet!"

Charlie roared with mirth as he recalled the incident, shaking his head slightly as he slapped a large paw down on his knee. "Oh, my god. There was a stink about that! If I recall rightly, they deducted the costs of repairing the door from the sailors' pay. But I'll say this for Rolls, he didn't fire anyone. After all, we all suffered when supplies were short."

I asked if they had ever tried eating whale meat when this

happened. "Oh, yes. When we were desperate enough!" he chuckled, then added, "The Chinese usually cut some large pieces of meat off the Sei or small Finbacks, and left these hunks to hang till the outside turned black. More than once, when only salt beef or pork were our alternatives, we bartered with them for some of this. If you trimmed off the blackened meat and sliced the remainder into steaks or roasts, and cooked it over a slow fire, it was as good as some of that stringy beef, and tasted about the same. Of course, we always tried our hand at fishing or hunting when the opportunity presented itself, but if you're busy chasing whales there isn't much time left for anything else."

Allan Heater disagreed with Charlie about the drinking habits of the old whalers. "I saw very little, if any, liquor around Rose Harbour during my time there, though I'd heard many stories of the wild drinking parties there during the earlier days. I guess everyone was watching his job just a little closer during those days. It wasn't uncommon, even at Rose, to have some guy come all the way up there from town, just to ask the skipper for a job."

The isolation of the stations usually prevented all but the most diehard alcoholics from finding a drink. They were usually built in remote areas that offered the shortest distance between the station and the known migratory routes of the whales. Built near the water on pilings driven down for footings, their timbers soon became saturated with oil from the whales they rendered down. Coal, their prime fuel, was piled high on the wharves to accommodate both the ships and the boiler house, which supplied steam power to run the station, and electricity to light it. The product of their endeavour was whale oil, and it was stored in large vertical tanks behind the stations, connected by pumps and pipes to the pierhead for delivery to the ships that transported it south to market. Gun powders and primers required by the whaling ships were stored in a powder shed, remote from work areas, while the accommodations for the station crew and management were favourably situated for a fair wind and a garden patch to grow fresh vegetables.

The station buildings were timbered and covered with corrugated iron; the sheds and houses were framed and clapboard-covered. Little consideration was given to creature comfort, as the station operated only during the fair weather months from April to late October. Water was usually piped in from a convenient high-level stream or dam, and stored in large, wooden water tanks which provided gravity

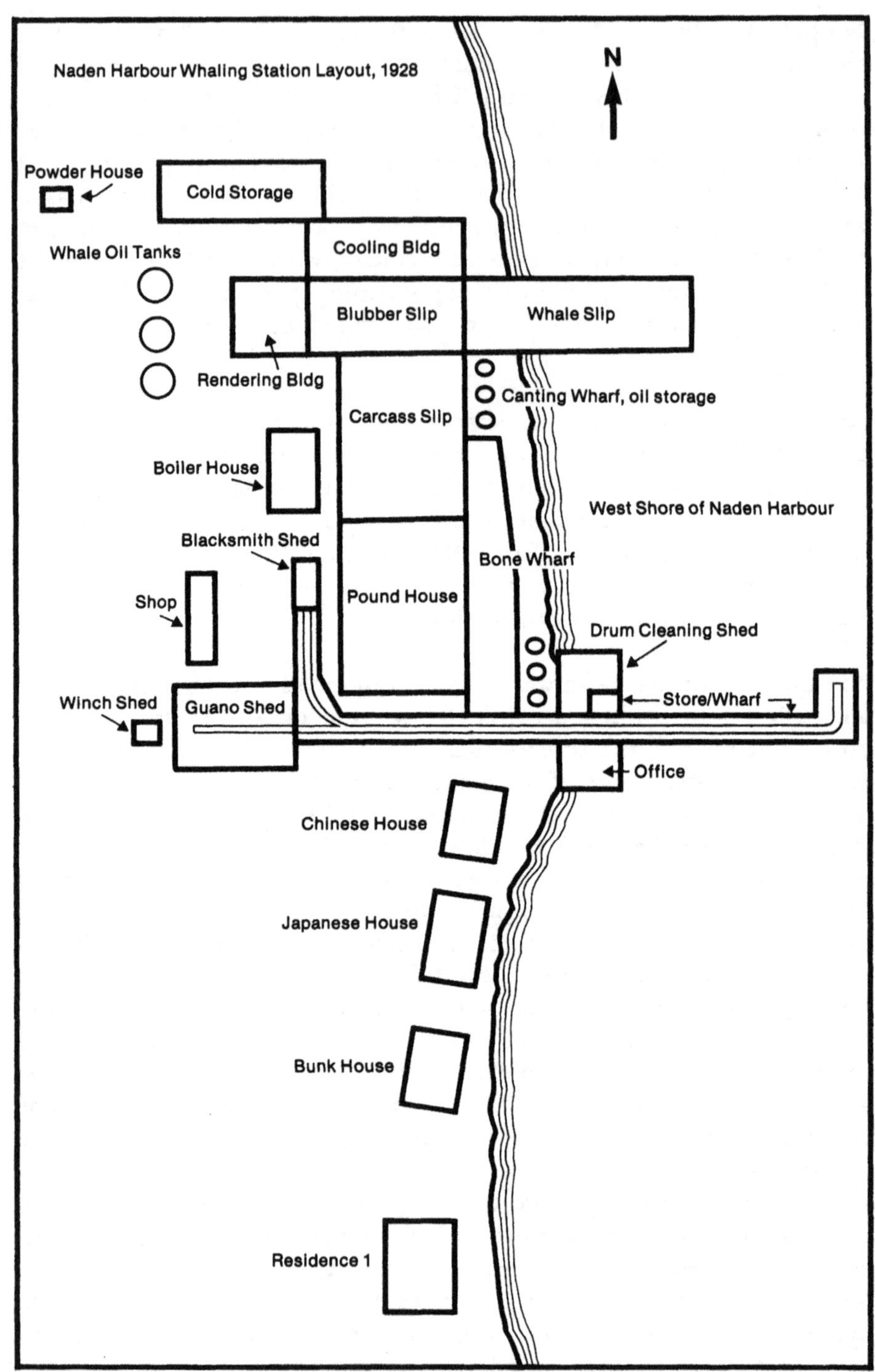
Naden Harbour Whaling Station Layout, 1928
N
Powder House
Cold Storage
Cooling Bldg
Whale Oil Tanks
Blubber Slip
Whale Slip
Rendering Bldg
Canting Wharf, oil storage
Carcass Slip
Boiler House
West Shore of Naden Harbour
Blacksmith Shed
Bone Wharf
Shop
Pound House
Drum Cleaning Shed
Winch Shed
Guano Shed
Store/Wharf
Office
Chinese House
Japanese House
Bunk House
Residence 1

feed to the houses and hose points. High-pressure service and fire points were supplied through steam-driven pumps. Outhouses were built on the outer end of piers that lay offshore, and steam heat was laid on to some of the buildings, while coal-burning stoves and heaters sufficed for the rest.

Each station had its slipway, a stoutly timbered and planked ramp that led up out of the water to the work decks and the buildings housing the rendering equipment, grinders, and driers required to convert the total whale into useful saleable products. Naden Harbour, built in 1912, was typical of most stations built before World War II, and offers a fair comparison with a modern station like that of Coal Harbour, which was built after the war.

Steam winches, fitted with heavy wire cables, dragged the whale up the wetted ramp, or whaleslip, till it reached the high water mark. The flensers climbed aboard the still-moving whale to begin slicing the blubber into strips with their long, wooden-handled, curved, flensing knives. These strips started at the head area and extended the full length to the tail, where the wire cable had been attached to haul the whale ashore. At the head end of the strip, a hole for the hook line was cut in. The strip of blubber was slightly undercut at the head end to allow it to fold back over itself. When it was pulled by the hook line from the stripping winch, it peeled back for the whole length of the whale with a sharp cracking sound that was not unlike that of an under-ripe banana being peeled.

Each strip was hauled up to the cutting deck and hacked into small chunks, then fed into the rendering kettles. The carcass was pulled up to the meat floor, where it was butchered into reasonably small chunks and placed in pressure cookers to render off the oil. Steam-powered saws cut up the bone. If the catch was a Sperm whale, the spermaceti was baled out of the head box, and the digestive tract was examined for ambergris.

After the cookers and kettles had rendered off most of the available oils, the bones were separated from the meat and stored on a bone pile, ready for grinding into bone meal during a lay day, or at the end of the season. The meat was ground, then dried in either flame-type or steam-jacketed rotary kiln dryers. In some stations, this dried meal was ground again to bring it down to the consistency of a powder, and was mixed with either the whale blood, which had also been dried and ground to a powder, or with the bone meal, to supply the various needs of the whale product market.

While baleen from the whalebone whales had declined in value, it still had a market of sorts during the period I whaled. In 1916 the

Naden Harbour station, Queen Charlotte Islands. The whale slip is at the right, meat house and cooker at centre, and the boiler house behind.

Victoria Whaling Company sold 42 tons and 250 bales of baleen or "gillbone" to England and France, for just over $10,000. It was probably worth less than five cents a pound in 1941, and in the post-war era it became a glut on the market and had to be dumped in the most economical manner. At Coal Harbour this meant trucking it down to a deep water pier and giving it the heave-ho. How ironic, when you consider that, during the height of the American Sperm whaling of 1820 to 1850, the baleen from one large Bowhead whale could net a market return that would pay the total cost of outfitting a ship for a year's whaling, and all the wages, too!

During the late thirties, a limited market for Sperm whale teeth existed in Japan, and the whaling company was able to get thirty cents a pound for them, landed at San Francisco. With the tightening export market to Japan during my time, and Pearl Harbour only a few months away, Sperm whale teeth were hardly worth the cost of removing from the jawbone. Our blacksmith, who was an expert scrimshaw worker, used both teeth and bone to perform his art, and many visitors came to Naden to view and purchase his work.

Winston R. Garcin is about my age, yet our experiences with the whaling company are from extremely opposite perspectives. He was born and raised in Victoria, knowing few wants, and the whaler's dock had been as familiar to him as his own backyard. His aunt married Captain Willis Balcom, nephew of Sprott Balcom, and his father had started as bookkeeper with the company before 1910, working for S.C. Ruck, the builder and first manager of the Kyuquot station, and general manager of the Victoria Whaling Company when it was owned by William Schupp. Alfus Garcin had few interests other than the whaling company, and, through the earlier years, had managed all the stations at one time or another. It was only natural that he should take his family with him each season, so Winston had intimate knowledge of both the Queen Charlotte stations, and fond memories of the Charlottes. He and his sister Nora had spent many school summer holidays up there when they were young.

In those years before I joined the whalers on the *Brown*, Alfus Garcin had become general manager and spent most of his time in Victoria, visiting Rose and Naden Harbours once in a while to oversee the station managers' operation. Win often accompanied him on these short field trips, and when he was not helping out around the station, would wander about the countryside, observing its beauty and variety of life.

"Rose Harbour was mostly built on muskeg. There were deep pilings sunk to support the station and the boardwalk. If you got off those boardwalks, you'd sink up to your knees in muskeg and water. You couldn't wander too far away at Rose!" Win laughed as he took a lunch break from work while I visited. "I used to get the watchman's boat and row around, looking at all the various small islands and rocks. There were seals, sea lions, gooney birds, and sea parrots. You know the ones, with big webbed feet, short fat bodies, black feathers, and an orange beak like a parrot. Then there were lots of muskrats, mink, otters, and fish, lots of fish and deer everywhere. I believe there were also cougar and wolves up in the mountains, but I'm not sure. Then we had cats, lots of wild cats. You know, domestic cats that had gone wild. I guess people had left them behind at the end of the season, and the cats had just wandered off into the bush and managed to survive on all the rodents that are there.

"We caught a cat while I was there. It had wandered into the station to gorge itself on whale meat and got caught in a rat trap, so I was given the job to deliver it to Cat Island. I don't know the island's real name, but locally it was known as Cat Island, and was a small bit of land a couple miles away from the station and well enough off shore so the cats couldn't get back again. I rowed out there with the cat secured in a net bag, hissing and growling at my feet, where I could keep a good eye on it. It was really wild and quite big, but once I got it ashore and cut the lashings on the net, it didn't stay to argue but bolted for the trees. There seemed to be enough food for them all on that island; I could hear them hissing and growling in the bush, but could not see a solitary one."

When I mentioned a small deer I had shot for meat, right at Naden, Win became awful silent for a moment. We had had a run of bad meat, and would be leaving the station before the supply ship arrived. I spotted a deer in the bush about 2:00 one morning, while Roy and I were picking up our repaired harpoons from the blacksmith shop at the rear of the station. The deer was standing not a hundred feet away, its large eyes mirroring the lights of the station. I borrowed the watchman's .22 rifle, and stalked it till our line of fire was clear of the settlement. Then I shot it, and we quickly dragged it aboard the boat.

Win looked at me with some reproach. "I think that was my pet deer you killed, Bill." He tried to smile to show there was no malice at this late date—thirty years after the fact. But I felt a twinge of remorse, and quickly apologized. To prove all was forgiven, Win began to talk of the beauty of Naden Harbour. As I had made a trip up the Naden River, partly by boat and the rest of the way on foot, I appreciated the picture his words conjured up. "There were flowers everywhere. Forget-me-nots, bluebells, snowdrops, and many others whose names I don't know. There were wild berries, huckleberries, blueberries, and wild strawberries. Underfoot was moss, lush moss, ankle deep and alive with shrews, moles, and all kinds of insects. The bushes and flowers were alive with bees, and the trees alive with birds. The place sang with nature's music. So warm and secure. The huge

Mr. and Mrs. Alfus Garcin and their son Win in 1941.

trees stood solid and tall against the sky, and the eagles...do you remember the eagles, Bill? Hundreds and hundreds of them, wheeling and diving, swooping and gliding silently away up in the sky. Remember all the black bears, and the duck and geese, almost as many as the seagulls. God, would I like to go back up there again and just wander around," Win laughed as we parted company.

Captain Alan Armour hails from one of the older Victoria families whose menfolk worked for the whaling company. His father was engineer/manager at Rose Harbour for many years, and his brothers sailed on the whalers. Alan joined the company only after being shipwrecked off the Atlantic coast aboard a steamer whose steering gear was frozen up in a cold winter gale. For the remaining years of the depression he sailed as winchman on the whaling tender *Gray*, under the venerable Captain Jim Hunter, and he spoke highly of both Hunter and of Harry Osselton, her chief engineer.

In the first years of the war he joined the five-masted schooner *City of Alberni*, carrying lumber from British Columbia to Australia, then sailed as third mate of the old iron-hulled barkentine *Daylight*, after she had been cut down to a simplified rig of foresails and staysails and was fitted with two huge Bolinder diesels as auxiliary power. His personal sea stories are worthy of a book all their own.

He nodded when I recounted Winston Garcin's account of living at the whaling station. "Well, you know, Win was younger than his sister Nora, and being a lad, found adventure where she could not. Nora often said how she hated spending her summers at the stations, and claimed her mother also hated it. But it was a job her father had to do, so they all bravely followed him aboard the *Gray* for their trip north each year. She did recall, and quite vividly so, the torment they suffered from mosquitoes and insects, and the loneliness and isolation of their station life. Even today, she recalls the odour that permeated everything, including their clothes and luggage. Claimed the odour was still there months later, whenever she had to wear the same clothes she had had at the station," Alan chuckled, having visited Nora Garcin a few hours previous to our interview.

They had all grown up together in Victoria. Winston was a bit younger than he, but Nora and Alan were the same age, and Alan had spent almost as much time at their home as he had at his own. "Not only was my father engineer at Rose," Alan added, "but he was also the manager, at least from 1933 to 1941, and Tom Storey was engineer/manager at Naden Harbour till he left to become chief engineer with the department of Transport."

This last item shook me, for Tom Storey had been one of my mentors in marine engineering. Billy Matheson on the *Sea Lion*, where I sailed as deckhand, had taught me engineering math and physics, and John Davidson, on the *Prince Rupert*, had hired me on the strength of that to learn about engines and boilers, but Tom Storey had taken me down below on the old twin-screwed steamer *Alberni*, and taught me to be an engineer. For a short time, when the wartime scarcity of skilled men was at its peak, he promoted me up to second engineer.

Tom Storey never mentioned whaling to me at anytime, and, until Alan Armour told me this story, I hadn't known Tom was a whaler, but he must have known I was. Captain Harry Ormiston, skipper of the *Alberni*, did, for he had hired me on as his quartermaster before Tom offered me the job down below. I now wonder if that was why he took such an interest in me, and taught me the skills that have stood me in such good stead during my life. I can't help but admire the man even more, now that I've learnt this fact of his life, but why he never told me himself I'll never know, for Tom died two years ago.

I talked to Alan Armour when he was on his way down to Portland, Oregon, to visit Joan Goddard, granddaughter of William Rolls, manager of Rose Harbour whaling station for several years. When Joan and I finally met a few months after that, we found we had much to talk about for she, belatedly, like myself, was trying to put together the stories of the whalers. Her mother had spent much of her youth at the whaling stations, and had valuable insight into the lives of the people who manned these lonely outposts.

"Do you know of Captain Halvorsen?" Joan inquired, after we had discussed the difficulties of following the whaling company's many name changes and reorganizations. I nodded cautiously, "That would probably be Canute Halvorsen, skipper of the *Brown* in Charlie Watson's days." Joan bobbed her head and gave an excited chuckle, "He was my mother's card partner. Whenever he came to the station they would play cards together. There was little else for entertainment. Few of the staff at the station did anything else but work or sit around reading or talking. There was little company for a young girl there. She said he was an excellent card player and could hold a good, interesting conversation."

As Joan's parents had been involved in the lumber business, I inquired how her grandfather had become involved in the whaling. "My grandfather came out from Newfoundland in the very early days, he and Gosney and several others, to work with S.C. Ruck. Most of the oldtimers were Newfies. My grandfather managed Sechart and Kyuquot before taking over Rose Harbour, but he had worked for them for quite a few years before becoming manager." Joan smiled as she recalled an observation of her mother's. "She said Captain LeMarquand was a lovely big gentle man, but very quiet and reserved. I think that was the strange part about them—they were a very close-knit group and stayed that way all their lives. They came out together from Newfoundland, worked together in the whaling, lived near each other in Victoria, and looked after each other. They were a big happy family, and only a few special outsiders ever really joined their group!"

Chapter Nine

Coal Harbour Station

Shortly after Schupp's American Pacific Whaling and Consolidated Whaling were auctioned off in 1947, a new group of people entered the whaling industry when Western Whaling was incorporated by BC Packers, Nelson Brothers, and Gibson Brothers. They had no difficulty securing a license to whale off the northwest coast of Vancouver Island. Through War Assets, they purchased the site and buildings of a former air force seaplane base at the head of Quatsino Sound in Coal Harbour. From Rose and Naden Harbours they brought over processing equipment and the whale winches. They converted wooden-hulled packers and towboats, fitting them with new breechloading cannons, nylon foregoers, wire whale lines, and hydraulic winches. Suitably ballasted, the ships performed well. The old *Sebastian* from Sprott Balcom days also joined these new whalers for a short time.

The Coal Harbour whaling station was, with the possible exception of the short-lived Page's Lagoon station, the only station built on this coast that was close to all the amenities and problems of civilization. It was located a few miles by good road from the logging and fishing village of Port Hardy. The availability of licensed pubs and a government liquor store lured many whalers away from their jobs.

Coal Harbour was equally accessible to the tourists travelling the regular shipping routes that called at Port Hardy, and the attraction of visiting a whaling station caused a two-way traffic that created many unusual problems for the newly founded Western Whaling Corporation. This easy availability of good copy also attracted the media, and more stories and pictures were published of this operation than of all the other whaling ventures on this coast.

The other major problem that confronted Western Whaling through its twenty years of operation was its distance from the whaling grounds. Located at the head of Quatsino Sound, where only a few miles of Vancouver Island separate the west coast from Port Hardy on the east coast, it was over thirty miles away from Kains Island at the entrance to the sound. The actual whaling grounds lay another hundred-odd miles northwest, from Cape Scott to Cape St. James. The towing of dead whales over these extreme distances, coupled with the unpredictable weather and the severity of low pressure storms in this area, created costly delays and waste, and caused irrecoverable expenses.

The manager of Coal Harbour station during its infancy was Douglas S. Souter. Though they processed 182 whales, to illustrate how six years of inactivity had lost local talent, they had to send all the way to Norway for a head flenser to come and show them how to cut up a whale!

"It was a very messy and difficult business," Orval Forrest, Coal Harbour's accountant, recalled as we discussed those early years. "Everything became slippery with blood and water—the concrete slipway, the large apron where the aircraft had been parked, and even in the former hangers where our equipment was scattered about. We had to use a great big forklift truck, "bull moose" it was called, to lift the blubber and meat up and dump it into the cookers and digestors. We had only temporary ladders and scaffolding to work from. Cables snapped, staging collapsed, and there were some damn close calls, but, thankfully, there were no fatalities. Gibson Brothers and Nelson Brothers backed out after that first terrible year, and we carried on alone.

"That winter we put in proper decking in the hangar buildings, and built heavy wooden ramps up to them from the main slipway. We installed better winches, and arranged equipment so that whole whale parts could be dragged right up to the cookers before being cut up. We installed freezing and cold storage buildings to supply what we hoped would be a market for whale meat. We couldn't have chosen a more unlikely time to venture into this domestic market. With beef and pork prices rising daily, it seemed a profitable alternative. But the packers flooded the market with horse meat, and stores dealing completely in this commodity sprung up everywhere. Few people were willing to try whale meat as an alternative, so we had to discontinue that venture and concentrate on the mink and pet food market."

By the time Hector Cowie took over as manager in 1951, the Coal Harbour station had become quite a modern operation, comprising four Kvaerner digestors, five Sharples Super Decanters, screen and deep bay cookers, a flame drier and meat cyclone, a meat press, four Sharples separators, a liver oil plant, and various settling, blowdown, and separating tanks. All liquids—blood, washdown water, body

Viner, *a whaling towboat built in North Vancouver, BC, in 1911. Used at the Coal Harbour station. This photo shows whale oil tanks, boiler house, and cooker building in the background.*

fluid, etc.—were collected and treated to remove solubles and oils. The effluent from this plant was touted as drinkable. Indeed, H.R. MacMillan, then president of BC Packers, drank a glass of it for the media, to prove Western Whaling's concern for the protection of the environment of Coal Harbour. This was almost complete usage of the whale, with only the smell and baleen being lost. Certainly it was a far cry from the old days of Akutan, when the number of floating whale carcasses constituted a hazard to navigation and prompted a national outcry.

It took twenty to thirty minutes to dispose of a large whale of sixty to seventy tons. Blubber was torn off in chunks that were one-quarter the girth, and the full length of the whale. Meat not used for mink food was hauled to the upper deck of the reduction plant, where it went through a pre-basher, a hasher, and finally into a screw cooker, before going through a press that extracted the oils. Looking like bits of dried bark, it was ground up into a fine powder, and sacked as a poultry and hog food additive.

The blubber, bone, and viscera were dumped into revolving digestors, pressurized with fifty pounds of steam, which reduced the material to a fine solid suspended in oil and water. This was blown down to centrifugal decanters, which precipitated out the solids. They were then dried into meal. The oil and water were separated in the centrifuges, the oils going to tankage, the water to a treatment plant to remove all solubles and oil.

Top: Coal Harbour, 1957. Getting started on a 45-foot Sperm whale. Note open lower jaw behind coveralled man.
Bottom: Removing left hand side of the whale.

Oil products from baleen whale oil (from Fin, Blue, and Humpback whales) were used for margarine, shortenings, and soap; the Sperm oils for lubrication, inks, and graphites; spermaceti waxes and oils for candles, gun oil, medicines, lipsticks, and face creams.

Hector Cowie, former manager of Western Whaling's Coal Harbour station, was a congenial, generous man, big in frame and heart, who donated much of his personal library on Western Whaling for this book. Typical of many of the men who had been involved in whaling, he had strong opinions about it, and many humourous anecdotes to tell of it. At no time while he was manager did he believe whaling to be a practical, profit-making business, and was on record many times during that period as advising BC Packers and H.R. MacMillan to discontinue their whaling venture.

"We had as modern a whale processing plant as you'll find anywhere in the world," Hector stated proudly, "but it wasn't in a good location. It was really too far removed from the whaling grounds, and too close to civilization. We had far too many tours of sightseers, and they were only interested in visiting when we were really too busy with whales. We had more government people underfoot than any other industry. Gordon Pike [a Fisheries research zoologist] and his crew were no problem, and we didn't mind waiting a few minutes while they got their measurements and data, but we were continually bothered by people. We were just too handy to the public, and we were always concerned lest one of them got hurt.

"We had a market for fresh whale meat, and to supply this market we used antibiotics in the air we pumped into the whale to inflate them, such as Aureomycin and Terramycin, to preserve the whale till we could get them into the station. The tow from the entrance of the sound to the station was a long one, almost thirty miles, with our whalers operating from Cape Cook to Cape Scott, and sometimes as far north as Cape St. James, and up to 150 miles offshore. We tried pick-up boats following the whalers to bring the whales to Quatsino Sound, and tow boats to bring the whales from Kains Island to the station. We even tried letting the whalers bring in their own whales. But it was too time consuming, and, with the variable weathers of that area, could easily be delayed not just hours but for days."

I asked him about the shut-down of Coal Harbour from 1959, when they landed 869 whales, to 1961, when they restarted and only landed 713. "Undoubtedly you are aware we had a problem getting whales, and an even greater problem getting good whaling crews. Fortunately we were finally able to get an experienced man like Captain Borgen to take over as fleet captain, and he brought in some excellent gunners, weeded out the drunks and troublemakers from the crews, and we began to increase our catch of whales.

"Just when we really got going, the whale products sales dropped right off, and at that time the union decided to demand increases we couldn't feel justified in agreeing to with those prospects. Believe me, it was a bitter pill for all concerned, but we had to shut down and wait to see if the market would improve. Many of our highly trained people drifted away to other jobs, and the idle equipment deteriorated, but we couldn't promise the share-holders even a marginal loss, that could have justified maintaining their investment till market conditions

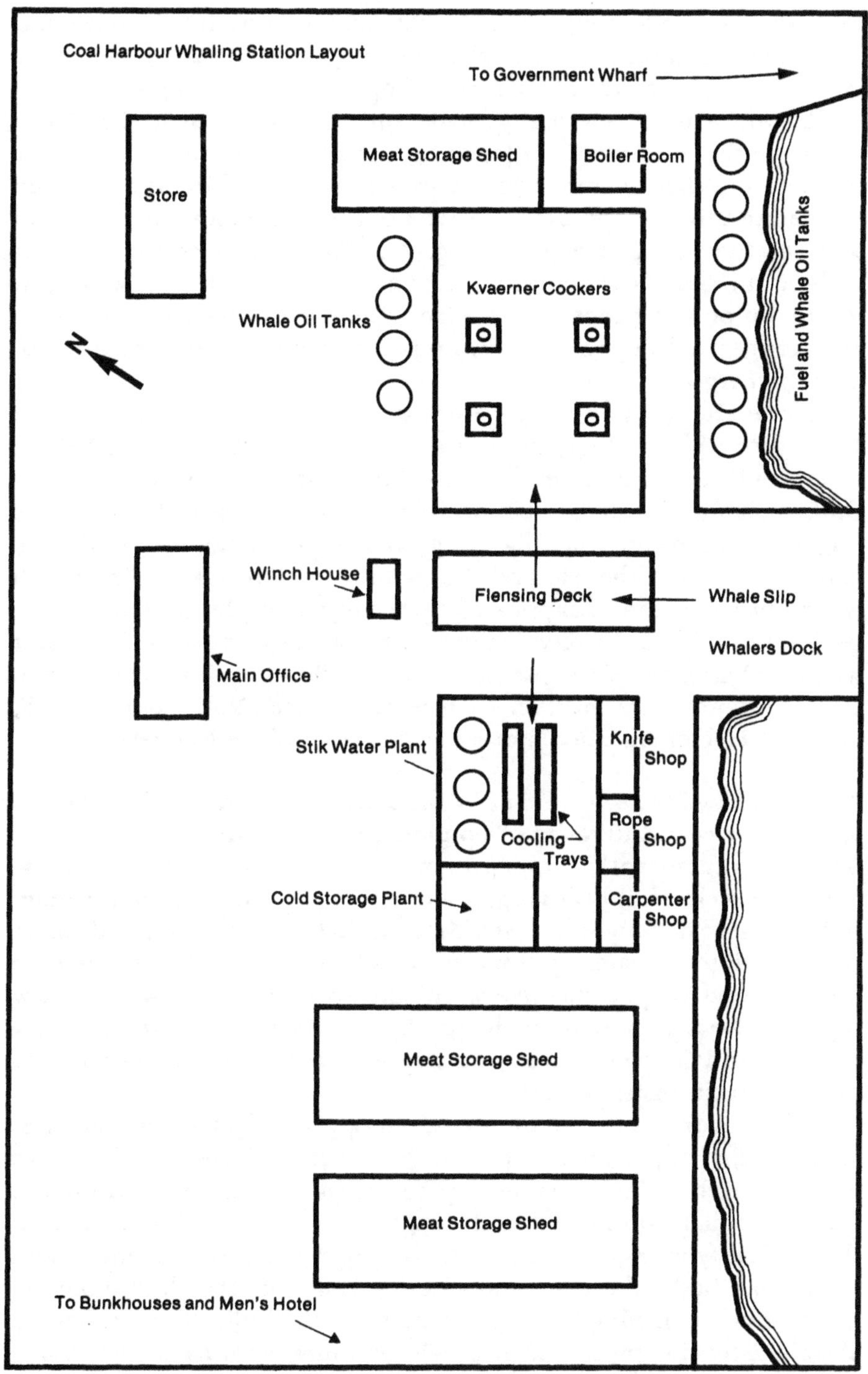

Coal Harbour Whaling Station Layout
To Government Wharf
Store
Meat Storage Shed
Boiler Room
Kvaerner Cookers
Whale Oil Tanks
N
Fuel and Whale Oil Tanks
Winch House
Flensing Deck
Whale Slip
Whalers Dock
Main Office
Stik Water Plant
Knife Shop
Rope Shop
Cooling Trays
Cold Storage Plant
Carpenter Shop
Meat Storage Shed
Meat Storage Shed
To Bunkhouses and Men's Hotel

improved. It would have cost over $200,000 to overhaul the ships and equipment for just a season of whaling, and about the same amount to get a union agreement, plus the cost of operations and wages.

"As you know, we finally made an agreement with the Taiyo Gyogyo Fishing Company in Japan to supply fresh whale meat to their market, and they in turn supplied us with modern ships and key men to operate this new venture. The whales were disembowelled at sea as soon as they were brought alongside. Then, with cold sea water rushing through them removing the body heat, they were towed right to the station and processed. We froze the meat in special containers, and refrigerated ships arriving from Japan came right to the station to load this cargo.

"Lorne Hume was manager during that period, and I'm sure that he'd agree with me that, under those conditions of selected whaling, where only the prime whales were taken, it could have become a profit-making business. Unfortunately, something changed the migratory routes of the big Blue whales we required, maybe an earthquake under the sea, and the feed for the Finback whales, which we might have used, disappeared rather mysteriously, so these whales were far too thin to be of value to us. Strange how things happen. Just when we had most of the problems licked, the whole business came to a halt. I doubt if we will ever see it revived again. Not in our lifetime, at least." Hector chuckled, not sadly, but certainly reflectively.

"So you know Hector Cowie of Western Whaling, eh? Well, I can tell you a story of a difference of opinion I had with that man!" Charlie Watson grunted with a touch of anger. "He insisted I allow those mechanic welders of his to repair a crack I found in the *Bouvet*'s main steam pipe to her engines. I wouldn't consider such a thing, and called the government steamship inspector down in town, and he backed me up one hundred percent. We were laid up over a week while a new pipe was bent and sent up to us. Cowie claimed it was extremely wasteful and frivolous. Even our skipper, Jack Hann, wouldn't back me up, but the inspector did."

Charlie looked over at me questioningly as he lit up a cigarette, gauging the importance I placed on a cracked steam pipe. This curved length of large diameter pipe brings the high-pressure steam from the boiler stop valve over the engine stop valve, and in the case of the vertical type engine of a whaler, is subject to all the movement and vibration, both thermal and mechanical, of the hull-mounted machinery. Depending on the flexibility of the hull, all movement is absorbed by this pipe, and it slowly becomes work-hardened. Good engineering practise is to remove it during major overhauls and have it checked for cracks or signs of metal fatigue, before it is annealed or replaced.

"The crack in the *Bouvet*'s pipe had developed right above the engine stop valve," Charlie snorted, convinced he now had my full attention. "Why, if that ever blew apart, that six-inch steel pipe would have straightened out like a fire hose under 250 pounds per square inch pressure, and emptied all the steam from the boilers into that engine room. It would certainly have killed every man below decks in seconds, and, I think highly likely, everyone aboard that ship. And damned if I didn't find they had let someone braze up a previous crack, right in the same area. You know, a seaman has enough to gamble with, without patchwork repairs. They took some awful gambles on those whalers, but I wouldn't, and I'll tell you why.

"A large ship carried away her main steam pipe sometime after I left the Victoria whalers, one of the Dollar Line vessels, if I recall rightly. Within seconds, all the men in her engine room and boiler room were dead. Men on her upper decks and in the cabins off this area were scalded so bad the skin hung in bags off their arms and faces. There were eight or ten men on watch below decks when it happened; they had to shovel their remains off the deck plates, like jelly draped in clothing, with just the white bones sticking out of them to indicate they once were in fact human beings. I know this for a fact, because I was one of those called there to carry out the repairs." Charlie took a last puff on his smoke, then butted it out and began another story to illustrate his point. "I was second engineer of the Union Steamship's twin-screw steamer *Venture*. And one afternoon in 1939 I was warming up the port engine—we were due to sail at 3 p.m. and this was about a quarter to three—when I heard steam hissing out from behind the lagging on the main steam pipe, right above the engine stop valve. Well, believe me. After the graphic example of the disaster caused by the Dollar Line ship failure still fresh in my mind, I didn't hesitate to have the fires pulled, and both boiler stop valves shut.

"The skipper and chief engineer were having a last minute chin wag with the company manager at the gangway on the dock, when I reported to them that the ship could not sail. Certainly they were shocked, but they also knew I was right. Can you imagine what might have happened if it had let go after we sailed? We had over two hundred passengers aboard, a full crew, and down to our marks with cargo. I'll say this for BC Marine, they had both those steam pipes out, new ones made, inspected, and installed before seven that evening, and we sailed a half hour later. Yes, you see, when we removed the lagging from the starboard engine's steam pipe, we found it also had cracks in it."

Charlie had very few fond memories of Western Whaling. Perhaps he is too critical, but as these observations are backed up by others I interviewed, his comments are indicative of the problems finally corrected by Arnie Borgen soon after Charlie left.

"When I took over the *Bouvet*, she had just lost most of her main and bottom end bearings, and scored her crankshaft, just because the second engineer had been more interested in the bottle than the lubrication. It cost over sixty thousand dollars to carry out repairs. You'd have thought they would have fired that man after that. But no, they kept him on, even though I told them I could get a better and more trustworthy engineer in a moment. I watched this guy pretty close after BC Marine completed the repairs and we sailed for Coal Harbour, but damned if he didn't let the intermediate bottom end overheat. Before I could get down there, most of the Babbitt had run out, but I eased her along on what was left and the web, till Jack Hann could get us back into Nanaimo."

Charlie shook his head slowly, like an old bear, and rumbled on as he lit another cigarette. "That man had a real drinking problem, and had just about run out of ships and companies to sail with. I couldn't rely on him, and didn't want him. But he had friends in the company, and our skipper just couldn't see any fault in him! Believe me, they were so busy covering up for each other, like a band of fraternity brothers, they didn't realize the trouble they were getting into. Arnie Borgen came after I left and straightened them out, but when I was there, there wasn't a whaler amongst them.

"Believe me, Bill. For someone like myself, who had been on the old whalers with men like Willis Balcom and Bill Heater, and then saw how those chaps out of Coal Harbour whaled, it left much to be desired, to say the least.

"Innar Ikaner was a towboat skipper who knew the score, but those other guys like Jack Hann and Jensen, they were strictly long liners who took up whaling without any real training. They were top-notch seamen I'd trust anywhere, but they didn't know how to shoot whales! I've seen Jack Hann shoot three and four times, just to hit the damn whale, and not a killing shot at that. He even shot a Right whale. As you know, they are a protected species, but he didn't even know the difference between it and any other whale!"

Charlie Watson sipped a little more tea to wet his parched throat after that outburst, then thumbed through his notebook. "Yes, well, let's see now. I have a list for that season. Harry Samson had the *Nahmint*, Olof Filing the *Tahsis Chief*, Innar Ikaner the *Polar V*, Innar Jensen the *Globe VII*, and Jack Hann had our boat, the *Bouvet III*.

"You know, sometimes we'd cruise for days and days, hunting for whales from Cape Cook to Cape St. James, then not be able to hit them with a harpoon when we did find them! It was heartbreaking, if not damn well ludicrous. I left there in mid-season, thoroughly disgusted. Thank god I'm too old to ever go whaling again. I wouldn't want to see a comedy like that again!"

"My father was a whaler," Captain Arnie Borgen stated matter-of-factly, as we sat in his comfortable living room facing out over south Vancouver. A well-built man, slightly stooped from a lifetime of looking down to others less tall than himself, his tanned attentive face was surprisingly free of wrinkles or lines, and his heavy eyebrows accentuated his seaman's eyes. "He managed a factory ship and three whale catchers," Arnie continued, after showing me a picture of

Captain Arnie Borgen on bridge of Westwhale 8. *Note stand for holding binoculars.*

himself and his father aboard a whaling vessel. "I was sixteen the year I went out whaling with him. That was 1933 and we were whaling off Spitsbergen. They were older vessels. Our factory ship was only five thousand tons, and without a stern slipway to haul the whales aboard. We had to cut-in the whale from staging slung down over the side at the water line, and each part had to be lifted aboard by tackle before it could be butchered and processed. I got sixty kroner a month as seaman. I guess that would be about fifteen dollars then, in Canadian money."

He chuckled when I asked if the whalers returning from the Antarctic spent their summers whaling in the northern oceans. "No, no. The regular whalers wouldn't do this kind of work! They were too grand and important for that. They spent the Norwegian winter down in the summer of the Antarctic, then came home to lay around during the northern summer in Norway."

I asked him how he came to whale in the Antarctic, and the story he told was so interesting, and so revealing of the man, that I thought it should be told here, if only to show the extremes of weather suffered by whaling men.

"Normally we worked from early spring to late fall in the waters around Greenland, Iceland, and Spitsbergen, before going into winter lay-up, but the year I started my Dad decided to take the fleet south for the winter. So, instead of laying-up the ships, we returned home for a brief refit, then sailed south for the Azores, then on to Monrovia, whaling all the way, before putting into Cape Town for another brief refit.

"Those were desperate days. Whaling was in a recession and the Antarctic was the only place making any money. My father decided to take the fleet further south through the roaring forties, and seriously considered sending me home before he left. Though he knew better than I what we faced, I managed to convince him to let me stay. You know, I've often wondered, in my later years, just what worrisome thoughts my father must have had at that time. I know he was very concerned, but I had no fear for our safety. I thought the ships were all very wonderful.

"But really, those ships were very old and very weak. They could never have got through a steamship inspection today." Arnie Borgen shook his head and smiled ruefully over at me, aware I had sailed in similar age-weakened ships.

"We were down there only a few months when the weather turned cold and a gale blew up, shoving the ice in around us. The catcher I was on got trapped, and the plates under the quarter were sprung by the pounding and squeezing of the ice, and she began to go down under our feet. Though the other catcher was nearby, the ice was so heavy she just managed to reach us as our ship slipped away beneath our feet. We stepped over onto their ship and looked back, and our ship was gone, just disappeared beneath the ice!

"You've no idea of the pressure and power of that drifting ice till you're caught in it. It would almost lift the ship right up out of the water, than another large piece would bash into you and the boat would slide backwards into the water, and it would start all over again. Our rescue ship was also suffering sprung plates and taking in water, but we had to break out of the ice and run back to the factory ship if we wanted to survive.

"I guess we were all worried we wouldn't make it, because everyone started looking around for a likely-looking ice floe to try and reach if the old ship sank from under us. But we were lucky and made the factory ship before the catcher sank. That left us with just one catcher vessel and the factory ship, and a couple dozen extra men. So my father headed north for South Georgia, where we found two newer catchers available for charter, and returned to the whaling grounds with them.

"But we'd been away from Norway for about eighteen months, and some of the men wanted to go home. My father wanted to stay a little longer, so he made arrangements for those who didn't want to stay to be shipped home. That's how I got my chance to be a gunner.

"Our old gunner, before he left to go home, had taught me well, and I felt sure I could carry out the hunting and shooting. But I was too young—I don't think I had turned eighteen yet—to be master of a whaling ship. It was decided to give me a chance, and I managed to hold my own, but I had to be signed on as the mate-gunner, not master gunner, because of my age. The regular mate was promoted to master because he was an experienced boat handler and navigator.

"I guess we were down there just over two years. We came north by way of South America and the Azores, whaling all the way. My studies had not been neglected during this time, and after our return I passed my examination for master. I had my own ship before I was twenty-one, and whaled off the coast of Labrador for several years before the Germans invaded Norway and I became a man without a country. I applied to Canada for a landing permit and, after granting it, they asked me to go to Cape Town and bring back several whale catchers interned there. These were turned into naval patrol and convoy vessels, and I had employment all through the war.

"I came out to the west coast in the winter of 1948 to inspect your herring fisheries and take recommendations back to Newfoundland," Arnie Borgen replied to my query of how he became Western Whaling fleet captain. "At war's end, Marine Oils Ltd. moved from Placentia Bay up to Williamsport and was renamed the Olsen Whaling and Sealing Company. They wanted to open up a herring fishery, so I was sent out here to approach BC Packers for information.

"They were most helpful, especially when they found out I was a whaler, and I was introduced to Bob Walker, Ken Fraser, and Dr. Roy Elsey, who told me about their venture at Coal Harbour. We agreed to trade information, so I went with them to a place near Seattle to look over some available whalers that were berthed there. I'm afraid I didn't think too highly of those ships. Compared to the old ships my father took into the Antarctic when I was just a lad, these were ancient and worn out, and more of a liability than an asset in the area they planned to whale. I told them to forget about these vessels, and suggested they consider rigging up fishing or towing vessels to take whales, till they could justify getting proper ships for the work. I even put them in touch with some of our suppliers for guns, harpoons, and other whaling equipment, and they in turn took me on a tour of their reduction plants, and a trip or two out on the fishing grounds.

"I went back to Newfoundland and whaled for a couple years, and they took my suggestion and rigged up several large, wooden-hulled, motor packers for whaling. They did very well. Some of them were still at it when I returned," grinned Arnie.

Getting the packers out in the first place was not so easy, though. George Willson, manager of Celtic Shipyards, and his superintendent Charlie Honour, remember the vessels and the problems of fitting out. "Let's see," drawled Charlie Honour when I spoke with him, "*Lavallee* and *Kimsquit* were first, then the *Nahmint*. These were good-sized wooden vessels of about 150 tons. We really had to ballast them after installing all that heavy deck equipment, just to make them stable enough to whale from."

"We tried sacks of rock salt first," laughed George Willson, perching on the corner of his deck, "but it wouldn't last long if it got wet. Then we tried sacks of sand, but when they broke open the sand got down into the bronze pumps, with horrendous results. Finally came up with the idea of casting concrete and steel punchings into shaped blocks that we numbered and fitted right into the hold. Worked fine. We'd just lift them out and store them in the yard during the fishing season, then remove the pen boards and put them right back in when they were going to go whaling. It was fast and easy, and they didn't shift."

Arnie Borgen nodded as I recalled that my skipper had gone down to Chile to bring up the *Bouvet*, one of the three steam whalers acquired before he joined the company. "In 1951, when the Newfoundland whaling closed down, I went back to the Antarctic for a couple seasons. The first summer I got back, BC Packers got in touch with me to say they were having a great deal of trouble at Coal Harbour. They couldn't get whales, nor could they attract or keep good crews on their whalers. They asked if I would come up and just look around and see if I could spot the trouble for them." Captain Borgen got up and paced slowly back and forth. "Well, we all realized that if I just came and snooped around, the whalers would get suspicious and give me a hard time, possibly cause the company more trouble than they already had. So the company offered me the title of whaling inspector with a carte blanche jurisdiction that would allow me to go and come anytime I wished and anywhere I wished.

"The boys were pretty good. They didn't resent my questions once they knew I wanted to help. They told me their troubles, and I listed them all out to the company. The outcome, of course, was that the company asked me to stay on in the role of fleet captain and try to expedite improvements.

"The *Tahsis Chief* had the most pressing problem. She had a good gunner, but he just could not hit a whale with that gun. They had tried all kinds of expensive ideas, but the gun just would not throw true. Well, I know there's a proper way to check if the gun is moving out of line during recoil, but you require certain special measuring tools, trammels and such."

Arnie chuckled and shook his head as he recalled his dilemma. "I had to improvise a trammel, but the results were so conclusive it justified all the time and effort spent on dreaming it up. I had a heavy wooden batten fitted so it just touched the base of her wheelhouse, and the other end almost touching the base of the gun. Into this end we drove a long nail, leaving its head standing proud so it just touched the gun base. Now, if the gun base moved during firing, we should be able to measure this amount of movement and correct it."

He stood up to describe the events that followed. "It's hard to believe, even now, what happened, but at the time I was utterly shocked. I loaded up the gun, put in a dummy harpoon for load, cleared everyone away from the area, and squeezed the firing lever.

"The batten sprang up between my legs and broke in several places, the nail literally buried in the end grain of the wood. That heavy gun base must have jumped back well over six or eight inches. When we checked the foredeck more closely, we found it was all loosened up, and so slack it moved about like an egg crate. We had the shipwrights refasten the foredeck, then strengthened the frames up under it with large channel irons and heavy gusset plates. After that, the base did not move, and you could lob a harpoon into a butter box ten to twenty fathoms away without problem."

While I flipped through some of his pictures of whaling, Arnie Borgen continued his story. "There was no doubt we needed better gunners to get more whales, and thus increase the bonus earned by each ship, if we were to attract the good seamen we required to man them. I managed to get several professional gunners and key crewmen to come out here from Norway and give me a hand. Most of them didn't stay long, but it was enough time for me to train the more professional-type seamen from here into damn good whalemen."

When we discussed the whaling ships, Arnie came up with the death of a theory I first heard back in the days when I fished with my father, when diesel engines were coming into vogue. "As you know, we had several diesel-powered vessels rigged out for whaling, as well as those three steam whalers. Often we were surprised that we could call in a motor whaler to stalk a spooky whale which the steamers could not get close enough to shoot. We felt it was the steady loud noise that lulled them, sort of surrounded them with noise that had no focal point for them to fear. Maybe it confused them, I don't know which, but a steamer was so silent that any odd noise it made, such as a fireman banging his shovel, or a loose bottom end, reached their ears like the report of a gun and they'd rush off in the opposite direction.

"It was the main reason why, when I went to Japan after we joined up with Taiyo Gyogyo, I selected only their diesel-powered ships. That old myth about diesel ships being too noisy is just a myth and nothing more."

I asked what his first reaction had been when Taiyo Gyogyo insisted those new ships be manned by their captains and engineers. "Well, they were just enforcing a condition, laid down in a Japanese decree that dated back to 1904, that Japanese whaling ships had to be commanded by Japanese seamen. Western Whaling tried to explain it as an in-breaking period to learn how to handle their new sophisticated equipment, but there was nothing there that our crews couldn't master in a short time, and, as a matter of fact, did. The company was just trying to save face and not upset a lot of people on this coast if they learned the truth. It certainly stuck in everyone's craw for awhile, but we soon got over it. Those Japanese were good men, and it wasn't too long till we were all whaling together, like a team."

We discussed the disposition of the vessels of Western Whaling, and

Mate Rusty Walco keeps watch while Wallace Anstey steers **Westwhale 8.**

Arnie concluded his story with these facts, "The *Tahsis Chief* was renamed *Lavallee*, and ended her days on the east coast, and I and the *Westwhale 8* went back to Newfoundland in 1968. I whaled with her for another five seasons out of Didlo, for H.B. Nickersons, before Canada ceased whaling. With our scheme there of selective whaling, I was getting more whales after five years than when I started. We took only prime whales of healthy species. Under those conditions, and working from a small local station such as we did at Didlo, whaling could be profitable and sustainable."

Chapter Ten

Men and Ships

As Arnie Borgen and Charlie Watson have pointed out, the success of a whaling venture depends not only on the availability of whales, but also on the efficiency of the whaling equipment. Ships, especially the ships of old, were like monasteries, their crews, like monks dedicated to their preservation and purpose. Each member performed an appointed task without error and without change, and the whole being of the ship was under the sole command of one man, the master. Of course in such closed communities there was bound to be occasional friction and personality clashes, and a wealth of anecdotes have come down through the years, tales of ships and the men that sailed them.

Dode MacPherson's memory held a variety of stories, including one that has a parallel to the story told me by the old doctor who pulled my tooth at Masset. "The whalers didn't go out in 1921. There was a surplus of whale products and a slow market, so whaling stayed down till 1922. During that time, I sat for and received my towboat master's papers. I got a job towing logs out of the Nitinat, which is a nasty river to tow out of because of the bar blocking the entrance. After that I began towing coal from Nanaimo, must have towed at least a million tons of that stuff, before I went up to the lakes and ran sternwheelers for the CPR," Dode paused, then chuckled when I recounted our experiences in keeping the tugboat *Master* in steam as a working artifact.

"When I didn't show up in '22, John Anderson took his brother-in-law, Jim Mathews, along as mate. Mathews was a small gruff Newfie who had sailed with Captain Anderson as mate years before. He was in his early seventies, and so short his head was barely visible from the deck above the bridge rail. I guess that was what saved his life!

"The *Blue* had been sent over from Naden to pick up the mail and supplies left at Masset by the *Prince John*, and some of her crew managed to get up town and buy some Jamaica ginger and vanilla extract. Soon the forecastle was roaring with loud voices, and as the ship made her way out of the inlet, one of the lads, temporarily off his rocker with this poison, decided to carry out a vendetta against the mate, and took aim with a rifle from the forecastle hatch. The shot creased the old boy's skull, knocking him out cold, but the fellow really believed he had killed the old son-of-a-bitch.

"The laugh disappeared from his face when he found John Anderson rushing up the deck at him, and he panicked and jumped overboard. They managed to fish him up after the cold water had shocked him sober. Then they returned to Masset where he was placed in jail. Mathews was found to be still alive, so the doctor that recently set up a practise there patched him up, and they were back at Naden before nightfall.

"It's a true story, and I can vouch for that. Not only did Captain Anderson tell it himself, but there is an account of it in the newspapers. But by the time it came up trial, everyone had cooled down a bit, so John Anderson spoke in favour of the seaman and he was released on a bond to keep the peace. You could do that in those days.

"That reminds me, you worked on the *Estevan*, didn't you?" he asked, and when I nodded, told this story about Allan Heater that Captain Heater had modestly brushed aside when I interviewed him. "Well, Harry Bilton was a friend of ours. Was he skipper of the *Estevan* when you were there?" I explained briefly that he had been a real friend to me on that ship, teaching me much. Dode nodded politely, obviously wanting to get on with his own story.

Whaler Blue, *1929, flying her chase flag as she closes a whale.*

"Right. Well, Harry was skipper of the old *Anyox* back in the late thirties. A lot of the fellows from the whaling company worked on the tugs or with the salvage company during the winter. Young Heater, Allan I believe his name is, Bill Heater's grandson, was sailing on her one winter when Harry lost the tow, a big old sailing vessel named the *Dunshire*, that had been knocked down into a barge. Well, they had put a couple of the younger crewmen aboard her to help the barge skipper steer her up the west coast, and one of those lads was young Allan Heater.

"You can understand how Harry must have felt. He and Bill Heater were old shipmates, longtime friends, we knew both of them well. Both of them have ate right at this same table you're sitting at now. Harry had searched the whole area where the wreckage of the *Dunshire* was found, without finding a trace of the crew. As they sailed back to Victoria, poor Harry was dreading the moment when he'd have to tell Bill that he had lost his grandson. But just as they were entering harbour, they received a radio message that all three of the barge's crew had turned up safe and sound, and were on their way back to Victoria.

"It was a miracle, really. There was a hell of a storm up there. Harry had tried several times through the night to send over a line; each time it carried away before they could send over the towing wire. By that time the *Anyox* was in amongst so many rocks, Harry was in danger of losing her, too. Though it broke their hearts, they just had to lay off and let that barge drift in on the lee shore.

"But the miracle was, the *Dunshire* surged unharmed, somehow, through all those rocks around Solander Island, and then paused for just a moment against one that was not quite covered with water. Allan Heater, realizing it was then or never, talked the others into jumping for the rock, and that's what saved them. The *Dunshire* drifted away and dashed herself to bits on the rocks a few miles down the coast, but at low water they were able to wade ashore and walk up the coast till they hailed a fisherman. It took them a couple of days, but the fisherman took them to Kains Island lighthouse, so they could radio out."

With barely a pause to catch his breath, Dode MacPherson continued on a new topic. "There was an old boy who sort of camped up near the whaling station at Naden, who made his living catching crabs off the dock. Some wag nicknamed him Uncle Billy. He had several large traps he had made, and he got chunks of whale tail from the station to bait them. He caught enormous crabs—they must have been twelve inches across the back—right off the dock. He'd sell us as many as we wanted for two bits a dozen. Twelve for 25 cents! That's what the crab cannery over at George Point was paying for them. Hard to believe, eh? But I've seen him land over a hundred dozen crabs in a day. That was good money!"

When I mentioned that the crab cannery had been operating when I was whaling, Dode said, "When I first came to Naden Harbour, Wallace Fisheries were still at George Point, and that year they allowed the fishermen to gillnet the salmon right in the harbour. My god, they caught so many fish the cannery was plugged solid, they just couldn't handle them all. Scow loads of salmon rotted. The Fisheries department never allowed them to net fish in the harbour again.

"By the way, talking about Wallace Fisheries, did you know they were one of the original partners in forming the British Columbia Packers? Wallace and Draney, to be exact. Draney had a cannery at Namu; Wallace had another in Rivers Inlet. I can't recall which had what, but they also each owned a cannery on the Skeena and the Nass. The *Gray* used to carry a lot of their freight, coal, cans, boxes, and lots of Chinamen to run their canneries, each season. She also carried a lot of copper concentrates down from Anyox to Tacoma each winter. Strange, the turnings of fate. BC Packers owned the last whaling company on this coast."

The steamer *Gray* was a typical U.K. fore and aft coaster of 707 gross tons and ninety nominal horsepower, built in Workington, England, in 1909. The former *Petriana*, she was added to the Canadian North Pacific Fisheries fleet in 1910 by Sprott Balcom, as a tender for their five whaling stations, carrying supplies north and whaling products as far south as San Francisco. When not employed at this, she was chartered out to various shipping companies, by the trip or by the month, and in 1939 was finally sold to one of these charterers, Frank Waterhouse of Vancouver.

After the Waterhouse freighter *Northholm* was lost with most of her crew off Cape Scott, the *Gray* took over her run, hauling pulp from Port Alice around the north end of Vancouver Island. Ray Perry, chief officer of the *Northholm*, and one of only two survivors from the sinking, made many voyages in the *Gray*, but in the mid-forties she too became a victim of this treacherous stretch of water, breaking her back on Nahwitti bar, east of the cape. Destined for the shipbreaker's torch, she was reprieved at the last moment to the role of breakwater at the logging operations on Oyster River, on the east coast of Vancouver Island, and was, for many years, a visible landmark in the area.

The *Gray* had many interesting voyages during her earlier years, when laws were less stringently enforced and the dire necessity of a livelihood was often excuse for desperate actions. The records and correspondence on her activities are as interesting and as extensive as those of the whalers.

From the beginning she carried a large crew of west coast Indians who manhandled the wooden barrels and, later, the metal drums of whale oil that were stowed in her holds each trip, along with the sacks of whale meal and bone meal. On her northern voyages, the empty drums and barrels were stowed on deck or in the hold, on top of the large cargos of coal she carried for both the stations and the canneries. All of this coal was unloaded by hand, shovelled into self-dumping buckets which her cargo winches lifted up to the high docks of these northern ports.

The number of feet and hands that were lost by her native help in the dangerous work of handling her cargos was appalling. She was probably the hardest working ship on the coast, and the list of lawsuits, court judgments, and claims against her was proof of her hazardous occupation. Only when more experienced people were employed, and oil tanks and pumps fitted, did these slacken.

Harry Osselton, her former chief engineer, was in his element when we discussed the *Gray*. "Oh, she was a good sea boat, and could carry about 1100 tons. Why, she had a big three-furnace Scotch marine boiler that only burnt about twelve tons of coal a day, yet she averaged a good nine and a half knots!"

When I mentioned trip number seven in 1915, when the *Gray* carried an unbelievable 79 passengers and 833 tons of freight, plus her coal, water, and crew, Harry gave an incredulous gasp. "Why, she only carried four boats, with a maximum capacity in each for twenty people, and when I sailed in her she only had accommodation for twelve passengers at the most. Why, they must have built temporary bunks for them in the hold. Eight hundred and thirty-three tons, you say. Certainly wouldn't have left much room below decks, not even for coolies!"

I asked him to recall what the accommodations consisted of, and he closed his eyes and cast his mind back to those days when I was still playing hookey from school. "Well, there were some cabins under the bridge, for the skipper and mates, and a larger one, where the steering engine was housed, that was fitted out with two berths and a large settee for special passengers. Aft on the port side of the boiler and engine fidley was the galley, and a companionway down to the stern quarters. The cook and steward were berthed there, and there was a

Steamer Gray, *ex* Petriana, *700 gross ton whaling tender from 1911 to 1942.*

Some of the crew of the Gray *at Rose Harbour in 1938. Left to right: Jack Craddock, winchdriver; Alan Armour; Reggie Owen, mate; Archie Bell, second mate; Gibbs, A.B.; Captain Hunter; one of the engineers; Bob Hurst, winchdriver; Hugh Burnett, fireman; Spence Walker, A.B.*

Harry Osselton, chief engineer of the Gray, *poses in the mouth of a Finback whale at Naden Harbour, 1935.*

couple of cabins for passengers, inspectors and such like, going to the station. The engineers had quarters on deck, aft on the starboard side. Nice and airy. The crew? Why, they were all quartered forward, in the forecastle."

We discussed the layout of the ship, and he explained, "She had long hatches, one forward in the well deck and one aft of the bridge. Her hold was full length of the ship, from the forepeak bulkhead to the cross bunker forward of the stokehold. She was a great ship for handling cargo. We'd make several trips to the stations or canneries with coal and supplies, and haul back whale meal or salmon, then we'd fit in the tanks to the hold and haul whale oil for a trip or two."

My ears pricked up, for this was the first time I'd heard of oil tanks on the *Gray*. All accounts I'd read, from the days of the old *Tees* to Charlie Watson's days on the *Gray*, had only mentioned barrels. These were rolled down the dock and loaded aboard with slings, to be stowed by hand in the hold or on the deck. It was hard, difficult work, made highly dangerous by the slippery oil and rain-soaked decks, and by the ungainly shape of the barrels. A slip often cost a finger or a toe.

Harry nodded agreement, and then described the innovation.

"They were large round tanks, about half their diameter high, that sat on their flats on the floor of the hold, all braced and piped together so we could pump independently or in groups, from any number of tanks at the same time. They were marked so that each tank went back exactly where it had been before. They were quick and easy to fit," he chuckled, then added, "You know, I was the first chief engineer to get paid overtime for pumping oil. We usually took out a load or two of oil, then removed the tanks to carry dry cargos, but sometimes we'd load freight right on top of the tanks. The bone meal was the last thing we'd take out of the stations."

Harry Osselton's report on the *Gray*'s good upkeep was in sharp contrast to descriptions of the condition of the whaling boats. The reason for this was twofold; first, as a cargo carrier, the *Gray*'s insurers and charterers would demand her seaworthiness be of prime importance. Secondly, she worked all year round, which kept her in better condition than the steam whalers that were laid up six months of every year. A cold ship is very vulnerable to the inroads of weather and the creeping paralysis of rust, corrosion, and dryrot, and the whalers suffered from all three, as the money to maintain them through the idle period was not forthcoming.

Graig Fergusson referred to the poor condition of the *W. Grant* while he sailed on her when he was explaining the lack of pictures for this time of his life. "The decks leaked so badly that my old box Brownie camera, and the exposed film I had taken of the whaling, were ruined. She was an old ship when I was on her. Rust shook down from the deckheads every time the old man fired the gun. The ship itself was almost worn out. She'd been worked hard, and during the depression years at least, I don't think anything had been rebuilt or replaced that could possibly be left. Our chief engineer, Niels Sladden, and his second spent a lot of time just on the winch. It was badly worn and needed continuous repairs. Old Cap was furious the day a pin broke and the whole damn thing came to a clanking stop with a jar that nearly took the mast right out of the ship. The harpoon was actually ripped right out of the back of the whale with the sudden jerk."

I nodded, recalling quite vividly those moments when I had been caught in the Brown's forecastle when the gun had been discharged, and a rain of dust, paint, and rust had showered down on me. While I had been a younger whaler than Graig, possibly a little less observant, and certainly a less knowing seaman in those days, my subsequent training for master mariner, engineer, and, for a short time, marine surveyor, has caused me to realize the borderline of seaworthiness those old whalers teetered on.

The sad condition of the whaling vessels by the mid 1940s had a lot to do with the future failure of the whaling company. There is little doubt that William Schupp spent no more on the company's equipment and ships than was absolutely necessary for them to get through the season's work. Nowhere have I witnessed, before or since, such frugality and austerity. There were absolutely no frills within the whaling company during my time, and the stories I've recorded here are also barren of such frivolities. The equipment had been good, and those repairs that had to be carried out during those difficult years had been done skillfully, though sparingly. But the lack of funds to replace worn-out equipment, and the necessity of husbanding the vital parts year after year while the elements slowly deteriorated them, was a plan of attrition that could only end, as did the one-horse shay, with the collapse of the whole, when all parts wore out at the same time. The whaling ships were a fine example of this theory in practise.

Yet those who knew them in their prime were unstinting in their praise.

"Best boats ever built," exclaimed Lawrence Balcom, when we discussed the colour ships.

Whaler White *at Naden Harbour dock. Note piles of coal on dock.*

"Unique in the annals of marine history, they are fitted with noiseless steam steering gear," the Victoria *Colonist* lauded in November 1910.

Certainly they had been the best ships of their time. A few years later Captain Dode MacPherson served in them and recalled, "Course the boats were in top condition in those days, they were only six or seven years old. You didn't have to worry about the gear too much, and we went after a lot of Sperm and Blue whales because of the higher bonus."

"They were beautiful engines, smooth as silk, and very easy to manoeuver," Harry Osselton recalled, after a trip out as chief engineer on the *Brown*.

He was echoing the words of Charlie Watson, who had sailed on the *Black* nearly ten years before as engineer, and who was unstinting in his praise of these small ships. "They were fine ships. God, were they lovely ships."

The unrelenting deterioration of the whaling vessels had, in the case of the American Pacific Whaling vessels, been delayed somewhat, due to certain innovations in their construction and, later, to American Pacific's much superior method of winter storage. However, this had not been realized at first. From 1912 to 1915 the American vessels, under the less-demanding requirements of Dr. Rissmuller, had suffered badly from frozen pipes, rusted fittings, eroded tubes, and rotting woodwork during lay-up. This sad condition came to light when Bill Kelly, the new marine superintendent for the Victoria Whaling Company, reported the state of the Bay City station and its whalers to William Schupp. His letter covered a hurried weekend visit to Hoquiam and Grays Harbor, and prompted Schupp to relieve Rissmuller of command and place Captain LeMarquand in the position of manager of American Pacific Whaling. Under this man's capable direction, the ships were drawn out of the water for dry land storage during the winter season, something their Canadian counterparts could not enjoy. He also instituted proper maintenance and overhauls, and ensured that laid-up equipment was properly drained and protected.

LeMarquand also instituted the conversion to oil firing for boiler heating, thus protecting the boilers from the high erosion factor of fly ash, and from the severe thermal stresses experienced by coal-fired boilers, whose heating surfaces are continually exposed to sudden drafts of cold air during firing or cleaning of the grates. The 1916 completion of locks to join Lake Washington with Puget Sound allowed Schupp to create a freshwater winter refit and storage facility

American whaler Unimak, *with whale alongside, at Akutan, Alaska.*

on the lakeshore at Bellevue, and he built his home on high ground overlooking this site, to keep an eye on his idle fleet.

This favoured place held by the American Pacific ships brought them such extras as electric lights and wheelhouses, things never seen on the Canadian ships, and showed in larger ways as well. The buying-out of the Alaska Whaling Company and the Tyee Whaling Company added three new ships to the American fleet, while the selling of the *Germania*, *Sebastian*, and later the *Orion* and *St. Lawrence*, reduced the Canadian fleet to six vessels, with the S.S. *Gray* acting as tender for both companies.

In 1924, Grays Harbor station was closed and a new station, Port Hobron, was created on Sitkalidak Island. Now American Pacific was the parent company, and even more attention and money was focused on its equipment, while Schupp's Canadian affiliate, now called the Consolidated Whaling Corporation, suffered more neglect. The austerity program demanded by Schupp continued after he had guided it back into a viable position, and was faithfully maintained by such diligent managers as C. Rogers Brown, S.C. Ruck, and Alfus Garcin.

It was a program that, by the end of World War II, had rendered the Canadian ships unfit for the rigours of whaling, much to the chagrin of Garcin and Ruck. They had already assigned the old *Brown* to Pete Bromson, the *White* to Oscar Luddvicksen, and the *Blue* to Andy Anderson. To overcome this setback, Marc Lagen, general manager of American Pacific, offered to reregister the *Kodiak*, *Unimak*, and *Paterson* under Canadian articles for their needs, with the promise to follow them with the *Tanginak* and *Moran* if the venture proved profitable.

The American boats were available for transfer to the Canadian sector for two reasons. First was the difficulty in putting the Akutan station back in operation after the departing Russians had stripped it of all the vital whaling equipment. There was also an absence of whales near the Port Hobron station. Unfortunately, Marc Lagen died before the transfer could be effected, and with the octogenarian William Schupp in retirement, payment in full was demanded for the Reconstruction Finance Corporation loan. American Pacific Whaling had to liquidate all its assets to satisfy its creditor, and American Pacific and Consolidated Whaling were put on the auction block.

Chapter Eleven

Rammed From Below

As the whaling ships deteriorated, the rigours of whaling took a proportionately greater toll on them each season, and they were less prepared to survive the hazards of the ocean. Of all the hazards faced by the whalers, none was more real to their minds than that of being rammed and sunk by the huge creatures they hunted. While we have many accounts of other mishaps, only two incidents of ramming are offered here. Both happened to my old ship, the *Brown*. The last time was when I was on her bridge; the first time twenty years earlier, and to tell that story we turn to the outspoken old marine engineer Charlie Watson, as he records his observation of those far-off days of 1923.

"Yes, yes. You know, it all comes back to me now, as we talk. God, those were quite the days. Old Alf Pepper, he was a humourous sort of a fellow. He'd take a sample of boiler water in a drinking glass and add a few drops of silver nitrate. If it turned the sample silvery grey, he'd grunt, 'Salty as Lot's wife's ass!' " Charlie shook his head slowly and chuckled, his eyes dancing merrily with humour of the historic jest.

Filling our cups with tea, he added more seriously, "You know, with all the manoeuvering we did, and the terrific concussion from the gun, we had a hard time keeping the condenser tubes tight. We'd salt up the boiler in no time if we didn't check it every watch. We'd treat with caustic soda to keep our pH up about 8, and blew down to remove the salt. If we got oil over from the engine, we'd add a little kerosene to the hot well and scum the boiler like hell till we got rid of it. But I know you want to hear more about whaling than engineering, so I'm going to tell you a story I don't think has ever been published, about how the old whaler *Brown* was rammed and almost sunk by a christly big Sperm, and believe me, I was right there and saw it all!" Charlie paused, took a swig of his tea, and glanced over to see if I was showing proper interest. Then, satisfied I was, he lit up a cigarette and began his story.

"Well, Canute Halvorsen was gunner of the *Brown* that year, and we were working with them out of Rose Harbour, and were cruising several miles apart in a southerly direction off Anthony Island. It was during the full of the moon, and the Sperms were all close inshore. Yes, you know how they seem to always appear a few days before and after the full of the moon. You also recall, no doubt, that we had a practise of hoisting an inverted blue ensign to the foremast when we were chasing Sperms, so the others would know to stay clear. Well, it was also a damn give-away that you had whale about, and was like waving a red flag to a bull; everyone would close up on you and sometimes you'd lose your whale because of them. So, few whalers hoisted the flag unless the other ship got too close to a whale you were stalking; then you did it to warn him off.

"Well, Canute hadn't bothered to hoist his flag when he got his first whale, but when the second one he was chasing swung towards us, he quickly put up his flag and rushed between us and the whale. Oh, some of those gunners were sly ones, always trying to beat the other guy out. Willis knew exactly what Canute was up to, so he pretended to haul the *Black* over to the other side of the *Brown*, as though he was going to try a long shot at Canute's whale."

Charlie Watson enjoyed an audience to his stories, and he paused while I changed tapes before continuing, so that not a word of this would be lost. "Willis was the best gunner in the fleet and noted for his long shots. This must have worried old Canute, for he suddenly tried a very long shot of his own to prove ownership of the whale, so we hauled up and turned away, leaving him to his fun. Well, my god. We could see the harpoon hit that whale. It didn't look like a very good hit to us, but he was fast to it, and that was for sure. What we didn't learn till later was that the bomb had not gone off, and that big Sperm was more startled than injured. Oh, my god, you had to see it to believe it! That Sperm took off like a shot. We roared with glee as the old *Brown* tried to get up speed to chase after the whale, her line smoking as it went out.

"It was like being on a seat at a grandstand, watching the action and enjoying the fun while the others did all the work. Just when it seemed that whale was going to tow the *Brown* all the way to China, it suddenly veered off in a great big circle that brought him back towards us. Well, Willis quickly swung the *Black* away to port to avoid Canute's whale, and the whale, coming up tight on the bight of the line, swung more sharply to the right till he was headed right back at the *Brown*'s starboard side. Canute and his boys were so busy loading up the gun and heaving in the line for a second shot that I don't think they noticed the whale's deviation or its evil intent. It took them all by surprise!"

Charlie wiped his flushed face with a handkerchief, and wet his throat with some tea. "Canute would never own up that he had lost track of that wounded whale, something a gunner must never do, but I was told that no one was watching the whale till the man on the wheel let out a cry of warning. By then it was too late. That sixty-ton whale, travelling at more than ten knots, hit them right abaft the stokehold, and rolled her far over to port. It must have been quite a blow, for a big cloud of black smoke shot up out of her funnel, and when she settled back down again she had a heavy list to starboard.

"Well, old Canute was certain they were finished, but he had no intentions of giving up his whale, so while the crew swung out the lifeboat, he called over to Willis and asked him to shoot their whale." Charlie paused long enough to light up a cigarette, then, talking through a cloud of smoke, continued, "God, it was no problem for Willis to shoot that whale. It was right under our bows and still dazed and spent from its attack on the *Brown*. You see, when we had backed away and denied that whale a ship to ram, it had rolled a beady eye up out of the water to find the *Brown*, and Willis, realizing the whale's intentions, had blown several warning blasts of the whistle as he rang down for full ahead and tried to come back up to speed to cut across the whale's path. After all, we owed old Canute that much at least. He had shot, unbeknowingly I grant you, our runaway whale just a few days before. So killing that whale was really anti-climax.

"Cutting loose their whale line, Canute decided to run towards shore where he could beach her. We picked up the whale and followed along with them. There was too much sea running for us to lay alongside and help pump out the water that was rushing in, so we gave them moral support by staying nearby as they headed in behind Anthony Island and squared away for the head of Louscoone Inlet where there was soft, safe mud to lay ashore. The tide was in the first hour of its ebb as we pushed her in towards the beach, and we felt her settle on the bottom and her plates rise above the water level. They had moved everything heavy they could lay their hands on to the port side of the deck, and this gave her sufficient list that way that she settled ashore against the raise of the beach. Alf Pepper and I went over to inspect the damage, and agreed with Fisheye and his second, Buster Brown, that if we could find enough bolts between us, the best repair would be to stitch her plates back together again before the tide turned to flood. While Alf Pepper went back out to the *Black* to scrounge up all the bolts, washers, nuts, and tools he could find, Buster Brown and I began knocking out the sheered rivets and shoring up the plates and frame from inside. The difficult part was to realign the rivet holes, after we had hammered the plates back, so we could put through the bolts and harden up the joint.

"The ramming had cracked a hull frame, and literally ripped some of the rivet holes out of the joint. But by using long bolts and large washers, then shorter bolts with grommets of lamp wick and red lead, we slowly pulled the joints together. I think, if I recall correctly, we also stitched strips of paint-soaked canvas in between the plates, passing the strips in and out of the rows of bolts, to form a watertight gasket when the joint was finally hardened up."

Charlie eyed the ash on the end of his cigarette with a concentrated squint as he tried to recall the events of the past. "Yes, let's see now, there was about three dozen rivets at least, horizontally, and, oh, say, a dozen and a half vertically, that we replaced with bolts."

He poured some more tea, and lit a fresh cigarette off the butt of the previous one, as I mentioned a similar incident we experienced on her twenty years later. Nodding agreement, he grunted, "But god, it was hard work! Cramped up inside that hull, working against the tide, hammering those damn stubborn plates back into line. We organized both crews into teams, and we'd take turns working from the lifeboat, hung in the falls over the side as a staging, pulling our guts out on those old spud wrenches and getting maybe a flat or two each time they hammered on the plates from inside. Then we'd take a breather while others had a go, then we'd go inside and swing the christly huge sledge Fisheye fished up from somewhere.

"We never stopped till the job was done, but we had her watertight by the time the tide flooded back. After it got dark, we hung lanterns over the side and down in the stokehold, so we could see. While the tide rose above our repairs, we fixed a cement patch, reinforced with steel rods, over the bolts, and shored up to support it. When the tide lifted her, we gave a pull with the *Black* and she came sliding right off, almost as good as new. There were some who thought the repairs so good they should return to whaling and wait to report it, but Canute wouldn't hear of it and left right away for Rose Harbour, to report to Victoria. We picked up their two whales and followed them back. I'll never forget the sadness on old Canute's face when Bill Rolls told him Victoria wanted him to bring the *Brown* back to town.

"I think he had hoped to get permission to keep whaling while the Sperms were there, and rightly feared, if the ship returned to Victoria, she'd be laid up and the crew paid off for the season. But, in all honesty, there was no way our temporary repairs were strong enough for her to continue whaling, especially with that broken frame and pulled holes. Everyone said good-bye, sure there would be no more whaling for the crew of the *Brown*. Fortunately, the company thought otherwise, and in less than three weeks the repairs were completed, and Canute and his boys were back whaling with us."

The second ramming took place during the season Roy and I spent on the *Brown*. Nearly two months had elapsed since the *Brown* had first arrived at the northern end of the Queen Charlottes in that spring of 1941. For Roy and I it had been a time of learning and now, with almost twenty whales to our credit, the novelty was wearing off. After a boiler washout at Naden, we headed out with the *Black* and *Green* to sweep the area westward of Frederick Island for the expected run of Sperm whales to this area. Stationed two to three miles off our quarter, the *Black* and *Green* followed us through an overlapping box sweep that had raised nothing more exciting than the odd small minke or sei whale.

Through the afternoon of the third day, the weather began to deteriorate, clouds scudding in from the sou-east dropped ever lower, and we could feel the damp push of the wind at our backs as we ran offshore. By supper time the *Green* was far astern and reported difficulty maintaining steam pressure, advising that she was returning to the station for boiler tube repairs. We watched her go with mixed feelings; the sky to the east, where she was bound, was foreboding with threatening black clouds, while ahead of us, the following sea and bright evening sky belied the weather that was building up. Just before nine o'clock, the crew of the *Black* reported they didn't like the look of it and were going to run for shelter in Port Louis, advising us to follow suit. She turned on her heel, rolling mightily as she took the seas on her beam, then, with the wind whipping the smoke off her funnel top, she stood off towards the distant shore.

A few minutes after Roy relieved me in the barrel and I had climbed down to take over the wheel, we spotted a whale. We had both been assigned to the skipper's watch, and Louis was looking astern as the *Black* shrank to a small dot on the horizon. Later he claimed he was about to tell me to haul round and follow her in, when Roy let out the loudest of yelps and hollers from the barrel. I don't know who was more startled, us or the whale. It was a large Sperm, getting his first breath after half an hour or more down in the depths of the ocean, and his blow, as he exhaled, was thrown back on us as we steamed over the spot where he had breached. A second or two sooner and we would have rammed him.

The whale gave a spurt of startled speed, but had not the breath in him for another dive, so he boiled off to starboard, attempting to

Sperm whale one cable ahead. Captain Louis Larsen at the gun on the Brown *in 1941.*

charge his lungs on the run. Louis gave an excited grunt as he slammed the telegraph over to full speed and ordered me to haul round and give chase. I steadied up on a course to port of the frantic creature, while Louis raced for the gun. By the time he had reached it, loaded his primer, and released the lock, we had closed the whale and were in an excellent position to fire.

Calling to me to ring down for slow speed ahead, he took aim from the wildly rolling gun deck as we ran almost beam-on to the heaving seas. Alerted by our sudden manouevering and the explosion of the gun, everyone rushed out on deck. And lucky it was that they did, for the shot went wild, the gun muzzle thrown high as the ship corkscrewed over a large sea. The shock drove the whale around to a more westerly heading, and he raced off with our harpoon stuck in his tail. Our mainline went shrieking out, burning the brake blocks that had been lightly set on the windlass.

His spurt was short-lived, as he was still taxed by his long dive, and within a half hour we had him close enough to fire our number two line across. This harpoon was better placed, but still was not a killing shot. Again the whale plowed off, blowing wildly, his blunt head bashing aside the seas as he pulled both lines away from the ship and headed for the distant horizon. There was no hope of heaving in the lines this time, and Louis called Roy down from the barrel to help load the gun. Everything was shaking and threatening to go by the board; even the brake blocks had caught fire, and Johnny threw buckets of sea water over them to keep them from burning up.

Urged by the skipper's shouted instruction, I had the ship at full speed following up the whale's wake, but it became obvious to everyone that, shortly, both lines would be gone—and the whale with them—if we couldn't ease the terrific punishment the ship and its gear were taking. Night was casting its gloom astern of us, and the evening sky had narrowed down to a low band of unreal orange light ahead. At that moment the Sperm plunged his head below the surface and tossed his tail high for a deep dive.

It was a sight right out of *Moby Dick*. The harpoon lines were draped across its broad back and over the wide spread of its tail, and this was all silhouetted starkly black against the orange brightness of the receding daylight.

The whine of the outgoing lines continued without hesitation while we ran up to where the whale had disappeared. Half a mile of line from each locker had disappeared down into the dark depths, and still the line ran out. It was now only a matter of feet before we would have to cut loose the whale or rip the gear out of the ship. Johnny and Finn John grabbed up cutting irons and were poised to slash the lines, waiting only on Louis's signal, when the outgoing rush of line stopped and silence fell over the ship. An eerie, dangerous silence.

The skipper shouted at me to stop the engines, and we coasted ahead with the speed of our mad dash still upon us, while everyone looked over the side. Quite suddenly, Louis and Finn John exploded in loud tones of argument. It took a few seconds for the meaning of their words to drift up to me on the bridge.

"The son-of-a-bitch is coming up!" roared Finn John, pointing over the side. "He's going to ram us!"

The frightening thought of being rammed from below in these darkening, stormy seas caused me to draw in my breath, but the look on Finn John's face chilled my heart. For an instant more, Louis remained frozen at the sharply-depressed gun, then he turned and shouted up to me, "Full astern! Give her full astern, Bill!"

Spurred by the sudden urgency in his voice, I threw myself at the telegraph and gave it a double ring over to full astern. It was as though Cec, our chief engineer, had heard the frantic call from the gun deck, for the engines were already racing astern before the telegraph stopped ringing under my hand. I put the helm hard a-starboard as the reversing propeller churned the sea to foam, and a passing sea tossed our stern high as we began to move sternway. But fast as we were, our belligerent whale was faster. It was a glancing blow, for in going astern with the helm hard over, our head slew to port, laying smooth water under our starboard bow as it drew away from the whale's direct line of attack.

There was a dull thud as he hit the turn of the bilge, lifting the ship slightly and rolling her to port. Then, as we rolled back to level keel, his broad snout rose up out of the water just ahead of the bridge, till it was as high as my eye. Blowing bloody froth and warm vapour over the bridge and myself, he fell over on his side and came within range of Louis's acutely angled gun. In a roar that thudded on my eardrums and blew smoke and powder dust over the bridge, our lance blasted into the stunned whale, and he died in a tangle of ropes under our bow, the scene masked from my eyes by the smoke and the evening's darkness, as we continued to go astern.

When hearing was regained after the concussion, and as the smoke cleared, I became aware of Louis calling me to stop the engines. Within moments the seas had pushed us beam-on, and we rolled lifelessly in a tangle of rope that threatened to foul our propeller. The seas were running too high to get the whale over to our port side, so we heaved it close to the damaged starboard side with the lance line and, after putting a chain around its tail, pumped air down into its abdomen to keep it afloat.

Then came the nightmarish job of heaving in both whale lines and stowing them in the lockers, a task that required all hands to complete. Through it all, as we worked below decks, the ominous thump of the whale hitting the ship's plates as we rolled together, and the report from the chief that we were making considerable water, urged us to feverish pace. By midnight we were again underway, moving slowly along at half speed towards the distant lee of the land.

During the last moments of my wheel watch, Cec came up to the bridge and reported that the water was gaining on the pumps. He suggested we drop the whale and run for the station, where he felt repairs could be made to stop the inrush of water. When Louis shook his head, Finn John strongly advised we keep the whale but haul back for Port Louis, where the ship could be beached if necessary, and the whale used to lay her over on. Louis argued we were now closer to Parry Passage than to Port Louis, and stated it was his intention to hold the best weather course possible to make it there.

There was no thought of going to our bunks when we came off watch. We huddled in the messroom, drinking coffee and listening to the older members of the crew discuss the pros and cons of our perilous position. At 2 a.m., his coveralls wet and coated with oil and coal dust, Cec climbed up to the bridge again to report to the skipper. Johnny, coming down to get a cup of coffee for Louis, gave us the gist of the chief's report. Coal was washing down into the bilges and plugging the pumps, and the water had risen till it was just about touching the cranks. Cec had been forced to put the main injection on the engine room bilge suction to hold it back. The skipper, claiming less than half an hour till we reached the lee of the land, refused to drop the whale and run for it. A few minutes later Finn John appeared and told us to man the deck pumps.

The whaling ships were fitted with flush-mounted, single-acting plunger pumps on either side of the deckhouse, used for keeping the bilges dry during the long winter lay-up. These slender tube pumps, fitted with foot valve and plunger valve, carried right down into the bilges under the coal bunkers, and this was where most of the sea water was coming in. With the aid of Finn John's flashlight, we removed the covers and primed the pumps with a couple buckets of seawater, then began to pump. When we lifted the pump handle up to chest height, the pump spilled two or three gallons of dirty water on the deck at our feet. Then we pushed the handle back down to deck level, to force the water through the plunger valve to the top of the plunger so we could lift it up to deck level. It was an up-and-down motion that quickly taxed our back and arms.

With both engineers and firemen below keeping the pumps cleared, and Johnny and the skipper on the bridge, Lee was told off to man the port pump with Joe, while Roy and I were sent to the weather side to man the starboard pump. It was desperate work, lent a chilling reality when we overheard Finn John mutter to Joe that, in his opinion, the punishment the deteriorated plates were taking could result in the whole side caving in, and us going down like a stone, no matter how close the land might be.

Dire misgivings were forgotten an hour later when, true to the skipper's predictions, we came under the lee of the land and the punishment on the hull eased. Leaving Joe and Lee on the port pump, Finn John had us open the starboard manhole covers into the coal bunker. Giving us shovels and a lantern, he ordered us down into the confined darkness to shovel as much coal as possible over to the port side, to help list the ship that way, and to expose the damaged area of the hull.

We soon reached the area of the leak, and from there on downwards as we worked, cold seawater and lumps of coal washed into our shoes, jamming in so tightly that, after a few minutes of torture, we had to remove our shoes and dump it out. It had grown daylight while Roy and I laboured in the coal bunker, but when we finally did come back on deck, we had succeeded in listing the ship several degrees. By stuffing a mattress over the worst of the leak, we reduced the water intake to a point where the bilge pumps could handle it.

By this time we had passed through Parry Passage, so Lee began to start breakfast while Roy, Joe, and I, under Finn John's direction, began moving every heavy piece of equipment and supplies over to the port side, returning to the coal bunkers to shift more coal over. We had such a pronounced list on her that, as we came alongside the dock at Naden, we had to ease into it to prevent our rigging from catching in the pilings.

The *Green* lay strangely silent ahead of us, and in a short while, with a hot breakfast resting comfortingly under our belts and the morning sun beginning to warm our tired bodies, we talked with some of her crew as they gathered on her fantail to hear about our mishap. On the dock, the station manager was discussing our position with the skippers of both ships, their muted tones not intended to reach our ears.

Roy and I were content to listen as the older members of each crew discussed possible cures for our woes. Slowly an optimistic plan evolved, the gist of which was that we would make sufficient repairs to the *Brown* to allow us to tow the *Green* over to Prince Rupert, where both ships could have more permanent repairs carried out—to our hull and to the *Green*'s boiler. Not too strangely, that was exactly the plan of action decided on by the manager and skippers, and a call was placed with Victoria to get approval. While confirmation was awaited, we began making temporary repairs to our hull.

More coal was shovelled over to the port side, and we filled our lifeboat with water to create a more severe list, till Willie's long arms could reach the sheered rivets from the workboat alongside. Pounding out these rivets, bolts with large washers fitted with grommets were forced through, and we pulled the joint together from the inside with nuts bedded on large, square, steel plates supplied by the blacksmith. When this was completed, Finn John brought oakum and a caulking iron down and rammed this into the joint till the water stopped coming through. Then the carpenter from the station built a wooden box around the area, suitably shored in place and fitted with reinforcing steel, into which we poured pails full of fast-setting cement.

By noon this had begun to set up, and we rested from our labours to enjoy large servings of Lee's stew and fresh bread with jam. We were sitting around after lunch in the warm sunlight, at peace with the world and satisfied with our endeavours, when the bad news came down from the manager's office. Prince Rupert Drydocks would not extend credit to the whaling company to repair its vessels.

The gloom that descended over both crews at this announcement caused considerable mutterings, and, in our case, accusing glances were thrown towards Louis's dejected and tiredly bowed shoulders as he stood hunched over the bridge railing, staring off into the distance, a cigarette pinched between tightly clenched lips. There was little doubt he was having bitter afterthoughts about his decision to shoot and lug home the whale that was now being flensed on the slip opposite us. For a couple of hours we sat around, gloomily aware that if repairs could not be realized, the whaling season was over for all of us. Even Roy and I, who had admitted to each other that whaling was a tough, oft-times miserable occupation which we would never follow again, did not want it to end this way.

At 2:30 the manager appeared at the pierhead and called up the skippers of both ships. Again they huddled in a circle, heads bowed and voices low. Then the mates and engineers were called up to join the meeting, and, finally, joshing each other in agreement, they climbed down to the ship. With a rueful smile, Louis explained to us the plan that had been agreed to. We were going back to Victoria for repairs, and as soon as these were completed, would return to Naden to commence whaling again. The reprieve got a growl of approval from all of us, and we set to with a will to ready the ship for her new role. We were going to tow the *Green* over eight hundred miles, from the north end of the Queen Charlottes to the south end of Vancouver Island, and we were going to ready our number one whale line to do so.

We put ashore our gun powders and primers, lightened the ship of all her spare gear and replaced its weight with more coal, topped up our water tanks, and took on provisions. Then we led our whale line out the stern fairlead and down the length of the *Green*'s hull to her bow, where we made it fast to her anchor shackle. After supper, with a line from our bow to the *Green*'s stern, we backed out into the harbour, towing the *Green* with us. Once clear of the dock, we slipped the bow line and swung away as the *Green* followed our towline.

Outside the harbour we eased out the whale line as the *Green* carefully let out her anchor chain. When she lay about 100 fathoms astern, we slowly came up to full speed and set the brakes on our windlass. Setting a course to clear Rose Spit and Butterworth Rocks, we set off for Triple Island and the sheltered Inside Passage, sixty

Roy Gustavson poses beside our unlucky Sperm whale. Note the list on the Brown *in the background.* Green *is alongside dock at Naden Harbour, 1941.*

miles away. Next morning we were in the long narrow reaches of Grenville Channel, and the following night entered Milbanke Sound.

It was evening as we eased out into Queen Charlotte Sound, and a fresh westerly warned of trouble ahead. Off Cape Caution the towline parted, and we hauled round in the boisterous beam seas to run back to where the helpless *Green* was drifting swiftly in on the crashing breakers. Heaving in the towline as we went, we flaked it down the full length of the deck. Everyone lent a hand, and in the confusion of ropes, seas washing over the decks, and everyone struggling to get all the line back aboard before it could tangle in our propeller, Joe burned his foot when a drain cock broke off and live steam roared out where he had placed his foot to brace himself as he drove the windlass. Unknowing, we shouted at him to run it faster, and he stayed stolidly at his post to carry out the orders.

Without steam to haul in their anchor chain and anchor, the *Green* had rigged a wire sling around the chain at their hausepipe. As we swept by under their rearing bows and sent over the end of our towline, they quickly passed it through the padded eye of the sling and made it fast as we steamed around in a tight turn to pull them away from the rocks. Once clear, we again eased out towline as they eased out more chain, creating an effective shock absorber of the heavy anchor which hung down deep between us on the towline.

The following evening we entered the warm humid climate of the gulf area through Seymour Narrows, and set a course down Georgia Strait. At nine next morning, with the bridge speaker mysteriously tuned in to the local radio station, and the strains of "Roll out the Barrel" echoing in our ears, we stood in for Brotchie Ledge and shortened up the towline, then slipped in past the breakwater to the calm of James Bay. Sliding under Johnson Street bridge, we eased over to the Victoria Machinery Depot and dropped the *Green* off at the jetty where the boiler makers waited. Then we picked up the dockmaster. The cradle was down and waiting, and the dockmaster and his crew quickly aligned us in over the keel blocks with winch-powered mooring wires. Moments later we were pulled up the inclined marine railway, till the cradle and the *Brown* stood higher than the surrounding buildings.

Chapter Twelve

The Last Farewell

The *Brown* stood tall and silent on the cradle at the depot, and all haste was made to get her back whaling. It took us a few hours to shovel the remainder of the coal over to the port side of the bunker, and then we removed the whale line from the locker so the yard men could assess the scope of work ahead of them, and prepare a plan of action to carry out the repairs.

By midafternoon, much of the internal woodwork in the way of the damage had been removed, and it now became obvious to all that the ramming had bent several frames and loosened some very suspect joints—joints that had held together more by the grace of God than by any mechanical means. She was indeed a most fortunate ship, and the yard figured to have her ready in three to four days.

Feeling the urge to see my parents, and with Roy agreeing to accompany me, we got permission from Finn John to be away a couple of days, and drew a fifty dollar advance from the office. We had little to pack: a few mementos, a change of underwear, socks, and a spare shirt. I hadn't begun to shave yet, so a toothbrush was my only article of toiletry. Smelling of the sea, of coal and smoke, and of the strange odour of whales, we climbed aboard the midnight boat for Vancouver.

We expected to endure the six-hour voyage on the crowded ship by stretching out on a chair or a bench, but we had no sooner been fortunate enough to find such than we were accosted by two rough-looking characters from the whaler *Green*, who were also headed for Vancouver. Montreal Mike, who made our fireman Willie look small, wore a black serge suit that failed to meet its obligation at cuffs and waist. His pal, Paper Nose Frenchie, wore the loudest set of plaids I'd ever seen, with a green tie knotted tightly over a light pink shirt with white collar.

They glared down at us with a belligerence that cautioned against refusal, and offered us a drink from brown-bagged bottles. They were so far gone that there were long pauses between their words, while they searched for the next one to spit out. Recognizing us as the young proteges of Finn John, they took a fatherly stance in warning us of the perilous road back to the ship if we were found by the ladies of the street to be carrying such a large sum of money as fifty dollars—about a month's wages for most people.

Tucking their bottles under their coattails, they motioned us to follow them back to their cabin and told us we could sleep in their bunks, which they assured us they had no plans to use. No sooner did we get there than two cronies of Montreal Mike's dropped in, and another bottle was produced from a leather suitcase. Roy and I were ignored as the four older seamen grunted and grumbled about their circumstances, the war, and what the paper hanger was up to. After excusing ourselves to go to the head, we made our way to a quieter part of the ship and let the booze drift us off to sleep.

We awoke to a silent ship, and groggily made our way ashore, only to recall our seabag and have to find our way back to the cabin to retrieve it. Our two protectors were stretched out on the settee, snoring loudly, so we quietly closed the door and gained the familiar CPR dock, where our adventure had started just over two months before. After a light breakfast of doughnuts and coffee, we caught the ferry to North Vancouver and the street car to Capilano, then walked down the long hill to my home on Marine Drive. We were spotted some distance off by my younger brother Bert, who let out a whoop of welcome and charged up to us on his bike.

My parents' welcome was more subdued but just as emotional. Mother kept talking almost without stop, chiding me for running off without word, then, in the next breath, thanking me for the money I'd arranged to be sent to her each month, all the while making coffee and hot baking-powder biscuits, and putting food on the table while she clucked her tongue in concern over my lanky gauntness. Roy, leaning back with a show of worldly wisdom, described for my father our many adventures on the whaling ship. Bert and his pals had worked themselves into the kitchen where they stood around, munching biscuits and hanging on every word, as Roy offhandedly told about our storm on the way up, the size of our first whale, and then casually dropped the bombshell that we had been rammed by a whale and had barely made it back alive.

Mom went to the bathroom and had a good cry when she realized the risk we were taking to get the money that was being sent home, and Dad later took me aside and advised me not to go whaling anymore, cautioning that we had been lucky this time; the next time we might not be. The harsh life of the whaler seemed far away as we talked, so different from the life at home that I was sorely tempted to agree with him. But something inside would not let me run away from a job that had yet to be done. Someone had to do it, I argued with him. He never asked me to reconsider; he knew what I meant. After all, he had come to Canada on a cattle ship from Norway at the age of sixteen, and within weeks had joined the First Canadian Battalion going overseas. Sent back as underage, he reenlisted in the second battalion as it was being sent over, and spent four years in the trenches as a machine gunner.

The hours at home passed quickly, but we got a shock when we tried to get tickets to return to our ship. There were none available. A movement of troops had cancelled two sailings, and the midnight boat was filled to capacity. We had to accept passage on the morning boat next day. Dad walked us to the dock and waved us off as the old *Princess Charlotte* backed away. At Portlock Point we were shocked to see the *Green* go sailing by us, heading north, and recalled Finn John's warning not to be away too long.

We recklessly paid for a taxi to the shipyard, only to find the *Brown* still high and dry, and a din of steelwork surrounding her. With more plates left to fit, no one mentioned our late arrival, and we whiled away the time by riding around with Willie and Johnny in a red

Johnny and Willie at the wheel of their girl-finding convertible in Victoria, 1941.

convertible as they looked for girls. Two days later, as we readied to sail the following morning, I realized Roy was not around. He had left the ship early with Willie, and, as I turned in, I thought it strange that he should still be ashore, but suspected he was with a girl and would return shortly.

I awoke to hear gasps and groans in the darkened forecastle, and vaguely made out the shape of a person sitting on the companionway ladder with his head bowed. Reaching out, I turned up the kerosene lantern we used as a night light, and was startled to see Louis Larsen hunkered down on the ladder, bawling his eyes out. It was the first time I'd ever seen a man cry, and my thoughts were dashed. Never had I seen such misery, such utter anguish, on a man's face.

I jumped up, got a wet cloth from the bucket of water we kept by the stove, and washed his face till he stopped crying, asking him what the trouble was, but only a torrent of unintelligible sounds came out. Easing him over to the locker seat in front of Harold's berth, I rolled him into the bunk and pulled a blanket over him. Slipping into my pants and shoes, I was about to climb up the ladder when his arm flipped out and he grabbed my hand. "Thanks Billy," he grunted, then fell back asleep, and his hand dropped from mine.

In a daze I climbed up to the darkened deck and moved aft to the galley, where I found Johnny and Willie silently sitting on the fidley. I stood in front of them for several moments before they took notice of me, and then I asked what was wrong with the skipper.

In a listless voice, Johnny replied, "We just got some mail from home. The Germans have retaliated against the underground. Louis has lost all his family. He had a son your age."

"Jesus Christ, God Almighty!" Willie snarled, springing to his feet and pushing roughly by me. As he passed the galley, he whacked the steel bulkhead with a blow that would have broken anyone else's hand.

"I didn't understand a damn thing he was saying," I stammered to Johnny, feeling very sad for our captain.

"That's OK, Bill, he was speaking to you in Norwegian. He went down there to tell you Roy wasn't coming back. That he had quit," Johnny muttered, starting forward.

"He quit? He didn't tell me he was going to quit. What the hell's going on here?" I groaned, feeling suddenly lost myself.

"I don't know, Bill, and what's more, I don't care," Johnny snapped, pausing to turn to face me. "All I know is that I have a young sister over there, and no one knows what's happened to her. . . ." His voice choked up and he turned away.

"Sorry," I called after him. "Really sorry to hear that."

The next morning we loaded out for the station, two new seamen joined us, and at noon we sailed. The skipper stood on the bridge, his cap pulled down over his eyes, his face expressionless. Johnny and Willie did their jobs without flaw, and the two new men, both more proficient seamen than I, took over their tasks without comment. As we steamed out of the harbour and Victoria receded astern, I stood alone at the taffrail, my mind in a turmoil that churned round and round like the tumbling wake below my feet. Why was I heading back to the whaling? Without Roy there'd be no fun in it. What the hell was I doing out here with a bunch of strangers? It was a terrible moment of indecision, and I could not find any answers. But whether I liked it or not, I knew I had to complete what I had agreed to do: a season of whaling. Just as I had not been able to let go of the steering wheel in the storm that almost overwhelmed us, so I could not quit now. I always made it a point, from then on, to keep busy and keep my mind occupied when leaving home port, never allowing myself time to reflect on why I was sailing away.

When we arrived back at Naden, the *Green* had already picked up a half dozen whales, and the *Black* a dozen more than she. We began whaling with a vengeance to catch up, sometimes lugging in three large whales at a time, and finally realized the gratifying grand total for the season of sixty-four whales. Gone were the hi-jinks, the little goofs of learning, and the spontaneous bursts of laughter that had been present when we brought the old *Brown* up to working efficiency. Now we worked with a cold discipline; there was pride in our ability, but there was no fun. Even Lee would no longer put up the noisy fights he had when Roy was there and we had the effrontery to ask him for another egg, or for more meat, please. In a way, we all missed Roy, but we were whalers, and the demands on our energies left nothing over for daydreams. Reality took all.

The summer weather slowly gave way to colder and darker nights, shorter days, and gales of wind that tore at us so that we had to steam up on our anchor all night to keep it from dragging free. There were more naval and airforce patrol vessels in the area, and once, when we were lying offshore, a whole fleet of American destroyers rushed by us, shepherding a couple of large cruisers that were plowing determinedly towards Alaska.

The signs of war were all around us, but the signs of the coming winter were also present. The fishermen began to move out. Soon the fish buyers' floats and barges in Parry Passage were towed away, and even the number of birds seemed to be reduced; only the gooney birds and seagulls remained. The bogey heater in the forecastle was now kept stoked with coal day and night as we tried to warm up and dry out after six hours on deck, exposed to the cold rain and wind. We were beginning to spend more time at anchor than out whaling when the call finally came to return to the station.

Lee immediately announced that this meant the end of the season, and forecast that, when we entered harbour, we would see the clouds of dust over the bonemill at the station, adding, for my benefit, that only at the end of the season did the station stop to grind up the whale bones. As we approached the dock I saw that he was right. After tying up, the word came down that we were to pick up all our harpoons from the blacksmith's shop, and were to load coal and provisions for the trip home.

By evening all this had been accomplished, and we had signed and received a copy of our earnings and whale bonus, less outstanding bills owed to the store, etc. The "etc." in my case was a bill, paid on my behalf to the hotel in Masset, for new sheets and pillow case to replace those I had soaked in blood when my tooth was extracted. I'm afraid my departure in darkness, and the lack of explanation for the great quantities of blood in the bedding, had caused some dire speculation as to the reason, till the good doctor had explained my calamity.

Not counting the money I had sent home each month, my net pay was in excess of $350—more money than I had ever seen in my life! With a half dozen candy bars to supplement Lee's cooking, and only three hours wheel watch every nine hours, the trip south to Victoria was passed in warm, lazy comfort, and late at night we tied up for the last time at the company dock at Point Ellice Bridge. Most of the crew vanished into the city, and I was left with the dock watch. In the morning I was startled to see a large group of strangers standing around the dock, as though they were waiting for something to happen. Upon more careful inspection I found them to be members of our crew, and others from the *Black* and *Green* who had got in before us, all dressed up in their shore clothes, clean-shaven, waiting for their cheques. I listened with anxious ears to the pessimistic talk of the whalers.

The company, they said, had no money to pay its debts; bills for the repair of the *Green* and the *Brown* were still outstanding at Spratt's Victoria Machinery Depot, and a lien on these debts was being processed in the courts. There was also talk that a bank loan to pay off the crews had been refused, and the cheques we would receive would bounce when we tried to cash them. At 9:30 we were ushered into the office to sign off articles and be paid. The *Brown* was the last ship to sign off, and I was third to last to receive my cheque. By the time I hurried down to the bank on Bay Street, a long line of whalers preceded me to the counter.

It was with immense relief that I watched the teller count off all the twenty dollar bills into my outstretched hand, and I hurried back out of the bank's gloom to the sunlit hustle-bustle of the street. Secured of my worth, I pinned most of the money inside my singlet and, shouldering my seabag, began my long walk around the harbour to the CPR dock.

Few of the men I sailed with that season were met again. The war scattered us younger ones around the world, and the older ones grew older and retired before we got back again. Cec Fletcher, our chief engineer, became chief engineer of the *Snohomish* after they raised her from a sinking in which I had been quartermaster. I spotted Finn John once during my naval days as he ambled along Douglas Street, but he disappeared before I could force my way through the heavy wartime crowds to greet him. Years later I sighted Louis Larsen at the wheel of the *G.N. #5* off Pine Island. I doubt if he realized the fellow waving his cap from the bridge of the new ship plowing by him was the same frightened lad who had stood with him on the bridge of the old *Brown* during a stormy night not more than twenty leagues to the west. He gave me a glance before turning his back upon us, but I silently wished him a safe voyage before returning my attention to piloting my own ship.

It was thirty years almost to the day before I saw Roy again. My eldest son was married, and I was starting to put together the notes for this story. As nonchalantly as he had left, he returned, and through these past years we have carried on the friendship that began with our introduction to the whales.

Chapter Thirteen

Sea Oddities

Sailors of yore, returning from their voyages over the mysterious deeps, were often charged with exaggerating, or falsely reporting, phenomena that supposedly more knowledgeable minds safely on the shore could readily explain by logical means. This skepticism was slowly altered by the credible reporting of such writers as Captain Charles Scammon and Captain Thomas Roys, the latter having the Roys whale named in recognition of his work. Though they were followed by zoologists equipped to dissect, measure, and record the creatures of the sea, these scientists' studies lacked the sense of romance. We had to await the work of the scuba diver with underwater camera and sound pick-up equipment, before we could finally see, in close focus, the life and death drama that Roys and Scammon had described from above.

Though stories of sea monsters are reported throughout the world, usually accredited to a particular body of water familiar to the storyteller, there is a consistency that suggests a thread of truth in all of them. For years, sailors reported giant octopi whose tentacles could reach up out of the sea as high as the rigging of becalmed ships. There are now reports of observations that may well prove these stories are not exaggerations, but are closer to the truth than many of us who travel the sea would ever wish to find out.

A normal large octopus, when measured from the tip of one outstretched tentacle to another, may reach a length of thirty feet. On those tentacles are suckers, four to five inches in diameter, which surround a bony ring of teeth. Scars from these ringbone teeth are commonly found on the snout and body of the deep diving Sperm whales, who have a preference for these tasty cephalopods, and for their cousins, the squid.

Yet there have been Sperm whale scars recorded that look exactly like these, but whose measurements reach the awesome proportion of eighteen inches in diameter. This gives rise to the speculation that there are giant squid and octopi, called "Kraken" or "Architeuthis," in the dark world where the Sperm whale hunts his prey. Some researchers believe these monsters may have twenty-foot bodies, thirty-foot tentacles, and a weight of more than fifteen tons. And if they exist, who is to say that these creatures do not journey up to the ocean's surface when undersea quakes or upheavals drive them away from their natural habitat.

Of all the wonderful stories told by Finn John, one was forgotten until I came across a photograph and news clipping years later while researching these notes.

Sperm whales, with their two stomachs, large throat, and biting jaw equipped with large teeth, have well-documented appetites. Sharks ten to twelve feet long appear to be swallowed as easily as Jonah was! Three undigested ten-foot sharks were found at one time in a large bull Sperm whale's stomach at Naden Harbour. Squid measuring over thirty feet long, and several hundred pounds in weight, were also found, nearly intact, in a forty-five foot Sperm whale's stomach.But for rare finds in a Sperm whale's stomach we must go back to 1935 at Naden Harbour, when the newspapers of the day reported that a small "Caddy monster" had been found in the upper stomach of a Sperm. Pictures of the creature were provided.

In British Columbia we have two fabled water monsters, one in Okanagan Lake and another in the Cadboro Bay area of Victoria. Both are similar in appearance, with a horse-shaped head, large eyes, and a long slender body not unlike that an eel. The undulations of this body cause parts of the creature's spine to rise above the water's surface in a series of humps. The Ogopogo or Cadborosaurus usually appears when the majority of the world is looking the other way. Much like the Loch Ness monster, they have their advocates and their detractors.

The best I can recall Finn John's description of this creature, he said it had a horselike head with large limpid eyes and a tuft of stiff whiskers off each cheek. Its long, slender body was covered by a furlike material, with the exception of its back, where spiked horny plates overlapped each other. It had skin-covered flippers and a spade-shaped tail, like a Sperm whale. But I must admit that his story had slipped my mind that evening in Pirate's Cove, thirty years after my whaling experience, when I met a living representative of the Naden Caddy find.

With my two sons and their grandfather aboard our centre cockpit sloop, we spotted a small surface disturbance in the calm anchorage where we had dropped the hook for the night. Lowering the dinghy, my youngest son Gerry and I rowed out to investigate. We found a small, eel-like, sea creature swimming along with its head held completely out of the water, the undulation of its long, slender body causing portions of its spine to break the surface. My first thought that it was a sea snake was quickly discarded when, on drawing closer, I noticed the dark limpid eyes, large in proportion to the slender head, which had given it a seal-like appearance when viewed from the front. When it turned away, a long, slightly hooked snout could be discerned.

As the evening's darkness made observation difficult, and the swiftness of the creature's progress warned that he could quickly disappear, I decided to attempt a capture and bring it aboard the sloop for closer examination. Reaching out with a small dip net as Gerry swung the stern of our dinghy into the path of the small vee of wavelets that were the only indication of the creature's position, I was pleased to find him twisting angrily in the net when I lifted it up.

Under the bright lights aboard the sloop, we examined our catch and found he was approximately sixteen inches long, and just over an inch in diameter. His lower jaw had a set of sharp tiny teeth, and his back was protected by plate-like scales, while his undersides were covered in a soft yellow fuzz. A pair of small, flipper-like feet protruded from his shoulder area, and a spade-shaped tail proved to be two tiny flipper-like fins that overlapped each other.

I felt the biological people at Departure Bay would be interested in this find, but without a radiophone to contact them, the next best thing was to sail up there in the morning. Agreeing on this, we filled a large plastic bucket with seawater and dumped our creature into it. We retired early, for I intended to leave at first light, but sleep would not come to me. Instead, I lay awake, acutely aware of the little creature trapped in our bucket. In the stillness of the anchorage I could hear the splashes made by his tail, and the scratching of his little teeth and flippers as he attempted to grasp the smooth surface of the bucket. Such exertion, I began to realize, could cause him to perish before morning.

My uneasiness grew until I finally climbed back on deck and shone

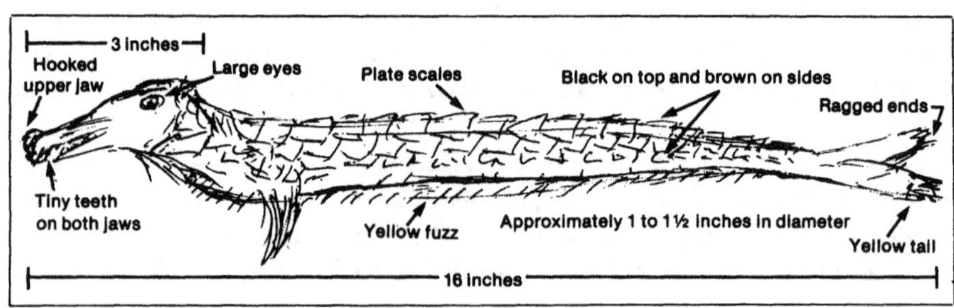

Page one, Vancouver Province, *October 16, 1937—Infant "Caddy" found in whale. The fisheries department's news bulletin today described a strange creature taken from the stomach of a pacific Coast whale, tallying closely with descriptions of the elusive Cadborosaurus of Southern Vancouver Island waters, but much smaller, possibly an infant. Officials said it was surprising to find such a large creature in a whale's stomach, as the mammals feed usually on squid, octopus, and sometimes shrimp. Discovery of the infant mammal was reported in the Daily Province in July. It was found at Naden Harbour whaling station, and its exact species has never been determined.*

Vancouver Province, *same day, on page 31—Officials reading the report of the Naden Harbour Whaling Station were surprised to find in it this description of an animal taken from the stomach of a whale killed off Queen Charlotte Islands: "About 10 feet long, having a head similar to a large dog, animal-like vertebrae and having a tail resembling a single blade of gill bone as found in whale's jaws."*

my flashlight down into the bucket. He stopped swimming immediately, and faced the light as though it were an enemy, his mouth opened slightly, the lips drawn back exposing his teeth, and the tufts of whiskers standing stiffly out from each side of his snout, while his large eyes reflected the glare of my flashlight. I felt a strong compassion for that little face staring up at me, so bravely awaiting its fate.

Just as strongly came the feeling that, if he was as rare a creature as my limited knowledge led me to believe, then the miracle of his being in Pirate's Cove at all should not be undone by my impulsive capture. He should be allowed to go free, to survive, if possible, and fulfill his purpose. If he were successful, we could possibly see more of his kind, not less. If he perished in my hands, he would only be a forgotten curiosity. I lowered the bucket over the side and watched him swim quickly away into the darkness, then returned to my bunk for a peaceful rest, my mind untroubled by the encounter.

It was Dode MacPherson who inadvertently caused me to remember, and to realize the similarities between, these stories of sea creatures, for it was while I was checking on some of his stories at the archives that I came across the news clipping of the Naden Harbour Caddy. My visit with Captain MacPherson opened a floodgate of fond memories, and, glowing happily, he cheerfully gifted them to this book. Here are two of those stories, about a whale with legs and a fortune in ambergris.

I had asked Dode if he knew anything about Cowboy Kean, a Vancouver moviemaker of the silent film era, who had been allowed by C. Rogers Brown to visit Kyuquot and make a film of the whaling. "Well, old man Brown had gone back to the States by the time I joined the company, and S.C. Ruck had been appointed by Schupp to take over as general manager. But, yes, I'd heard about it. Before my time, mind you, but it seems to me it was either Bill Heater or Willis Balcom who took him out to get the action shots of the whales," Dode mused, pinching his lips in concentration. "But mind, Kyuquot, you know, probably had more interesting incidents, one way or another, than any other whaling station on this coast."

Holding up his left hand with the fingers spread apart, he pinched each finger as he listed all those incidents he could recall. "Let's see now, they had the first cannery for processing whale meat for human consumption. I think they only put up fifty or sixty thousand cases, but it was a first, on this coast at any rate. There was the largest whale ever caught and recorded here, ninety-eight feet long, I believe John Anderson said. It didn't weigh in as heavy as the Right whale taken at Port Hobron the first year they opened; that one produced well over two hundred barrels of oil, but the Kyuquot Blue was longer. I heard the Tyee Whaling Company landed some well over a hundred feet long, but there is no official record of that," Dode chuckled. "Let's see now, where was I? Oh yes, Willis's three whales with one harpoon, that was out of Kyuquot, and the old *St. Lawrence* brought in the largest number of whales at any one time. Ruck was manager there then, and I believe it was seven or eight large Humpbacks she lugged all the way in by herself. They said you could hardly see the ship with all the whales ballooned up around her, just her smoke. But, say, I'll bet you didn't know about this," he chortled, pinching the thumb on his left hand. "Willis Balcom brought in a big whale with legs!"

It was my turn to chuckle, but Dode was quite serious. "It's the truth. People came all the way from New York to inspect and

Visitors have their picture taken on the belly of a large Blue whale, Kyuquot station, 1922.

photograph it. John Anderson told me all about it. Willis had a heck of a time lashing the big sulphur bottom alongside because of the queer protuberances that poked out from the whale's side, so he told his boys to hack one of them off. My god, John Anderson said, you should have heard the howl from the shore people. He said there were zoologists crying all over the place about the great loss to science. But, at any rate, if you want to check up on it, go down to the museum; you'll see parts of that whale with legs on display there."

Pinching a finger on the other hand, Dode's voice took on a deeper timbre as he leaned towards me and chuckled, "You ever find any ambergris, Bill?" When I smiled skeptically and shook my head, he grunted as though that was what he had expected, but quickly flashed a boyish grin and told this story.

"The year before I sailed with him, John Anderson shot a large Sperm outside Kyuquot, and when they cut it open, they found a large lump of yellow greyish, waxy-like mucus in its intestines. It was so tough they had to chop it into pieces with a heavy fire axe. I think Ruck was still manager there at the time, but it might have been Captain Gilmore. Doesn't matter much at this time. It weighed over five hundred pounds, and I guess was worth about five to six dollars an ounce. Quite a find, at any rate. Especially when you consider that skilled tradesmen were only earning three to four dollars a day, top wages. If I recall correctly, Captain Anderson said he got a bonus of about four hundred dollars for bringing it in. Not much really, when you figure it was worth over fifty thousand dollars."

Dode shook his head at the memory. "They didn't dare put it all on the market at one time, Schupp was too smart for that. They cut it up into fifty pound lots, sealed it in tin containers, and shipped it to the bank here in town, where they sold a little each year. That kept the market price at top level. They were still selling some of it when I was with them." Dode leaned back and, rubbing his large, bony nose, slyly asked, "You know how to recognize ambergris?"

I again shook my head and quickly checked the tape recorder, for the sparkle in his eye alerted me of his intention to leave me ignorant no longer. "Well, you take a knife with a sharp blade and scrape it across the stuff, like this," he explained, dragging the edge of one hand across the back of the other so that it pushed a small wave of flesh ahead of it. "If it runs off the blade like an oil it's probably just a piece of rotten blubber, but if it sticks on with little hairlike fibres hanging from the edge of the blade, there's a good chance you got yourself some ambergris. There's lots of people who could have saved themselves some bother if they'd known that."

Dode passed around a little vial of ambergris for us to see, then continued. "Not all whales sink after they die, you know. And if a dead whale happens to float around long enough in the hot sun, the gases inside expand till they swell up like balloons and explode, and pieces of this rotten blubber float for weeks in the area.

"Sometimes we'd lose a whale. We'd put a buoy on the tail and drop it to go after another whale, then when we got back, we'd be unable to find the damn whale. If they were left like that for long, especially in the summer heat, they'd swell up till they burst, then the skeleton would fall out of them and leave the blubber floating around to rot.

"Usually about two or three weeks after a whale was lost, some fisherman from the area would lug in gobs of smelly grey stuff and try to sell it to the company, believing he'd found a fortune in ambergris, when all he had was some rotten blubber!" Dode laughed, slapping his thigh with glee.

Ambergris, in the form of grayish gobs of greasy residue, has been found from times long past, either washed up on shore or floating at sea. It was believed to come from sick whales, and it wasn't till Captain Hussey and other whalers began catching Sperm whales that the mystery was solved. They found residues of this matter in the intestines of some Sperms, and realized it was a protective coating created to cover an irritant ingested into the whale's digestive system.

Often this irritant lodges in, or pierces, the walls of the intestines. Other than the Gray whale, which is known to eat mussels and clams and will sometimes form a mucus to cover the undigestible portions of these tidbits, the Sperm is the only whale to create ambergris. This is probably because the Sperm devours sharks and seals whole, and squid and octopus in liberal chunks. Sharks themselves are devourers of almost anything that moves underwater—even wood or metal objects have been found in their stomachs, and these could certainly cause the Sperm a problem. But, in most investigations, it has been found that the beaks of octopi have been the irritant that caused the mucus to form.

Like butter or water, ambergris can hold an odour many times its own volume till temperature and viscosity allow it to be released into the air. The scent of lilac or orange blossoms, for example, can be stored in a fluid containing ambergris, and when this mixture is spread thinly on the skin, the body heat will cause it to evaporate slowly, producing an alluring aroma that masks other not-so-alluring body odours. Ambergris became widely prized by perfume manufacturers as a fixing agent.

Many stories and myths revolve around the Sperm whale, but other BC cetaceans demonstrate interesting characteristics as well. The Blue whale, for example, is the largest of all whales and attains lengths of up to one hundred feet, with corresponding weights of over one hundred tons. Often referred to as a sulphur bottom, this latter name is derived from the appearance of Blue whales in deep southern oceans near the ice, where the skin on the lower portion of their bodies becomes covered with a yellow spore from the heavy growth of plankton that abounds in these waters during the almost perpetual daylight of the Antarctic summer.

The Humpback is the whale most often seen along the British Columbia coast. It is a coast crawler, whose visits to the kelp and rocky reefs encourage the growth of barnacles, sea lice, and crustaceans on his skin. The irritations of these parasites must be very maddening to the whale, and to rid himself of these annoyances he appears to disport himself playfully by leaping full length out of the water, or rubbing himself fearlessly against sharp rocks.

The Gray whale, also known as the Devil fish, or KoKo Kujaira as the Japanese call him, is a visitor to both eastern and western shores of the northern Pacific ocean, and is not only the most aggressive of all whales, but is also the ugliest. He is heavily covered with external parasites, and wears a head bonnet, like that of the Right whale,

Humpback whale.

which is crawling with whale lice. The Gray whale is one of the few species of whale that mates while lying on its side in the warm shallow waters of a lagoon. A mating couple is usually accompanied by a third whale, who will assist the pair by bracing himself behind the female.

The Right whale is a very timid and slow-moving creature, wallowing along at four knots or less. Its only defense from whalemen is to dive swiftly under the lee of an ice floe, or deeply down under the surface of the sea. They have been known to break their own necks upon striking the sea bottom in shallow waters when diving frantically away from a whaleman's harpoon. The Right is a filter feeder, eating swarms of small crustaceans and pteropods or sea butterflies (pelagic molluscs). Lowering its huge lower jaw like a massive coal scuttle, it swims through the feed, scooping it up. Satisfied it has a mouthful, the whale closes its jaw and, using the tongue like a pump plunger, forces the sea water out of its mouth through the thick layers of baleen. The feed trapped on the sieve-like whalebone bristles is then licked back by the tongue, and the throat is opened to allow the food to be swallowed.

Although not the prey of whalers, there are fascinating stories told of BC's killer whales, too. The Pacific Killer whale, Orcinus Orca, can be easily identified by its tall, triangular-shaped dorsal fin, and by the conspicuous white markings on its otherwise jet-black body. The Killer whale averages a length of twenty to thirty feet, and each jaw is armed with a dozen pairs of strong, large teeth. The species is the only whale known which habitually preys upon other warm-blooded animals. Its diet includes seal, walrus, other whales and porpoises, fish, squid, and sea birds.

Right whale. The top photo shows the tongue swollen, as it is when, after scooping up a mouthful of shrimp, the whale closes his jaw and swells his tongue, pumping the sea water out of his mouth through the baleen, while holding the feed in. At bottom, the eye at corner of jaw, and bonnet on top of upper jaw, are visible. Baleen can be seen hanging from upper jaw.

Front view of a Killer whale shot at Coal Harbour.

Many true stories of this creature's ferocity are recorded, yet no story can portray to the reader the terror this creature causes in whales many times his bulk. Sixty-ton whales have been known to run themselves aground on reefs or shoaling beaches in an attempt to escape this savage pursuer. So respected is the Killer whale that the coast Indians usually gave him top billing on their tall cedar totem poles, and most Indian folklore includes a legend of some of his exploits.

There are also stories recorded of this enormous dolphin attacking man, either in the water or on ice floes. History relates the experience of Thomas Edge and the survivors of the Moscovy Company's ship, *Mary Margaret*, in 1611, when she was wrecked in the east Greenland seas. It also tells the misfortunes that befell Ernest Shackleton and his men during their 1914–16 Antarctic expedition. In both those instances, Killer whales lifted their heads above the water to eye the men trapped on the ice floe, then dove under the floe and tried to dislodge the men by butting the underside of the floe with their snouts.

Thomas Edge recorded how these whales ate the men so unfortunate as to fall in the water.

Killer whales are best known today because of recent attempts, both successful and otherwise, to capture and display alive this most contradictory of sea creatures. In captivity it appears to lose its ferocity and becomes very playful with humans. Some people claim it will become amorous or aroused when in contact with human playmates of the opposite sex. When a Killer whale was cruelly harpooned off the British Columbia coast a few years ago, it meekly allowed itself to be towed into a drydock and nursed back to health. It even ate food from the hand of the man who had shot it, which shows a very great capacity for forgiveness.

Most Killer whales in captivity respond very quickly to training, and can be fed from their trainer's hand, or stroked and played with by knowing swimmers. Some will perform stunts few of us who have seen him as a killer would ever believe possible. The keen intelligence of the Orca enables it to understand what is expected of it, and his eagerness to please is not just a trick for a fishy handout, but the very human enjoyment of being the star.

Graig Fergusson related a story to me concerning the late Gordon C. Pike, a fisheries research zoologist whom I knew, and who worked out of Coal Harbour whaling station for the government. Gordon put together the statistics and identification brochures that have been so useful to everyone interested in whales and dolphins. He is credited by Edward D. Mitchell as a source of information for his much more comprehensive work, *Status of the World Whales*.

Graig Fergusson joined the air force shortly after leaving the whaler *W. Grant*, hoping to be assigned, after basic training, to their marine division. Instead, he ended up in a flight crew as navigator of a bomber flying over Germany. Shot down, he became a prisoner of war in East Prussia, and later transferred into Poland and then central Germany. When he was in Stalag 6 he met Gordon Pike, also an RCAF flight crew member, who took a great deal of interest in Graig's stories of whaling.

For entertainment, Graig often related interesting facts about the whales and their habits to his fellow prisoners, little realizing he was kindling a future pursuit for the young zoology major who asked so many questions. Graig's storytelling soon encouraged others to tell interesting facts about their own experiences, and this became an evening ritual to fill in their lonely hours. Graig and Gordon struck up a bond of friendship that followed them back into civilian life after the war, when Gordon joined the Fisheries Research Department, and Graig the marine division of Shell Oil.

Harry Osselton made a trip on the *Brown* as chief engineer when Finn John was skipper, and he wasn't very generous in his comments about my mentor. "Finn John was on different boats, the *Black* mostly, but he wasn't a crack gunner, you know. Harry Anderson on the *White* was top gunner when I was there." He grinned at his wife before adding, "Bill Heater was good—a bit of a religious hypocrite—though he did take his grandson out whaling with him for a couple of seasons."

Getting up, he walked over to the fireplace mantel and fingered a large Sperm whale tooth. "Did you ever hear the story about the purloined jaw bone?" he chuckled, carrying it back to the table where I sat. "Well, you see, some of the boys wanted a Sperm whale's tooth to take home or make into a cribbage board, and Garcin wouldn't allow anyone to take one because he was selling all he could get to a buyer in San Francisco. Well, this got the fellows mad. After all, one lousy tooth! How cheap can you get? So one night, when a couple of the boats were tied up at the dock and they had just finished cutting up a large Sperm, some of the lads slipped up into the station and stole the whole lower jaw bone, complete with all its teeth.

"They lugged it back to the ship and worked most of the night, sawing it into chunks and boiling it up in barrels down in the stokehold, till they could pry out the teeth. Boy, was old Garcin on the rampage over that one. Course he couldn't prove anything. He searched everywhere and not a tooth or piece of bone could he find. After all, you see, most of the bone had been dropped over the side. That which wasn't, and the teeth, had been divided out between both ships and hidden away in the most devious places!" Harry laughed heartily, the hard-won justice of those yesteryears still worthy of a chuckle. Then, with a twinkle in his eye, he handed me the tooth. While I admired the etched carvings and the polished cribbage board drilled on one face, he asked, "What do you think of this tooth? Worth the effort?"

As a reward for bringing in the first Sperm of the season, the manager at Naden allotted each of us on the *Brown* a piece of the jaw bone and a couple of Sperm teeth. The box of whale teeth was duly divided, but the allotment of whale bone proved to be one piece short, and a larger piece than the rest was given to me to saw up and share with our cook. Lee immediately protested the manner in which I was going to cut it, and snatched the bone away. I just as quickly grabbed it back from him, and commenced sawing what I thought were fair portions, prepared to offer him first choice.

Lee burst forth with a protest of Chinese, amply punctuated with Anglo-Saxon cuss words, and again wrested the chunk of bone away from my saw. This time when I gave chase, he ran pell mell towards the stern, the bone safely pocketed in his apron, which he held chest high, while his long skinny legs galloped across the deck fittings. Jumping up on the after gratings, he glared down at me as I paused in uncertainty, his blackened yellowed teeth exposed in a defiant grimace, while his breath whistled out of flaring nostrils. Overcoming my hesitation, I jumped up on the grating and reached for the bone that was still held in his apron. Quick as a flash, he spun round to the rail and, dropping his apron, allowed the bone to roll out and over the side.

I gazed down in disbelief as the bone slipped into the murky depths, then, still aghast, asked him why the hell he had done such a thing. His reply made little sense to me then, but later, as I gained maturity, his logic became more understandable. "When bone causes trouble between shipmates, get rid of bone!"

Speaking of whales, there was one favourite story my boys often asked me to tell as they settled in to go to sleep. With a certain literary license on my part, our boys knew it as "The Dance of the Whales." Few people have seen this phenomenon, and never have I seen accounts of it written, but it was perhaps the most thrilling sight I have ever seen. If I were a painter, I could paint its details in stark shades of colour, for the picture of it is still etched in my mind.

It was during the latter part of the afternoon watch, on a day that had been wet and squally, and I was cold and miserable as I stood my trick on the wheel. Finn John, smoking his old stubby pipe and wearing his brown Indian sweater and his battered old brown fedora, scanned the ocean as we rolled along on an outward sweep, skirting a northerly storm front that had kept us in its frigid grip all day. My eyes automatically came up from checking the compass to search the horizon opposite the direction the mate had swung his head. I snapped alert as my weary eyes spotted a strangeness there that warranted greater concentration.

To the southwest, the storm clouds were lifting and breaking apart as the wind backed around to that quarter. Fingers of sunlight poked down through these rents in the clouds to illuminate the grey heaving sea, turning the cresting waves a translucent green, and their foaming

Humpback whale.

tops a milky white. Between these shafts of warm yellow were the dark curtains of rain squalls sloping down to the sea. What had caught my eye were small dark shapes that appeared and disappeared in those dark areas of the rain squalls. Undoubtedly fish-shaped, they were so far away that only once in a while could I actually see their tails. This placed them well over five miles away, and the only fish I knew that could be seen five miles off were whales. But I'd never seen whales behaving like this before. Almost a hundred feet in length and as many tons, they were propelling themselves up, completely out of the water.

I can not recall what sort of hail I made to get Finn John's attention, but when he turned to look, they were gone. He looked back at me, a little bemused, after scanning the area for a good five minutes through his binoculars without sighting a thing; even the sunbeams had disappeared. But he showed respect for my judgment and keen eyesight by hauling the ship around to a heading I indicated and, still at cruising speed, we moved towards that distant spot where the two winds came together.

Twenty minutes later we were amongst the rain squalls, and the wind tore the clouds apart with a fury that rent the silence with several long rolls of thunder. It was like the beat of drums, signalling that the curtains were rolling back and the play beginning. Sunbeams poked down onto the sea ahead of us with a brilliance that caused my eyes to water, the dark vertical lines of the rain squalls retreated northward, and the heaving, cresting sea came alive with colour. Then, before us, not more than ten or fifteen cables off, the surface of the sea erupted as sleek black whales nearly as big as our ship hurled themselves up out of the water, some standing as high as our mast, their tails beating the surface into a frothy foam to maintain their momentary posture.

Never had I seen anything like it. Finn John got so excited he literally jumped up and down. Pulling his pipe out of his mouth, and tearing off his hat, he beat it against the weather dodger of the bridge as he roared at me, "Jesus Christ, God almighty! Vill you look at those god damn sulphur bottoms yump and dance!"

He rang down for slow speed, but there was no need to call anyone up; the noise made by the whales had brought them all out from the supper table. There must have been a dozen or more whales in sight at any one moment, and as they dropped back into the sea, others took their places. God only knows how many whales were there, perhaps a hundred. Some of the smaller ones leaped so far out of the water I could see the horizon under their tails, and they terminated their leap in a curve that brought them back to the surface in a thunderous fountain of spray as they landed full length. Sometimes they would rise together in pairs, facing one another, and pause like two huge dancers before our startled eyes, their tails beating the sea into a froth that rumbled louder than any propeller rising to the surface.

Bounding up to the bridge, Loùis scowled over at the whales like a tiger held at bay, his jowls quivering, his mouth opening and closing, and his hands clenching and unclenching on the handle of the telegraph. His gunner's instinct to let fly with a couple of harpoons warred with his master mariner's regard for our old ship's aging gear.

Caution won out and, ordering John to skirt the pod of Blue whales, he began looking for more suitable whales for our taking. The display lasted less than fifteen minutes, then the sea became strangely silent. Before anyone could retire, however, we sighted several Humpbacks breaching to starboard, and pounced on them so swiftly they were lashed alongside before we went to our supper. On our way into the station, we heard that the crew of the *Black* had not resisted the temptation when the pod of Blues had surfaced near her, and they were now returning to repair her windlass and replace the whole length of her mainline. There was no doubt they rued their impulsiveness.

During supper, Finn John attempted to explain the phenomenon we had seen by stating the whales were merely throwing themselves out of the water to create an impact of sufficient force to dislodge the encrustations and parasites they hosted on their skin. He said these parasites became more active and worrisome to the whale the further inshore, to the warmer and less salty waters, they came.

But Jacques-Yves Cousteau, in *The Whale, Mighty Monarch of the Sea*, states that both Finback and Blue whales couple by facing together like humans, and, to achieve this, they swim up from the depths together, trying to achieve penetration and climax before reaching the surface. I believe that what we had seen was the grand finale, after climax had been achieved, and the inertia of their swift passage upward rocketed them above the surface, where the tail wagging was a burst of ecstasy, signalling fulfillment of this great desire.

Perhaps someday the dance of the whales will be performed within range of a camera, and this amazing spectacle will be recorded for all to behold. Nothing less would convey the true magnificence of these great creatures.

Epilogue

In 1947, when the Consolidated Whaling Corporation was auctioned off piece by piece, only fifty persons came down to the Point Ellice wharf to witness the end of the Canadian whaling fleet. One of those in attendance was an ex-sealer named Max Lohbrunner. He incorporated himself as the Deepsea Fishing Company and bought the S.S. *Green* with a modest bid of three hundred dollars.

Most of the other ships quickly disappeared under the breaker's hammer (the *Aberdeen* escaped and sailed down to California to whale for the Del Monte pet food company), but the *Green* was transported across the harbour to the garbage dock and moored to the iron rings in the granite bluff at the foot of Herald Street. She remained there for the next twenty-odd years, to the great embarrassment of the city fathers.

Max Lohbrunner had been head seal hunter with Harry Balcom, whom he revered both as a sealing master and as a friend. The saving of the *Green*, in his eyes, was a saving of his friend's identity. In the days of Max's youth, when Victoria was the main port of the Pacific sealers, large fleets of schooners moored during the off-season at iron rings set in the granite bluffs around the Inner Harbour, with set anchors offshore so the vessels could raft up together. The Herald Street bluff had been much favoured by the sealers, and many pictures still exist that show them moored off this point. Under the protective conditions of the 1911 treaty, Max claimed the right of a sealer to moor his vessel at this spot, and the city fathers were unable to find cause by which to remove him.

Max was a bit of a romantic at heart, and dreamed of the sealing treaty being rescinded and of himself sailing off once again into the North Pacific. He insisted to all who would listen that the *Green* would be converted into a sealer under his command. While he may have been guilty of being a dreamer, he became deadly serious when he swore that he would "never let those people get her." "Those people" were the numerous promoters, both charitable and otherwise, who approached him with schemes to display or preserve the old *Green*.

Max Lohbrunner was destined to attract much attention over the years till both he and the *Green* were gone, but it is sad to think that he will be remembered more for his stubbornness than for his thoughtfulness.

The *Green* lay on the north side of the city dock, with her mooring cable sent ashore from her bow fairlead, and one line attached to the piling of the dock. The city, wishing to enlarge the dock facilities from which their garbage scows were loaded, were thwarted by Max's oratory and arguments at City Hall. Each time such an endeavour was mounted, Max would appear at council meeting laden with legal data to support his right to remain, and the city fathers would again be advised not to take legal action. In desperation they resorted to a form of slow attrition, dumping fill under the dock. This sediment gradually seeped over and entombed the unsuspecting *Green*, and dust from the workings settled so thickly over her topworks that wild seeds sprouted up in a dozen places on the old ship.

Max also had a talent for gathering junk. Valuable junk, no doubt, to him, but embarrassing junk to everyone else. His own little troller became burdened with it, as did the log float he had moored alongside the old *Green*, and finally it spread to the old ship herself. As the years rolled by, this junk rusted and rotted, as did the vessels beneath it.

Left: Whaler Green *at the Victoria garbage dock, 1960.*
Right: Last remains of the Green. *Her mast has been removed, and the gun is about to be blown off. Detonating scow is nestled under the stern of the train ferry* Canora.

Tourists in search of Beautiful Victoria avoided the foot of Herald Street.

Through the years, when I came to visit him or just paused to look over the bluff at his holdings, I became more concerned that each time would be the last. When I cautioned him about an opening in the *Green*'s plates just inches above the water line, he scoffed, claiming she took in no water, and stuffed some cotton wadding in the crack to ease my concern. In the late 1960s, on a minus tide, she settled on the bottom that had filled in under her during the years, and laid over enough to take in water. She never rose again. The last time I saw Max, he sat bare-footed in the warmth of the summer's setting sun, reading the evening's paper on the cabin of his troller. Only the mast, funnel, and snout of the old *Green* were visible above the water beside him.

My last visit to the foot of Herald Street was after Max's death, when the lookout barrel on the mast and the gun on the snout were blown off the old ship with explosives, for display at the new Maritime Museum a few blocks away.

At the very least, they should have given credit to Max for preserving them that long, for without his efforts, Victoria would not have had even these whaling artifacts to display. But, as they did not see fit to do so, we will remember him here, with the whalers he so admired. Though he never sailed with them, he alone had been willing to put up the hard-earned money and effort to preserve a tribute to them. Few, if any of us, have done more.

Appendix

Whaling Companies Mentioned in Text:

This table indicates the years of operation of each company. Owners' names are in brackets, followed by the home port and the location of the company's stations.

1905–10: Canadian Pacific Whaling Company (S. Balcom and W. Grant) Victoria, BC—Sechart, Kyuquot, Page's Lagoon

1907–17: Tyee Whaling Company (I.N. Hibbard) Seattle, WA—Sitka

1909–10: Queen Charlotte Whaling Company (S. Balcom and G.A. Huff) Victoria, BC—Rose Harbour

1910–15: Canadian North Pacific Fisheries (Mackenzie and Mann) Victoria, BC—Sechart, Kyuquot, Rose and Naden Harbours

1910–14: American Pacific Whaling Company (Mackenzie and Mann) Victoria, BC—Bay City

1911–12: Alaska Whaling Company (L. Christensen) Minneapolis, MN—Akutan

1912–15: North Pacific Sea Products (K.B. Birkeland) Minneapolis, MN—Akutan

1912–23: United States Whaling Company (Principals unknown) Huron, SD—Port Armstrong

1915–22: North Pacific Sea Products (W. Schupp) Seattle, WA—Akutan, Alaska

1915–22: Victoria Whaling Company (W. Schupp) Victoria, BC—Sechart, Kyuquot, Rose and Naden Harbours

1915–48: American Pacific Whaling Company (W. Schupp) Seattle, WA—Bay City, Akutan, Port Hobron

1922–53: Consolidated Whaling Corporation Ltd (W. Schupp and estate) Victoria, BC—Rose and Naden Harbours

1948–present: American Pacific Whaling Company (W. Lagen) Seattle, WA

1947–69: Western Whaling Corporation Ltd (BC Packers Ltd) Vancouver, BC—Coal Harbour

The Whaling Ships

Vessels are registered by length/beam/draft in feet
NHP—nominal horsepower
HP—horsepower
GT—gross tons
NT—net tons
RT—registered tons

Canadian Pacific Whaling Co/Victoria Whaling Co/Consolidated

Vessel	Dimensions	Power/Tonnage	Service
Orion 1904, Christiania, Norway	94.1/17.4/10.6 ft	42 NHP/109 GT/104 NT/22 RT	1905–30 whaling; renamed *Pluvius*, Vancouver's fireboat—1945
St Lawrence 1903, Christiania, Norway	93.2/16.9/10.6 ft	50 NHP/111 GT/106 NT/24 RT	1907–30 whaling; 1931–48 towing
Germania 1903, Christiania, Norway	94.3/16.8/10 ft	30 NHP/106 GT/101 NT/26 RT	1909–16 whaling; 1916–26 towing
Sebastian 1904, Christiania, Norway	93.5/16.8/10.3 ft	102 GT/98 NT	1909–16 whaling; renamed *Saanich* #117323; 1916–47 towing; 1948 whaling for Western Whaling
W. Grant #126517 1910, Victoria, BC	93/18/10.3 ft	103 GT/98 NT/37 RT	1910–42 whaling; 1942–48 towing
Brown #131358 1910, Christiania, Norway	91.8/18/11.2 ft	46 NHP/102 GT/100 NT/37 RT	1910–47 whaling

Blue #131357
1910, Christiania, Norway — 91.8/18/11.2 ft — 46 NHP/102 GT/100 NT/37 RT — 1910–47 whaling

Black #131337
1910, Christiania, Norway — 91.8/18/11.2 ft — 46 NHP/102 GT/100 NT/37 RT — 1910–47 whaling

Green #131339
1910, Christiania, Norway — 91.8/18/11.2 ft — 46 NHP/102 GT/100 NT/37 RT — 1910–42 whaling; 1947–68 laid up, sunk at her moorings, Victoria

White #131338
1910, Christiania, Norway — 91.8/18/10.6 ft — 46 NHP/102 GT/100 NT/37 RT — 1910–47 whaling

Gray #124395
1909, Workington, England — 182.7/27.9/12.3 ft — 90 NHP/707 GT/511 NT/280 RT — former *Petriana*; 1911–42 whaling; 1942–47 Waterhouse Steamships; breakwater at Oyster River

American Pacific Whaling Co

Moran
1911, Moran yards, Seattle, WA — 87.3/18/11.4 ft — 36 NHP/120 GT/77 NT

Paterson
1911, Moran yards — 87.3/18/11.4 ft — 36 NHP/120 GT/77 NT

Westport
1912, Seattle Construction & Drydock, WA — 88/19/11.5 ft — 36 NHP/116 GT/77 NT — lost 1936 in Alaska

Aberdeen
1912, Seattle Construction — 88/19/11.5 ft — 35 NHP/116 GT/59 NT

Tyee Whaling Co

Tyee Jr. #204458			
1907, Moran yards	97.9/17.7/11.8 ft	151 GT	renamed *Tanginak* for NPSP-APW; twin screw, compound engines

Alaska Whaling Co/North Pacific Sea Products

Kodiak			
1912, J.F. Duthie, Seattle, WA	100/19.2/12.4 ft	41 NHP/146 GT/99 NT	
Unimak			
1912, J.F. Duthie	100/19.2/12.4 ft	41 NHP/146 GT/99 NT	

United States Whaling Company

Star I			
1912, Seattle Construction	106.1/21.2/13 ft	53 NHP/196 GT/133 NT	1925 Hvalfanger-Sandefj'rd, Norway; 1963 owner R.J. Hamilton, New Zealand
Star II			
1912, Seattle Construction	96.1/19.5/12.3 ft	143 GT/97 NT	1925 Hvalfanger-Sandefj'rd, Norway; 1933 renamed *Taratahi* for Stewart Island Fresh Oyster Co., Invercargill, New Zealand
Star III			
1912, Seattle Construction	96.1/19.5/12.3 ft	143 GT/97 NT	1925 Hvalfanger-Sandefj'rd, Norway; 1932 owner P. Feron, Lyttelton, New Zealand

Western Whaling Corporation Ltd

Saanich			
1904, Christiania, Norway	93.5/16.8/10.3 ft	102 GT/98 NT	former *Sebastian*: 1948 whaling

James Carruthers 1912, Beverly, England	118/22/11.5 ft	400 HP/233 GT/97 NT	1948 whaling
Nahmint 1943, San Francisco, CA	98/21.3/9.4 ft	500 HP/172 GT/119 NT	1948–59 whaling (diesel powered)
Polar V 1931, Oslo, Norway	119/24/13 ft	1200 HP/278 GT/110 RT	renamed *Westwhale 1*, 1951–65 whaling
Bouvet III 1930, Tees, England	116.2/24.2/12.8 ft	850 HP/246 GT/88 RT	renamed *Westwhale 2*, 1951–65 whaling
Globe VII 1935, Moss, Norway	116.4/24/13.5 ft	900 HP/251 GT/113 RT	renamed *Westwhale 3*, 1951–65 whaling; engines to film company
Tahsis Chief 1942, Tacoma, WA	129/24.6/10.3 ft	1200 HP/254 GT/150 RT	renamed *Westwhale 4*, 1948–69 whaling; renamed *Lavallee 2*, 1969–72 Newfoundland fishing (diesel powered)
Katsu Maru 1942, Muroran, Japan	143.6/25.6/13.7 ft	1600 HP/383 GT/185 RT	renamed *Westwhale 5*, 1962–69 whaling (diesel powered)
Seki Maru 1939, Moss, Norway	130.6/25.1/13.2 ft	1600 HP/307 GT/137 RT	renamed *Westwhale 6*, 1962–69 whaling (diesel powered)
Toshi Maru 21 1953, Arendal, Norway	158.6/29.6/15.3 ft	2013 HP/581 GT/278 RT	renamed *Westwhale 7*, 1963–69 whaling; renamed *Pacific Challenger*, towing

Toshi Maru 22 1953, Arendal, Norway	158.6/29.6/15.3 ft	2013 HP/581 GT/278 RT	renamed *Westwhale 8*, 1963–69 whaling; 1969–72 Newfoundland fishing
Fumi Maru 8 1950, Shimonoseki, Japan	167/28.3/12.7 ft		renamed *Westwhale 9*, 1967–69 whaling; renamed *Samarinda*, 1971–75 towing (diesel powered)
Lavallee I 1943, Vancouver, BC	114.3/22/10.3 ft	375 HP/167 GT/99 RT	1949–52 whaling; 1970 Newfoundland fishing; total loss by fire (diesel powered)
Kimsquit 1944, Nanaimo, BC	104/23.2/10.2 ft	167 GT/99 RT	1949–52 whaling (diesel powered)
Speed Mac no data available			PT style motor vessel powered with twin Hall-Scott gas engines
Retriever no data available			powered landing barge with A-frame
Tow Mac #179458 1944, Bellingham, WA	157.6/33.5/16 ft	642 GT/166 NT	renamed *Pacific Salvor*, four cylinder triple expansion engines 16 x 26 x ⅔2 inch cylinders and 24 inch stroke
Viner 1911, North Vancouver, BC	45.7/14.5/5.7 ft	220 HP/28 GT/16 RT	1951–59 towing whales to station
Walter M 1925, New Westminster, BC	54.6/15.4/6.6 ft	220 HP/41 GT/28 RT	1951–59 towing whales to station

Annual Catches

Date	BC Stations	Alaska Stations	Bay City Station
1905	200		
1906	nr		
1907	nr		
1908	569		
1909	672		
1910	812		
1911	1199		182
1912	1109		265
1913	705	186	211
1914	573	175	192
1915	229	163	334
1916	413	150	268
1917	379	285	209
1918	500	310	189
1919	432	419	174
1920	493	290	187
1921	no	nr	nr
1922	187	325	163
1923	455	355	136
1924	414	nr	
1925	351	nr	
1926	269	583	
1927	258	nr	
1928	305	nr	
1929	407	nr	
1930	320	355	
1931	no	nr	
1932	no	nr	
1933	209	nr	
1934	350	394	
1935	202	nr	
1936	378	385	
1937	317	376	
1938	310	173	
1939	no	171	
1940	220	no	
1941	328	no	
1942	163	no	
1943–1947	Wartime, no whaling		
1948	182		
1949	255		
1950	314		
1951	437		
1952	465		

ANNUAL CATCHES, CONT.

Date	BC Stations
1953	539
1954	630
1955	630
1956	375
1957	635
1958	774
1959	869
1960	no
1961	no
1962	712
1963	578
1964	880
1965	865
1966	721
1967	456
1968	no
1969	no
1970	no
1972	Whaling ceases in Canada and United States

Notes
nr — no record
no — not operating
Alaska stations records:
from 1913-16, only Port Armstrong reported
from 1917-20, only Akutan reported
from 1926-37, both Akutan and Port Hobron reported

Bibliography

Cousteau, Jacques-Yves and Philippe Diole. *The Whale, Mighty Monarch of the Sea*. New York: Doubleday, 1972.

McDonald, Lucile. "Whaling on Washington Coast." In *Sea Chest*, Vol. 6, No. 1. September 1972.

Mitchell, Edward D. "The Status of the World Whales." In *Nature Canada*, Vol. 2, No. 1. 1973.

Newell, Gordon. *H. W. McCurdy's Marine History of the Pacific Northwest*. Seattle: Superior Publishing, 1965.

Ommanney, Dr. F.D. *Lost Leviathan*. London: Hutchinson & Co., 1971.

Ormsby, Margaret A. *British Columbia: A History*. Toronto: MacMillan of Canada, 1958.

Pike, Gordon C. "Guide to Whales, Porpoises and Dolphins." Fisheries Research Board of Canada, Circular #32 (revised). August 1956.

Robertson, R.B. *Of Whales and Men*. New York: Alfred A. Knopf, 1954.

Sanderson, Ivan T. *Follow the Whale*. Boston: Little, Brown & Co., 1956.

Schmitt, Fredrick P. *Mark Well the Whale!*. Port Washington, 1971.

Index

Photo Credits

Alan Armour, 149 (B); Hector Cowie, 130, 131, 185, 186; Cowie/Hudson, 42; G. Ellis, 190; Win Garcin, 77, 125; Gustavson, 171; Gustavson/ Hagelund, 29, 167; William Hagelund, 7, 195; Allan Heater, 81, 93; William S. Lagen, 54, 67, 69, 73; D.B. MacPherson, 107, 108, 122 (T); McPhee/Borgen, 137, 143; Harry Osselton, 150; G.C. Pike, 184; Provincial Archives, 11, 27, 50, 59, 82, 149 (T); San Francisco Maritime Museum/New York Public Library Collection, 43; Spearing/Balcom, 57; Vancouver Maritime Museum, 16 (Garcin), 25 (Hagelund), 34, 35 (Hagelund), 47, 53, 55, 61, 62, 63, 91, 115, 122 (B), 145, 152, 154 (Garcin), 161 (Hagelund), 179 (Boorman), 181; Charlie Watson, 99, 105; Joe Williamson, Winslow, 49.

All drawings by Gaye Hammond except drawing on page 178 by author.

www.ingramcontent.com/pod-product-compliance
Lightning Source LLC
Jackson TN
JSHW071703170426
101040JS00022B/486

9781550177602